Gus Dur and the Indonesian Economy

Gus Dur and the Indonesian Economy

edited by
Anthony L. Smith

INSTITUTE OF SOUTHEAST ASIAN STUDIES
Singapore

First published in Singapore in 2001 by
Institute of Southeast Asian Studies
30 Heng Mui Keng Terrace
Pasir Panjang
Singapore 119614

Internet e-mail: publish@iseas.edu.sg
World Wide Web: http://www.iseas.edu.sg/pub.html

ISEAS Library Cataloguing-in-Publication Data

Gus Dur and the Indonesian economy / edited by Anthony L. Smith.

1. Indonesia—Economic conditions—1945-
2. Indonesia—Economic policy.
3. Fiscal policy—Indonesia.
4. Banks and banking—Indonesia.
5. Debts, External—Indonesia.
6. Economic stabilization—Indonesia.
7. Wahid, Abdurrahman.

I. Smith, Anthony L.

HC447 G98 2001 sls2000062570

ISBN 981-230-115-1

Cover photograph courtesy of TEMPO/Robin Ong.
Printed in Singapore by Seng Lee Press Pte Ltd.

Contents

List of Tables

List of Figures

List of Contributors

Anggito Abimanyu	Faculty of Economics, Gadjah Mada University Yogyakarta, Indonesia
Aris Ananta	Department of Economics National University of Singapore
Jusuf Anwar	Jakarta Initiative Task Force for Corporate Restructuring, Indonesia
Mark Baird	World Bank Country Director, Indonesia
Faisal Basri	LPEM-FEUI, University of Indonesia
Boediono	Faculty of Economics, Gadjah Mada University, Indonesia
Anthony S. Chan	USAID, Indonesia
Howard Dick	Department of Management Australian Centre for International Business University of Melbourne
H. S. Dillon	Executive Director of Center for Agricultural Policy (CAPS), Indonesia
Joshua Felman	International Monetary Fund, Jakarta
Noor Fuad	Director-General, Ministry of Finance Republic of Indonesia
Farid Harianto	Deputy Chairman, Indonesian Bank Restructuring Agency (IBRA)
Mohamad Ikhsan	Associate Director, Micro Economic Division LPEM-FEUI, Jakarta
Jusuf Kalla	Former Minister for Industry and Trade Republic of Indonesia

Bambang Kusumanto	Ministry of Finance Republic of Indonesia
Anwar Nasution	Dean and Professor of Economics, Faculty of Economics, University of Indonesia; and Senior Deputy Governor of Bank Indonesia
Mohammad Sadli	Chairman, Indonesian Forum Foundation
Emil Salim	Head, National Economic Council (DEN)
Gunarni Soeworo	Head, Indonesian Bankers Association (Perbanas)
Anthony L. Smith	Fellow, Institute of Southeast Asian Studies (ISEAS), Singapore
Sri Adiningsih	Gadjah Mada University, Indonesia
Sri Mulyani Indrawati	LPEM-FEUI, University of Indonesia
Laksamana Sukardi	Former Minister for Investment and State Enterprises, Republic of Indonesia
Franky Widjaja	Group Managing Director Sinar Mas Group

Abbreviations

ADB	Asian Development Bank
AFTA	ASEAN Free Trade Area
AMU	Asset Management Unit
APBN	Anggaran Pengeluaran dan Belanja Negara (government budget)
APEC	Asia Pacific Economic Co-operation
ASEAN	Association of Southeast Asian Nations
Bappenas	Badan Perencanaan Nasional (National Development Planning Board or Planning Board)
BCA	Bank Central Asia
BDI	Bank Dagang Indonesia
BI	Bank Indonesia
BII	Bank Internasional Indonesia
BIS	Bank for International Standards
BLBI	Bantuan Likuiditas Bank Indonesia (Bank Indonesia Liquidity Assistance)
BPK	Badan Pemeriksa Keuangan (State Auditing Agency)
BPS	Biro Pusat Statistik (Central Bureau of Statistics)
Bulog	Badan Urusan Logistik Nasional (National Logistics Board)
CAPs	Centre for Agricultural Policy
CAR	capital adequacy ratio
CDs	certificate of deposit
CGP	Consultative Group on Indonesia
CPF	Central Provident Fund
CPI	consumer price index
DPR	Dewan Perwakilan Rakyat (People's Representative Assembly)
EPF	Employees Provident Fund
FX	foreign exchange
GDP	gross domestic product
HDI	human development index

IBRA	Indonesian Bank Restructuring Agency
IMF	International Monetary Fund
INDRA	Indonesia Debt Restructuring Agency
IPO	initial public offering
JITF	Jakarta Initiative Task Force
KKN	korupsi, kolusi, dan nepotisme (corruption, collusion and nepotism)
KLBI	Kredit Likuiditas Bank Indonesia (Bank Indonesia's Special Credit Scheme)
KUT	Kredit Usaha Tani (farmers' credit scheme)
LIBOR	London Inter-Bank Offered Rate
LIPI	Lembaga Ilmu Pengetahun Indonesia (Indonesian Academy of Science)
LoI	Letter of Intent
LPEM-FEUI	Lembaga Penelitian Ekonomi dan Masyarakat — Fakultas Ekonomi Universitas Indonesia (Institute for Economic and Social Development — Faculty of Economics, University of Indonesia)
MAI	Multilateral Agreement on Investment
MOA	Ministry of Agriculture
NGOs	non-governmental organizations
NIEs	Newly Industrialized Economies
NPL	non-performing loan
OFG	One-Stop Facilitation Group
PAN	Partai Amanat Nasional
PDI-P	Partai Demokrasi Indonesia-Perjuangan
Perbanas	Indonesian Bankers Association
PKB	Partai Kebangkitan Bangsa
PLN	Perusahaan Listrik Negara (National Electricity Company)
REEF	Real Effective Exchange Rate
SAM	Social Accounting Matrix
SBI	Sertifikat Bank Indonesia (Bank Indonesia Certificates)
SMEs	small and medium enterprises
SOEs	State-owned enterprises
SSN	Social Safety Net

SUPAS	Five-yearly Population Census
SUSENAS	Indonesia Socio-Economic Survey
TNI	Tentara Nasional Indonesia (Indonesian Armed Forces)
UNDP	United Nations Development Programme
VOC	Vereenigde Oostandische Compagnie (Dutch East India Company)
WTO	World Trade Organization

Preface

The chapters in this volume started life as conference papers at the Institute of Southeast Asian Studies' (ISEAS) Indonesia Forum entitled "Abdurrahman Wahid's First 100 Days: An Economic Agenda" held on 17-18 January 2000. The Forum drew together Indonesian government ministers, senior civil servants, representatives of bilateral and multilateral organizations, and academics. The record of these proceedings is valuable in order to assess the views of decision-makers and academics (some of whom are advisers to government in a formal or informal capacity) concerning the overall economic direction of Indonesia. It should be noted that the two cabinet ministers here, Laksamana Sukardi and Jusuf Kalla, subsequently left cabinet under controversial circumstances. However, they were government ministers and representatives of the Wahid government at the time of writing their respective papers. The papers were presented in January 2000 but a decision was taken not to attempt to alter the details in each chapters for publication. Some aspects have dated, but the challenges, dilemmas, themes, and analysis of the overall economic prospects for the Wahid administration identified by the contributors have not. The Introduction will help update the reader through to the end of 2000.

The editor thanks Dr Leonard Sebastian, formerly a Fellow at ISEAS (now with the Institute of Defence and Strategic Studies, Singapore), who co-ordinated the Forum. Appreciation is also extended to Anggito Abimanyu of the Faculty of Economics at Gadjah Mada University, Yogyakarta, Indonesia, for his assistance with aspects of the conference and the resulting publication.

Anthony L. Smith

1

Introduction
Abdurrahman Wahid's Economic Agenda: The Views of Leading Decision-makers and Commentators

Anthony L. Smith

INTRODUCTION TO THE INDONESIAN ECONOMY

When the Dutch finally left Indonesia in 1949, founding president Sukarno and his fellow nationalists undertook the task of building a new nation. The Dutch bequeathed little to the new government in terms of economic structure, while at the time Indonesia did not really cohere as a single economy. For Sukarno, and others in the independence movement, colonialism and global capitalism were the twin evils of the colonial order (although moderates, like vice-president Mohamad Hatta, were less radical on this issue). To avoid the "neo-colonialism" of the west, including the Netherlands, Sukarno eventually turned to self-reliance on the domestic Indonesian economy. His policies, a cross between economic nationalism and socialism, involved the nationalization and public ownership of key assets. Barriers to trade were erected, while foreign investment was discouraged. By the 1960s, the Indonesian economy had become a "basket case", as Hal Hill describes it, with inflation as high as 1,500 per cent by mid-1966 through an extremely liberal monetary policy (i.e. the printing of money) and interest repayments on debts exceeded returns from imports.[1] Sukarno engaged in "borrow-and-hope" policies by fuelling government expenditure through overseas debt, and by the end of his tenure debt servicing was costed at US$530 million in 1966, while export earnings were only $430 million.[2] A vast amount of spending was wasted on a defence build-up, including the disastrous military campaign against the Federation of Malaysia from 1963-66, and a number of "showpiece" buildings and monuments in Jakarta.[3]

Soeharto's ascension to power in 1965–66, saw a dramatic turnaround in Indonesia's economic fortunes. Anne Booth considers that Soeharto's stabilization programme was one of the most successful undertaken anywhere in modern history.[4] From 1969 to 1994, Indonesia embarked upon its first development phase, which saw absolute poverty go from 60 per cent of the population to 14 per cent.[5]

The new administration, staving off further crisis, brought in the so-called "Berkeley Mafia" of technocratic liberal economists, under professors Widjojo Nitisastro and Ali Wardhana based at Bappenas (the National Planning Board). Opening the economy to foreign trade and investment was seen as necessary, while inflation was brought under firm control. The New Order also tried to balance its books with an explicit commitment to a modest surplus. Hal Hill has pointed out that this was something of a "fiction" as the official budget did not include the off-budget expenditure (many industrial projects and some military funding was achieved through state banks), while aid and external borrowings were officially listed as revenue.[6] Debt remained a problem for the Soeharto regime, probably at a cumulative US$100 billion at peak, while Indonesia continued to be dependent to some extent, on foreign aid. Inaccurate record keeping remains a feature of Indonesia's budget. Nevertheless, even if most years saw a small deficit, it was a far cry from the chronic deficits of the Sukarno era. In most years after 1966 Indonesia recorded economic growth rates between 5 per cent to 7 per cent, while maintaining a favourable balance of payments. According to these measures, many economists judged the economy under Soeharto to be based on sound fundamentals.

Indonesia's economic management has shown a trend to undertake sensible steps during crisis years, but once significant economic growth returns, economic rationalism is often abandoned. From the mid-1960s to the early 1970s, Indonesia sought sound macroeconomic policies. However the 1973 global oil shock was a boon for an oil rich state such as Indonesia. These new found riches were not necessarily channelled wisely as the state oil company, Pertamina, actually managed to become virtually bankrupt forcing a government bail-out. Pertamina had attempted a massive commercial expansion into other industrial projects under the leadership of Ibnu Sutowo. Pertamina's debts of US$10.5 billion doubled the public sector debt at the time to about 30 per cent of GDP.[7] A recession in 1984, partly caused by declining oil prices, prompted more crisis management, but the "technologs" (meaning statist or mercantilist officials), led by the Minister for Research and Technology, B. J. Habibie, gained the upper hand in the late 1980s and managed to secure funding for large scale industrial projects. Habibie sought to create strategic industries to jump the technological gap with the west, which included heavy investment in steel, armaments, and ship construction.[8] Growing economic fortunes, over time, also saw the growth of other state owned enterprises like the electricity company (PLN) and IPTN (Industri Pesawat Terbang Nusantara), which infamously tried to build passenger aircraft at great expense to public funds. Increasingly Indonesia engaged in import substitution in order to develop the domestic market and domestic technologies — the latter involving questionable heavy industrial projects.

A GROWING CONCENTRATION OF WEALTH

The Soeharto regime was quite openly nepotistic, and increasingly so towards the end. The growing economy provided opportunities for the Soeharto family and its close associates to create monopolies and toll-gate enterprises. The Soeharto regime resembled a feudal system of capricious law changes to suit family members and the gifting of lucrative sectors of the economy to favoured family and friends. The World Bank has stated that the business empire linked to the Soeharto family during the New Order amounted to 417 listed and unlisted companies, and particularly through state controlled companies, while total assets were measured at US$24 billion.[9] One measure of wealth concentration that the World Bank engaged in was to measure the corporate share of the top ten families, with Indonesia and the Philippines topping the list in Asia with 57.7 per cent and 52.5 per cent respectively (by comparison Japan is at 2.4 per cent, South Korea, 26.8 per cent and Taiwan, 18.4 per cent).[10] One Indonesian conglomerate, the Salim group under businessman Liem Sioe Long, was estimated to control a massive 16.6 per cent of market capitalization (and was said to represent 5 per cent of the Indonesian GNP by early 1990[11]) by the onset of the financial crisis.

Increasingly the Indonesian economy, under Soeharto, was falling between two stones. Rhetorically Soeharto espoused the language of free trade to the international community, most famously when Soeharto managed to broker the APEC Bogor Declaration in 1994, calling for complete free trade in the Asia Pacific by 2010 for developed nations and

2020 for developing nations.[12] However, the openness of the Indonesian economy in earlier times was not sustained due to the lack of political commitment. Instinctively, the regime saw economic nationalism as a long-term goal: “There remains a deep-seated mistrust of market forces, economic liberalism, and private (especially Chinese) ownership in many influential quarters in Indonesia.”[13] The free market was seen by many in the Indonesian political élite, and possibly by Soeharto himself, as being a pretext for the domination of foreign and non-*pribumi* (non-indigenous) interests — although co-opting these interests was clearly useful at times. In March 1990 Soeharto appealed to ethnic Chinese to share their wealth with the masses, adding to a dialogue of the ethnic division of labour: “The use of terms like ‘social gap’ took on distinct racial connotations. The gap referred to was the gulf between rich Chinese and poorer indigenous Indonesians.”[14] Soeharto, without consulting his cabinet, called on thirty-one major businesses owned by ethnic Chinese to divest up to 25 per cent of equity to co-operatives.[15] The picture that emerges of the Soeharto administration is that it was a curious combination of free market and mercantilist — a chimera — while in more confident economic times the true intentions of the regime were revealed as that of economic nationalism.

THE FINANCIAL CRISIS

In a sense, Indonesia’s stability under Soeharto was bought at a high cost given the civil chaos surrounding succession. Michael Vatikiotis argues that “[o]ptimism about the business scene was tempered by doubts about the capacity of the existing political structure to sustain a healthy commercial environment”.[16] While the problems of Indonesia’s economy were many, including massive corruption, monopoly control over the economy and the prevalence of bad loans in the banking sector, Valerie Cerra and Sweta Chaman Saxena argue that Indonesia “has been viewed as the clearest case of contagion, as it had the least severe macroeconomic imbalances”.[17]

At the time of the crisis, in late 1997, Indonesia had a healthy balance of payments situation, strong export growth, and an official target of 1 per cent of GNP budget surplus.[18] Through most of the latter half of 1997 it appeared as though Indonesia would actually ride out the crisis relatively unscathed. But Indonesia experienced a significant economic meltdown which began in December 1997. The contagion effect stemmed from depreciating neighbouring currencies (and export competitors) and the withdrawal of short-term foreign investment from the entire region in response to the financial crisis in other Asian currencies. “Hedge Funds” and "Emerging Market Funds" often linked investments for a portfolio holder in several regional economies — their withdrawal impacted on all the host countries.[19] Anticipating a fall in currency prices, the withdrawal of short-term investment became a self-fulfilling prophesy. The tremendous growth of financial flows was also a complicating factor — being worth an estimated 1 per cent of GNP of developing countries in 1989, but expanding massively to 5 per cent just prior to the financial crisis.[20] On 1 July 1997 the rupiah was 2,432 to the U.S. dollar, but by 24 January 1998 it was 14,800 — sinking to its lowest point during the crisis.[21]

There is no doubt that the growing ostentatious nature of first family favouritism also added to a growing perception that Soeharto had come to view this as more important than the health of the overall economy — the failures to close down one of Tommy Soeharto's banks and the continuation of the IPTN aircraft programme and the Timor car projects in defiance of IMF conditionalities. While commentators are still pondering and debating the causes of the crisis, and its impact on Indonesia, Indonesia's structural problems, while not the cause of the crisis, served to deepen the impacts and cause an economic meltdown.

The International Monetary Fund (IMF) bailed out Indonesia with an aggregate US$43 billion package, which involved disbursements of, on average, US$1 billion per month. There were conditionalities attached to the various letters of intent signed with the IMF, including a balanced budget (initially), reduction of subsidies, a reduction of tariffs, withdrawal from strategic heavy industry protectionism, rationalizing the financial sector and so on. The IMF's role in bailing out the economies of Thailand, South Korea and Indonesia was essentially a prescription of policies based on the tenets of neo-classical economics. While the general direction of these reforms was helpful in Indonesia's case, legitimate criticisms were made that the IMF approached these economies with a single approach (sometimes called a "cookie-cutter" approach by the media). However, the IMF did learn from some of its earlier mistakes, notably it has done a U-turn on the issue of a balanced budget, with a modest deficit now seen as the best short-term measure.

The effect of the crisis was quite mixed, with urban areas being affected far more than rural areas — the urban middle class saw substantial reductions in their overall incomes, while large numbers of urban poor fell below the poverty line. Unemployment rose to approximately 20 million. While Java was badly affected, Sumatra, Sulawesi and Maluku, amongst other regions, showed fewer negative impacts, as exporters of some primary products found that their goods were suddenly very competitive with the rupiah's free fall. Industries with imported inputs faced soaring production costs.

THE SLOW ECONOMIC RECOVERY UNDER HABIBIE

Signs that the economic troubles had already bottomed out were evident during the transitional Habibie administration which came to power after the resignation of Soeharto in May 1998. While in 1998 the economy contracted by 13.2 per cent it stabilized at a modest 0.2 per cent growth rate for 1999, according to data from the Asian Development Bank.[22] Recovery was aided by improvements in the agricultural sector and mineral exports. Perhaps the success story of the Indonesian post-crash economy was the control of inflation: At 58.5 per cent in 1998, it declined to 20.5 per cent in 1999, with December 1999 recording an inflation rate of 2 per cent.[23] Although inflation levels are now up to 7 per cent, a level expected to continue for some time, inflation remains under control. The central bank's tight monetary policy — and the complete resistance to the temptation to print more money — is a large part of the reason for taming inflation. Falling rice prices and the appreciation of the rupiah were also helpful in this regard. The continuing financial sector problems did, however, see a declining formal services sector. The impact of the crisis on official unemployment and underemployment continued to be felt rising to 6.3 per cent unemployment in August 1999 (up from 5.5 per cent the previous year), while underemployment rose from 60 to 63 per cent with more young people coming into the workforce each year.[24] Real wages have remained 20–25 per cent below that of pre-crisis levels. Nevertheless, macroeconomic stability has returned to Indonesia and the key indicators show modestly positive signs. The exchange rate has stabilized with the rupiah generally falling between 7,000–7,500 to the U.S. dollar, with the recent peak being 6,775 on 1 July 1998 and the trough 8,260 on 10 September 1998.[25] Wahid's accession to power saw the currency stabilize to between the 7,000–7,500 mark, although subsequent difficulties have seen the currency fall.

While Habibie's transitional government was able to implement some of the needed reform, it was undermined by evidence of corruption. In particular, the US$70 million paid from Bank Bali to Habibie aides allegedly to bolster Golkar's election war chest for the June 1999 ballot. $250 million was also unaccounted for at Semen Cibinong. This growing evidence of KKN (corruption, collusion, and nepotism) in the Habibie administration, particularly the Bank Bali scandal, in which Habibie is believed to have interfered with the debt restructuring agencies (IBRA, INDRA and JITF)[26] coupled with the TNI-backed militia violence in East Timor, caused the IMF to suspend instalments towards the end of 1999.[27] The World Bank also suspended its budget support during this time. The ambivalence of leading multilateral lenders further tarnished the image of Indonesia's commercial sector in the eyes of foreign capital. This highlights the need for a stable political environment, together with the promotion of good governance, as a *sine qua non* for the return of investor confidence and smooth transfers of IMF disbursements.

The Habibie administration also showed signs of economic nationalism, with Habibie's Minister for Co-operatives, Adi Sasono, promoting the Ekonomi Rakyat (people's economy) by giving government assistance to co-operatives. Ekonomi Rakyat had connotations of promoting *pribumi* interests as the capitalist class were assumed to be ethnic Chinese. In fact Adi Sasono sparked an argument with Singapore when he publicly criticized Singapore for allegedly harbouring "economic criminals", by which he presumably meant prominent Chinese Indonesian businesspeople who had fled to Singapore after the May 1998 riots.[28]

The Habibie administration could not shake its image as a product of the Soeharto era. Habibie's description of Soeharto as "Super Genius Soeharto" or "SGS" did not help this impression. Furthermore, Habibie could not entirely escape his past as a technolog or economic nationalist — or in the words of the *Economist Intelligence Unit*, he was unable to undo "his reputation as a profligate spender on high-tech 'white elephants'".[29] The Bank Bali scandal also demonstrated that Habibie was not entirely above the KKN problem, and in fact presided over the emergence of a growing neo-KKN at the very highest level.

THE ECONOMY UNDER WAHID

As the chapters in this volume conclude, Indonesia's economy has shown the beginnings of a modest recovery. Many commentators expect a growth rate of 4 per cent for 2000, and 5 per cent for the year after that. A healthy balance of payments due to rising exports, low inflation, and markedly lower interest rates are all positive signs. After Wahid's appointment there was a resurgence in the Jakarta Stock Exchange (JSX) to a peak in December 1999 of US$63.7 billion, although this has declined a little in the subsequent months (the market capitalization of the JSX steadily increased since the 1990s to a high of US$102 billion in June 1997 and crashed to 20 per cent of that level by January 1998). Scandals and growing concerns over stability, have seen a slight slump in the recovery. In June the rupiah fell again below the 7,000–7,500 level, and was trading at 8,395 to the U.S. dollar on 3 June 2000. This slide has continued with the rupiah settling at over 9,300 towards the end of 2000. This is a depreciation of 35 per cent in the year 2000.

In 2000, Indonesia and the IMF signed two Letters of Intent (a process that a number of contributors to this volume participated in). The January agreement included the following: the elimination of VAT exemptions, improvement of taxation laws and a four tier classification,[30] clarification and standardizing tariffs and customs administration,[31] assessment studies on the impact of the autonomy proposals, targets for loan recovery from debtors, individual restructuring targets for banks, the improvement of audits and general oversight, and improvements in company law.[32] While the IMF is still the subject of suspicion and criticism from a wide array of Indonesian subnational interests, pragmatism has ensured that the current cabinet see international assistance as vital. Co-ordinating Minister for Economic Affairs, Rizal Ramli, has remarked: "we remain committed to the International Monetary Fund programme and its role in supporting Indonesia's economic recovery".[33]

In October 2000, the Wahid administration unveiled a budget that showed some major difficulties. Largely constrained by debt repayment and subsidy spending, the assumptions of the budget were incorrect (which were that the rupiah would remain at 7,300 to the U.S. dollar, and interest rates at 11 per cent, when they have climbed to nearly 14 per cent). The budget was optimistic about the generation of revenue (petroleum, taxation, and assets sales), although high oil prices have helped to offset the shortfall. Privatization remains a problem for Indonesia, with an estimated 70 per cent of the economy in the government's hands, now that many banks and indebted corporations have been effectively nationalized. The sale of Astra in April 2000 to Singapore GLC Cycle and Carriage was seen as the first of many deals to recapitalize the teetering state-owned enterprises. The Indonesian Government is also close to privatizing Bank Central Asia, with a first tranche sale of around US$100 million. The sale of SOEs has been very slow, and is surrounded by political controversy.

DEBT AND RESTRUCTURING

While debt remains a significant problem for the Indonesian economy, declining budget deficits are forecasted. As this volume shows, there is a commitment from the Ministry of Finance to reduce the deficit from its current 5 per cent of GDP (used as a medium term economic stimulus measure) over the next few years. The overall 5 per cent deficit was announced as part of the FY2000 budget and presented to Parliament on 20 January 2000. Interestingly this issue shows that the International Monetary Fund (IMF) has had a change of heart on its earlier prescription of greater fiscal austerity, which is now widely credited with deepening the crisis. The current deficit was undertaken on IMF advice. Debt is a major issue now for Indonesia, with public debt levels estimated by the Asian Development Bank at 95 per cent of GDP, which is a fourfold increase from early 1998.[34] Debt servicing now consumes over 50 per cent of government revenue, and will continue to do so over the next few years. This seriously constrains the government's room for manoeuvre: "the debt burden is so large that the actions needed to reduce it will severely strain policy making and Indonesia's institutional capacity for implementation".[35] Good news came from the Paris Club this year — in April 2000 the Club rescheduled US$5.8 billion worth of debt until 31 March 2002, which was more than Indonesia was hoping for. In June, at the London Club, a further reschedule of US$340 million for the same time period was a welcome supplement to the original deal.

It is well known that Indonesia's banking structure, due to ineffective oversight mechanisms, has over-extended itself. When the economic crisis struck, the high percentage of non-performing loans helped to deepen the crisis and create a credit crunch. Untangling the web of Indonesia's bad loans from a vast number of private and public banks is going to be a formidable task for the Wahid administration. Non-performing loans (NPL) increased from 14 per cent prior to the crisis to 50 per cent at the height.[36] As such, recapitalization of the financial sector — to be funded by a domestic bond issue — will cost around US$90 billion or 60 per cent of GDP. The interest payable on the domestic bonds will be covered by receivership assets taken by the Indonesia Bank Restructuring Agency (IBRA). IBRA has had a lot of trouble with debtors not paying up and the whole process has lost some momentum. Since reforms to the industry in 1988, the number of banks exploded by doubling to 136 between 1988 and 1991,[37] and the number of banks had swelled to 222 by 1998. Failure to close insolvent banks by guaranteeing loans and deposits increases the moral hazard problem and fails to undertake long-term reform of the industry. However, closing down the insolvent banks can create panic among the general public causing severe bank runs, while there is a disruption of payment flows, losses (whole or partial) by account holders, and illegal removal of funds by staff. In November 1997, under the

Soeharto regime, sixteen banks were closed, including some of those connected to the Soeharto family, only to see one of his children take over a small bank soon after and resume international trading. This incident was indicative of the level of corruption that existed in the New Order. Improvements were made subsequently, but not without some substantial mistakes. In late-January 1998 a blanket guarantee of deposits and loans only deepened the NPL problem. In February fifty-five banks (fifty-four of them private banks) were determined to have a capital asset ratio (CAR) below 5 per cent and were brought under the aegis of the Indonesia Bank Restructuring Agency in the beginning of a process that Anwar Nasution describes in this volume as the virtual nationalization of the banking industry (these banks represented 40 per cent of banking sector capital[38]) and Hadi Soesastro calls the process "nationalization by default".[39] Bank Danamon became a "bridge bank" whereby the assets and liabilities of other banks could be deposited into this institution. While figures differ, the bank recapitalization programme, according to the estimates of Standard and Poors, will amount to US$80 billion, or 82 per cent of GDP.[40]

On evidence that nearly all the private banks were practically insolvent on 26 September 1998, the Governor of Bank Indonesia (BI) announced a threefold categorization of banks:[41] "A" banks, with a CAR greater than 4 per cent (Indonesia's minimum requirement as of 1998); "B" banks between –25 per cent to 4 per cent; and "C" banks below –25 per cent. Under this "triage" policy,[42] the "C" banks were to be wound up, while the "B" banks were deemed potentially worthy of recapitalization. On 13 March 1999 38 banks were closed under this scheme, 7 were taken over and 9 were considered eligible for recapitalization. Throughout this process BI and IBRA acted independently and were able to undertake their objective largely without political interference in contrast to the half-hearted attempts to reform the banking sector under Soeharto's regime. As Anwar Nasution mentions here, the aim is to raise the CAR to 11 per cent by 2003 to overcome structural flaws in the banking system in the long term.

The Jakarta Initiative Task Force (JITF) was also established to undertake negotiations between corporate debtors and creditors about restructuring loans along the lines of the so-called "London Rules" developed by the Bank of England to facilitate out-of-court settlements. By December 1999 JITF was assisting in 323 cases of restructuring worth an estimated US$23.4 billion. The Indonesian Debt Restructuring Agency (INDRA) provides some insulation against currency fluctuations for companies with debt denominated in overseas currency.

THE PROBLEM OF CORRUPTION

Cleaning up corruption[43] in the Indonesian system, estimated by the Berlin-based corruption watch group, Transparency International, to be amongst the most widespread of any country in the world, is a very complicated process.[44] This remains a monumental challenge to the Wahid administration. At the heart of the problem is a substandard legal system. Overlapping and terribly confusing laws delivered the power of discretion to officials. Coupled with a murky taxation system, the opportunities for personal enrichment were great. It was often said that Indonesian justice belonged to the highest bidder. The June 2000 court decision that went *against* former president Soeharto in his bid to sue *Time* magazine over reports of his family wealth, was seen as a positive sign of improvement in the judiciary.

In 1999 the Clean Government Law required civil servants to declare their assets, while the Eradication of Criminal Acts of Corruption Law defines what constitutes corrupt practice. Corruption in Indonesia is not just a question of the avarice of "bad people" (to use Howard Dick's phrase in this volume), and that by somehow removing the "rotten apples from the barrel" that it will fix the problem. To some extent, individuals must be prosecuted where corruption occurs, but equally the problems that beset Indonesia have also been structural — that is to say that extra payments to bureaucrats has been a necessity given the low salaries paid to civil servants (Adam Schwarz calls the salaries of Indonesia's civil servants a "retainer"[45]). Soeharto's New Order turned a blind eye to the *pungli* (informal taxes) collected by bureaucrats who wished to supplement their meagre incomes. An overall 20 per cent rise in income in 2000 for top level civil servants is designed to undercut the need for under the table payments, thus helping to evolve the bureaucracy into a more transparent institution. The problem of corruption is that it compounds income inequalities (as it favours the rich) and it acts as a distortion on the operation of the free market.[46] Clearly, recent scandals that have forced the resignations of government officials show that measures are being taken to control the problem and strengthen the judiciary to handle these issues. Kwik Kian Gie, the previous Co-ordinating Minister for Economic, Financial and Industrial Affairs, even stated that the military's involvement in commercial enterprise will come under investigation in due course, particularly Kartika Eka Paksi, which is a military front company for a range of business activities.[47]

Recent cases of corruption in the Wahid administration, or involving those close to Wahid, reveal that this problem remains a serious one.

Wahid's brother, Hasyim Wahid (or Gus Im), it was revealed in May 2000, had been appointed to IBRA secretly on 1 December 1999. Newspapers questioned his credentials to sit on the important restructuring body and generally described him as a "university drop-out". He claimed that he was able to bring nine out of twenty leading debtors to the negotiating table but has also revealed another motive: "I want to be his [Gus Dur's] Don, collecting money to finance his political activities."[48] While he promised to resign by 1 June 2000 once his "cover had been blown", there was strong disappointment over evidence of nepotism in this case. News of the appointment, when it surfaced, drove down the value of the rupiah to 8,170 against the U.S. dollar.[49]

There is also the Bulog-gate scandal when presidential aide and the then acting State Secretary, Bondan Gunawan, resigned over an attempt to divert around US$3.5 million to "humanitarian projects" in troubled provinces like Aceh. The Indonesian media have begun to suspect that there is a power struggle within the cabinet as the various political parties try to seize resources to enrich their parties for the funding of future election campaigns. Wahid's masseur is also thought to have embezzled money from Bulog (Badan Urusan Logistik Nasional (National Logistic Board)).

Indonesian Corruption Watch (ICW) also criticised Wahid for accepting a US$2 million donation from Sultan Hassanal Bolkiah of Brunei as a personal donation and putting it through unofficial channels. The president claimed the money was to be used for humanitarian projects in Aceh, but some members of parliament claimed that the bulk of the money was in the hands of those close to Wahid.[50] There has also been criticism of the slow pace of investigations into the alleged abuse of power by former president Soeharto — in any event Wahid has made it plain that he will provide a full pardon, in the interests of national unity, if Soeharto is found guilty.[51] A question mark also lingers over why the Attorney General, Marzuki Darusman, controversially chose to suspend the investigation of Marimutu Sinivasan of the Texmaco conglomerate when he reportedly refused to pay back US$1.3 billion in outstanding loans.

A major political argument is also underway, at the time of writing, about the reinstatement of Central Bank Governor, Sjahril Sabrin. Sjahril Sabrin has been under house arrest for his alleged involvement in the Bank Bali scandal. However, in the absence of a guilty verdict, he is allowed to return to his position as Indonesian law gives autonomy from government interference to the Bank.

However it is plain that corruption scandals, while clearly not going away, have been dealt with in an entirely different manner to that of the Soeharto period. Investigations by the Attorney-General have caused political embarrassment and resignations — a small measure of accountability wholly absent from the New Order. Both the Habibie and Wahid administrations, the foibles of some individuals notwithstanding, have sought to reduce the rampant corruption which was officially tolerated under the Soeharto regime, achieving greater transparency, and making the civil service less dependent on illegal payments.

SOCIAL COSTS AND SUBSIDIES

The 1999 SUSENAS survey, using a sample of 10,000 households, estimated that the poverty line fell from 11.3 per cent prior to the crisis to 20 per cent in more recent times, while UNICEF has drawn a similar conclusion (this is despite initial reports of figures reaching 50–60 per cent in some quarters of the media). Indonesia does not have what the Western world would call social welfare or social security. The "safety net" for the poor in Indonesia is an array of subsidies on basic food stuffs and fuel. In the FY1999-2000, subsidies consumed Rp50 trillion or 25 per cent of expenditure.[52] Blanket subsidies, of course, also benefit those who do not need them, and there is some debate in Indonesia over whether this government involvement really does assist the poor, as they are often not the *main* beneficiaries. Nevertheless, the issue of subsidies is a highly politicized one, as Soeharto found to his peril when his decision to remove kerosene subsidies (causing a 71 per cent fuel increase) sparked riots that ultimately lead to his departure from office. There is acknowledgement in the cabinet that there is a need to re-examine this issue and the latest budget saw a 12 per cent increase in fuel prices as the result of a decrease in that subsidy.

Political Decision-Making

In October 1999, Abdurrahman Wahid (popularly known as Gus Dur) came to power as a minority candidate, but quickly assembled a loose coalition with other parties through the "Cabinet of National Unity" including Megawati Sukarnoputri as vice-president and members of her Partai Demokrasi Indonesia-Perjuangan (PDI-P, or Indonesian Democratic Party—Struggle) as well as cabinet ministers from the military, Golongan Karya party (Golkar), Partai Amanat Nasional (PAN, or National Mandate

Party) and the president's own Partai Kebangkitan Bangsa (PKB, or National Awakening Party). The initial relevant cabinet appointments were as follows: Kwik Kian Gie, the overall Co-ordinating Minister for Economic, Financial and Industrial Affairs, and Laksamana Sukardi, Minister for Investment and State Enterprises, are both members of PDI-P. Jusuf Kalla, Minister for Industry and Trade has Golkar affiliations, while Economics Minister, Bambang Soedibyo is with PAN.

While all present cabinet ministers and main political parties broadly support the economic direction taken by the Wahid administration, there is still a lingering concern over party and personality conflict within the government. This was evidenced in the sackings of two ministers, Laksamana Sukardi and Jusuf Kalla, the former on unsubstantiated claims of corruption.[53] The replacements were Rozy Munir as Minister for Investment and State and Luhut Panjaitan as Minister for Trade and Industry.

Wahid, having initially stated that he wanted an eighteen-member cabinet, ended up with a thirty-three-member executive but was able to scale this back to twenty-six when a new cabinet was unveiled on 24 August 2000. Unlike the first cabinet, Wahid chose to appoint a cabinet largely composed of those from his own party or close supporters from outside his party. The relevant appointments are as follows: Co-ordinating Minister for Economic Affairs, Rizal Ramli; Minister of Finance, Prijadi Praptosuhardjo; and Minister for Trade and Industry, Luhut Panjaitan. Wahid's reshuffle was remarkable in the sense that he defied all expectations of either a multi-party or a non-partisan technocratic cabinet and opted for an executive mostly drawn from his party and supporters. The markets initially reacted badly to the cabinet, principally due to the inclusion of Prijadi Praptosuhardjo as Minister for Finance after he earlier failed a "fit-and-proper" test to run a minor bank. Given that the president's party, the PKB, took less than 13 per cent of the vote, although this current cabinet is more solidified, it will struggle to appease a greatly empowered legislature in newly democratized Indonesia.

Gus Dur has also turned to alternative sources of economic advice — not being an expert on the economy himself — and has established two circles outside cabinet. The first, an advisory team, is headed by the architect of Indonesia's post-1966 recovery, Widjojo Nitisastro, and includes Faisal Basri. The second is the official National Economic Council (DEN) headed by experienced Soeharto cabinet minister and subsequent critic of the New Order, Emil Salim, and also includes Sri Mulyani Indrawati. These prominent advisors are known as the "whisperers" and appear to be growing in influence. For example, when elements of the bureaucracy publicly flirted with the idea of a Malaysian-style currency board, Wahid rejected this idea on the advice of Sri Mulyani Indrawati and others.

Continued demands for independence in Aceh and Irian Jaya, inter-communal violence in South Maluku, and rising levels of crime, have served to give financial investors the jitters over returning to Indonesia. The regional autonomy, which gives greater powers to the districts and some provinces, seems unclear and its revenue sharing provisions ill-defined. International investors, rightly or wrongly, continue to have negative perceptions about the long-term stability of Indonesia. Wahid's greatest challenge is to re-establish confidence in the governance of Indonesia. Wahid must work within a political environment much different to that fostered by Soeharto. Now, the executive is answerable to an invigorated parliament. While this will have the benefit of a greater check on presidential power — something sorely lacking in the New Order — it will also make it more difficult to push through unpopular economic changes that may be needed for long-term stability.

DECENTRALIZATION

The reality is that power has already shifted to the provinces since the fall of Soeharto. Local government machinery, heavily manipulated under the New Order regime, has gained greater power since Indonesia's democratization. Law No. 22/1999 and No. 25/1999 passed in May 1999 and not in full force until May 2001, state that power will be devolved mainly to the district level (not to the thirty-two provinces) under an arrangement in which central government retain the functions of defence, foreign affairs, justice, overall monetary and fiscal policy, religion and the development of natural and human resources. While the demands for greater autonomy are a response to the perceived Java-centric policies of Soeharto, the reforms entail a number of problems. Cornelis Lay, from Gadjah Mada University, argues that on available evidence, the devolution of power will not undermine the problems of corruption and abuse of power. This is so ingrained that the shifting of power also means the shifting of the "locus of KKN" (corruption, collusion and nepotism) from the bureaucracy to local parliaments.[54] It is also true that many districts will not have the necessary human capital to run government services. Furthermore, the law, as it stands, is still ambiguous in a number of areas and funding allocation is not clear. However, to take the case of Riau, which produces 50 per cent of Indonesia's oil, received only Rp821 billion (US$108 million) of the wealth generated in the last financial year, or 1.4

per cent of the total returns from the oil resource.[55] The fact that 98.6 per cent of returns go to Jakarta has increased demands for greater autonomy over resource use. Wahid has promised to allow Riau to keep the profits from oil exploitation when it renegotiates the contract with PT Caltex Pacific in 2001.[56] An official of the Bappenas has argued that under the current proposal ten provinces would be bankrupt while four resource rich provinces will make "enormous gains".[57]

CONCLUDING REMARKS

Kwik Kian Gie stated while he was Co-ordinating Minister for Economic, Financial and Industrial Affairs in Wahid's last cabinet: "If I were a foreign investor, I wouldn't come to Indonesia."[58] This frank, off-the-cuff, admission by a senior cabinet minister is quite revealing. Confidence in the Indonesian economy remains low as the economy is not growing as fast as expected due to corruption scandals and the perceptions of growing political instability. A survey of Indonesia's economy shows a disturbing trend towards sound economic management during recession, followed by mismanagement when economic growth returns. In this sense the economy is also path dependent. It remains to be seen if the Wahid administration can break this cycle, however the recent evidence suggests that while Wahid seems to be personally above questionable dealings, the same cannot be said for many close to him.

THE CHAPTERS

The sharp-eyed reader will note, as the editor has, that there are some minor discrepancies over some key economic data — inflation levels, interest rate levels, growth levels for the coming year, the estimated inflation rate for 2000, the overall government deficit, and levels of indebtedness. Partly, there is dispute over some of these indicators given the opaque nature of Indonesia's record keeping — something that most contributors recognize as requiring great improvement as Indonesia attempts to bring about greater transparency. However, this data does not vary markedly, which is to say that the contributors are in general (but not specific) agreement on the data at hand. A choice was made not to try to "correct" these differences as they are part and parcel of the position statements from each contributor. Furthermore, the contributions found here are also reflective of the debate in Jakarta and the different perspectives on the direction that the Indonesian economy should take. By reading the chapters the reader can ascertain the nature of this discussion.

This introductory chapter is designed to give the general reader a starting point to the topics dealt with by the subsequent chapters of this volume. While many of the details here will be well-known to specialists, it is important to establish a picture of the Indonesian economy and specifically explain some of the themes that are referred to by the contributors.

The chapters written by Anwar Nasution and Boediono provide a comprehensive overview of Indonesia's macroeconomic situation. Anwar Nasution is cautiously optimistic about the prospects for a recovery and gives a survey of improving economic indicators. Boediono generally shares these conclusions but expresses the concern that complacency will set in amongst Indonesian decision makers slowing down the speed of much needed reforms. Bambang Kusumanto follows on from this by outlining the problems inherited by the Wahid administration and explaining the main methods of the Ministry of Finance's economic stabilization policy — a mixture of monetary restraint and an expansionary fiscal policy. Anthony Chan, from USAID's Indonesia office, stresses in his contribution that improving governance, including the legal system, enforcement and audit mechanisms, corporate and banking restructuring and so on, will be the primary means by which to attract foreign capital back into Indonesia. Joshua Felman, from the IMF's Indonesia office, praises Bank Indonesia (BI or the central bank) for its rapid and effective control over inflation with a base money policy. He refutes speculation that BI may be insolvent.

Sri Mulyani Indrawati examines the nature of the official budget and questions the government's overall fiscal policy, including whether a 5 per cent deficit was really the right level. She also questions the use of off-budget expenditures which makes the true record of Indonesia's government spending a murky picture. This chapter also discusses some of the problems of budgetary allocation in the proposal to decentralize authority in Indonesia in 2001. The issue of corruption is discussed by Howard Dick. He concludes that the only way to control the problem of corruption is to undermine the root causes rather than to focus on individuals. Rent seeking behaviour by firms is seen as far more serious than widespread low level corruption by civil servants. Mark Baird argues that there are five crucial issues for the economy: the fiscal deficit, civil service salaries, subsidies, decentralization, and the development programme. Noor Fuad, Director General of the Indonesian Ministry of Finance, and speaking for his minister, outlines a series of steps that the ministry will take to improve the economic performance, including, improvements in taxation, increasing civil service remuneration to reduce inflation, a reorientation of public expenditure, funding for poverty alleviation and SMEs, and a reduction in the budget deficit over the medium term.

Social issues form the basis of the next three chapters. Anggito Abimanyu produces a comprehensive set of data to show the impact of the financial crisis on the lives of ordinary Indonesians. Amongst his findings is that fact that the impact of the crisis was uneven across Indonesia, with some outlying areas remaining relatively unaffected. He concludes with recommendations about how to try to alleviate the effects of poverty. Mohammad Ikhsan echoes Anggito's findings on poverty after the crisis but also maintains that improvements in social conditions are evident with an improving economy. Aris Ananta upholds people-centred development, as exemplified by the United Nations' Human Development Index (HDI), as necessary to supplement more traditional economic indicators. To improve human capital, Aris Ananta argues that three things are needed — education, health and "freedom from fear". While others in this volume express reservations about what decentralization will mean, Aris Ananta strongly advocates this as a solution to some of Indonesia's pressing problems.

The two contributions by two authors who were cabinet ministers at the time of writing give the reader an insight into some thoughts of those who sit in the executive. For His Excellency Laksamana Sukardi, Indonesia has been poorly served by the authoritarianism of Soeharto which is responsible for poor governance and regional tensions. He also supports a more aggressive approach to the sale of state assets. His Excellency Jusuf Kalla argues that the scrutiny of parliament, the media and multilateral financial institutions means that the Wahid government must undertake consistency in action and deed. Kalla does go against the prevailing wisdom to argue that there are no major problems in the real sector, and that private businesses are avoiding paying back their loans but this is due to businessmen keeping their money in bank accounts rather than to a shortage of capital.

The details of bank restructuring are the focus of the next three chapters. Farid Harianto, deputy chairman of IBRA, gives an insight into the options available to the Agency to achieve proper CAR levels in the various banks. To complete the picture, Gunarni Soeworo, the head of the Indonesian Bankers Association, gives a practitioner's view of the problems that beset the banking industry. Both agree that there is a serious problem, and that the revival of a strong banking sector is essential for long-term economic stability in Indonesia. Sri Adiningsih completes the picture and argues that a proper legal infrastructure will be necessary to ensure the long-term liquidity of the banking sector.

Corporate debt, an issue linked to the debt problems in the banking sector, is the theme of the next two chapters. Jusuf Anwar, director of the Jakarta Initiative Task Force (JITF), and Franky Widjaja, managing director of the Sinar Mas Group, provide two contributions from their different stations. Jusuf Anwar stresses the desire to create "win-win" situations where creditors regain significant capital while at the same time businesses stay afloat. JITF, it is argued, wishes to achieve a number of out-of-court settlements. Frank Widjaja, from his perspective in the private sector, argues that the solution to the problem rests with government as foreign investment and credit ratings will be contingent on Indonesia's overall performance.

The next two chapters offer the reader an insight into the debate over industrial policy. H. S. Dillon argues that the growth in the agricultural sector after the financial crisis should be further encouraged by the abandonment of the cheap rice policy. Dillon argues that Indonesia needs to move back to farming, which he sees as being a strength of the Indonesian economy. Faisal Basri disagrees with this orientation, arguing that although agriculture has risen as a percentage of GDP, the long-term future is in the promotion of the secondary and tertiary sectors. To Faisal Basri there is a need to promote SMEs, not through the picking of state favourites, but through the availability of capital, a reduction in bureaucratic red tape, and the creation of regional autonomy.

Last of all, two of Indonesia's most respected and influential economic commentators, Emil Salim, head of the National Economic Council, and Mohammad Sadli, chairman of the Indonesia Forum Foundation, give their final thoughts on the Indonesian economy. Emil Salim gives a lot of credit to the Habibie administration for laying the framework for the modest economic recovery. He states that Wahid is favourably disposed to foreign interests and suggests that Indonesia will not consider cutting itself off from the outside world. Mohamad Sadli gives the reader an insight into the role of advisors in Indonesia — both under Soeharto and Wahid — revealing something of the prominent role that Emil Salim is now playing in the Wahid administration, but from behind the scenes. He awards the Wahid administration a "B average" for its overall economic performance but states that this will improve if Wahid successfully tackles corporate debt.

December 2000

Notes

1. Hal Hill, *The Indonesian Economy*, 2nd ed. (Cambridge: Cambridge University Press, 2000), pp. 1, 32.
2. H. W. Arndt, "Survey of Recent Developments", *Bulletin of Indonesian Economic Studies*, no. 8 (October 1966), p. 4, cited in Anne Booth, *The Indonesian Economy in the Nineteenth and Twentieth Century: A History of Missed Opportunities* (New York: St Martin's Press, 1998), p. 73.
3. Anne Booth, *The Indonesian Economy in the Nineteenth and Twentieth Century: A History of Missed Opportunities* (New York: St Martin's Press, 1998), p. 71.
4. Ibid., p. 178.
5. Leonard C. Sebastion and Reza Y. Siregar, "Indonesia: Setting the Stage for Soeharto's Re-election", in *Southeast Asian Affairs 1996* (Singapore: Institute of Southeast Asian Studies, 1996), p. 181.
6. Hill, *Indonesian Economy*, pp. 43-62.
7. Adam Schwarz, *A Nation in Waiting: Indonesia's Search for Stability* (NSW: Allen & Unwin, 1999), p. 55.
8. These ideas are outlined in B. J. Habibie, *Ilmu Pengetahuan Teknologi dan Pembangunan Bangsa: Menuju Dimensi Baru Pembangunan* (Jakarta: Cidesindo, October 1995).
9. World Bank, "Who Controls East Asian Corporations — and the Implications for Legal Reform", *Public Policy for the Private Sector*, [not dated].
10. Ibid.
11. Michael Vatikiotis, *Indonesian Politics Under Suharto: The Rise and Fall of the New Order* (New York: Routledge, 1998), p. 177.
12. It is reported that Soeharto even put pressure on Malaysia's Prime Minister, Dr Mahathir, to sign the agreement.
13. Hill, *Indonesian Economy*, p. 95.
14. Michael Vatikiotis, *Indonesian Politics Under Suharto: The Rise and Fall of the New Order* (New York: Routledge, 1998), pp. 170-71.
15. Hal Hill, *The Indonesian Economy Since 1966: Southeast Asia's Emerging Giant* (Cambridge: Cambridge University Press, 1996), p. 261.
16. Michael Vatikiotis, op. cit., p. 165.
17. Valerie Cerra and Sweta Chaman Saxena, "Contagion, Monsoons, and Domestic Turmoil in Indonesia: A Case Study in the Asian Currency Crisis", *IMF Policy Discussion Paper*, March 2000, p. 5.
18. Although this last figure is misleading. Indonesia has had a practice of operating extra-budgetary expenditure, while including overseas assistance and loans as income, which gives the appearance of balanced books. In reality, a small deficit was incurred in the years during the run up to the crisis.
19. Paul Krugman, *The Return of Depression Economics* (New York: W. W. Norton and Company, 1999), p. 97.
20. Ramkishen Rajan, "Currency Basket Regimes for Southeast Asia: The Worst System with the Exception of All Others", Seminar at Institute of Southeast Asian Studies, Singapore, 1 June 2000.
21. Manuel F. Montes, *The Currency Crisis in Southeast Asia*, Updated Edition, (Singapore: Institute of Southeast Asian Studies, 1998), p. xv. In fact the rupiah sunk to its lowest

point around the time that Habibie was nominated as Soeharto's vice-president. When Lee Kuan Yew, Singapore's Senior Minister, predicted that this would be the case, he sparked a bilateral dispute between Indonesia and Singapore.

22. Asian Development Bank, *Asian Development Outlook 2000* (Hong Kong: Oxford University Press, 2000), p. 90.
23. Ibid.
24. Ibid.
25. World Bank, *Indonesia: Macroeconomic Update*, 31 January 2000, p. 1.
26. See Hadi Soesastro, "The Indonesian Economy Under Abdurrahman Wahid", in *Southeast Asian Affairs 2000* (Singapore: Institute of Southeast Asian Studies, 2000), p. 140.
27. Nick Freeman, "Economic Outlook 2000-2001: The ASEAN-6", in *Regional Outlook: Southeast Asia 2000-2001*, Daljit Singh and Nick Freeman, eds. (Singapore: Institute of Southeast Asian Studies, 2000), p. 52.
28. Adi failed to name individuals or make further clarifications, leading to suspicions in Singapore that ethnic Chinese businessmen and women would be targeted. He did warn Singapore that the relationship would undergo a substantial change under a "new Indonesia in the making": "... there won't be a Liem Sioe Liong or Anthony Salim or those connected to Soeharto to give concessions in Bintan anymore, for example. Indonesia will change and Singapore has to adjust to that fact." "Adi wants extraction treaty with S'pore", *Jakarta Post*, 26 December 1998, p. 2.
29. "Country Profile: Indonesia: 1998-99", London: *Economist Intelligence Unit*, 1998, p. 5.
30. Hal Hill argues that during the Soeharto years that so many wealthy people were able to avoid paying taxes that rather than being progressive, tax collection "may even be regressive". Hill, *Indonesian Economy*, p. 64.
31. During the Soeharto regime tariff levels and products covered by tariffs were nearly impossible to determine. Customs procedures were similarly opaque.
32. Duplication and lack of clarity has, in the past, given enormous discretionary power to individual bureaucrats. It is widely acknowledged that this is a leading cause of corruption. Clearly defined institutions, with proper transparency, can considerably assist the reduction in incidents of corruption.
33. Rizal Ramli, "Nurturing Growth and Democracy", *Asian Wall Street Journal*, 23 October 2000.
34. Asian Development Bank, *Asian Development Outlook 2000* (Hong Kong: Oxford University Press, 2000), p. 92.
35. World Bank, *Indonesia: Macroeconomic Update*, 31 January 2000, p. 2.
36. Soesastro, op. cit., p. 136. Other estimates put the figure at anywhere between 60-90 per cent of GDP.
37. Schwarz, op. cit., p. 57.
38. Charles Enoch, "Interventions in Banks During Banking Crises: The Experience of Indonesia", *IMF Policy Discussion Paper*, March 2000, p. 9.
39. Soesastro, op. cit., p. 136.
40. Dan Murphy and Ben Dolven, "Now, Back to Work", *Far Eastern Economic Review*, 24 June 1999, p. 51.
41. Enoch, op. cit, p. 19.
42. Ibid., p. 28.
43. Defining corruption is not altogether easy. James Scott argues that corruption should

be defined as a deviation from accepted standards of behaviour or breaching the rules of office with the objective of improving one's personal wealth or status. James C Scott, *Comparative Political Corruption* (Englewood Cliffs, N. J.: Prentice-Hall Inc., 1972), pp. 3-4.

44. See <www.transparency.de/documents/cpi/index.html>. Transparency International rank Indonesia 96 out of 99 countries surveyed, only polling better than Cameroon and Nigeria, and drawing level with Azerbaijan. Transparency International admit that the ranking of countries in terms of levels of corruption is methodologically problematic, nevertheless Indonesia's position does point to a rather serious problem.
45. Schwarz, op. cit., p. 136.
46. For a good overview of the effects of corruption, see Kimberley Ann Elliott, ed., *Corruption and the Global Economy* (Washington, D.C.: Institute for International Economics, 1997). Elliott notes in her introduction that the IMF and the World Bank announced revisions to their previous views in June 1996 of corruption — which was to tolerate it — arguing that it was an impediment to growth. This pre-dates the crisis, but there is little doubt that the economic crisis solidified the resolve of these multilateral institutions.
47. The military has also suffered from low pay, while military expenditure as a whole has been partly undertaken through TNI business ventures. In East Timor, for example, a military front company took control of coffee production in order to generate extra income for high ranking officers and help fund the military operation in the territory.
48. Interview with Gus Im in Susan Sim, "My brother the president", *Straits Times*, 7 June 2000, p. 24.
49. "Gus Dur's brother joins bank agency as an expert", *Straits Times*, 11 May 2000, p. 19. Gus Im went on to state that his role as an "arm twister" was necessary as "Indonesia is now more corrupt than Chicago in 1929".
50. "Donation from Brunei questioned", *Jakarta Post*, 13 June 2000.
51. See for example, "Suharto to be pardoned if guilty", *Sunday Times*, 12 March 2000, p. 21.
52. Soesastro, op. cit., p. 143.
53. There is wide suspicion that Megawati's husband, Taufik Kiemas, wanted the removal of Laksamana who was regarded as being "too zealous" in pursuing good governance. Peter Montragnon and Tom McCrawley, "Signs of recovery belie strain in Gus Dur's govt", *Straits Times*, 18 May 2000, p. 81.
54. Cornelis Lay, "Centre-Regional Relations in Indonesia", Seminar at the Institute of Southeast Asian Studies, Singapore, 28 April 2000.
55. Margot Cohen, "Chorus of Discontent", *Far Eastern Economic Review*, 17 February 2000, p. 24.
56. "Riau 'to manage its own oil fields'", *Straits Times*, 1 May 2000, p. 19.
57. Cited in Harold Crouch, "Indonesia: Democratization and the Threat of Disintegration", in *Southeast Asian Affairs 2000* (Singapore: Institute of Southeast Asian Studies, 2000), p. 126.
58. John Aglionby, "Indonesia gripped by violence", *Guardian Weekly*, 1 June 2000, p. 1.

SECTION I
The Macroeconomy in Year 2000

2

Meltdown of the Indonesian Economy
Causes, Impacts, Responses, and Lessons

Anwar Nasution

INTRODUCTION

Since 1998, Indonesia has suffered from twin interrelated crises, namely a political crisis and an economic crisis. The politically weak and technically less competent governments of President Soeharto and President B. J. Habibie could not take bold, daring, but sometimes unpopular, demand- and supply-side measures, that are normally required by a short-run stabilization programme. Medium and long-term economic reforms were equally difficult.

The present economic crisis is a combination of a banking crisis and an external debt crisis, and it has been sparked by a combination of both external and internal factors. The external factors include: (a) regional recession, currency realignment, contagion effects, and the loss of business confidence that have induced capital flow reversal; (b) the abnormal weather phenomena that has seriously affected food output and agriculture incomes in the rural sector; and (c) negative terms of trade. Until recently, the price of oil had dropped to below US$10 per barrel, the lowest price in the past twelve years.

CAUSES OF THE ECONOMIC CRISIS

The home-grown problems, which are the focus of this chapter, include: a fragile financial sector; monetary and exchange rate policies that accommodated an excessive growth of money supply and bank credits; allowance of the rapid accumulation of private sector's external debt; and the reduced quality of investment. Slow response and policy mistakes stifled the reform process and magnified the existing difficult problems.

The "strong" economic fundamentals (a low inflation rate, high economic growth and a respectable growth in non-oil exports), as boasted by the authorities prior to the crisis, turned out to be artificial. The low inflation rate came at a high price in the form of subsidies to state-vended products. The high rate of economic growth (6 per cent or more per annum) was mainly generated by the non-traded sector of the economy — such as land based industry, physical infrastructure and the financial system. The majority of growth in the non-oil export sector during the 1990s consisted of those sectors which relied least on domestic inputs and were associated with foreign firms. In contrast, those which were domestically owned, and relied on domestic inputs, fared poorly.

STRUCTURE OF EXTERNAL DEBT

The external debt problem in Indonesia revolves around private sector debt, not public sector debt. A few years prior to the crisis, the authorities had maintained the formal budget in "surplus" between 0.5 to 1 per cent of the GDP. The consolidated budget of the public sector, however, may be in deficit due to the large "extra budget" (popularly known as "non-budget") expenditures of the public sector at large. The extra budget items include the financial transactions of state-owned enterprises, and contingency liabilities of government sponsored projects owned by well connected private sector companies or the one time former Minister for Research and Technology (later President) B. J. Habibie.

The external debt of Indonesia grew rapidly following the reform of the economy, particularly the banking sector reform in October 1988 (see Table 2.1). Over 60 per cent of the debt was owed by the private sector and nearly 90 per cent of this was to the non-banking private sector. Most of the private sector external debt was short-term in nature and unhedged. In the final analysis the private sector debt was turned into public debt as domestic firms were protected from bankruptcy procedures and external takeovers.

The key element that turned the debt problem into the external debt crisis was the sudden change in the rate of net resource transfers from positive to negative. The reluctance of foreign lenders to roll over short-

TABLE 2.1
Indonesia: External Debt Outstanding, 1989–99
(In US$ millions)

	1989	1990	1991	1992	1993	1994	1995	1996	1997	1998	1999[a]
External Debt Outstanding	51,974.7	62,820.6	65,697.2	73,358.9	80,591.8	96,500.1	107,831.9	110,170.8	134,794.3	150,886.1	142,415.2
Public Sector	39,576.9	45,100.2	45,724.7	48,768.7	52,461.4	58,615.6	59,588.2	55,302.6	53,865.0	67,328.2	70,786.0
Private Sector	12,397.8	17,720.4	19,972.5	24,590.2	28,130.4	37,884.5	48,243.7	54,868.2	80,929.3	83,557.9	71,629.2
The Structure of Private Sector External Debt (%)											
By Debtors											
1. Banks	**6.4**	**14.8**	**17.1**	**23.4**	**27.6**	**21.7**	**20.9**	**16.5**	**17.7**	**12.9**	**13.4**
- State-owned Banks	3.4	6.4	7.0	10.3	11.1	7.3	8.0	5.4	7.3	5.7	6.0
- Private Banks	3.0	8.4	10.2	13.1	16.5	14.4	12.9	11.1	10.4	7.2	7.4
2. Non-bank	**93.6**	**85.2**	**82.9**	**76.6**	**72.4**	**78.3**	**79.1**	**83.5**	**71.2**	**80.8**	**82.1**
- State-Owned Enterprise	26.0	17.6	16.8	18.4	18.0	13.4	10.0	6.8	4.9	5.0	5.8
- Foreign Investment Enterprise	26.4	26.4	25.8	22.7	21.2	25.3	27.0	29.9	29.0	38.8	41.8
- Domestic Investment Enterprise	23.0	23.0	22.5	19.8	18.5	22.1	23.5	26.1	20.4	24.1	21.3
- Financing Institution	3.9	3.9	3.8	3.3	3.1	3.7	3.9	4.4	4.2	2.5	2.2
- Others	14.4	14.4	14.1	12.4	11.6	13.8	14.7	16.3	12.6	10.4	10.9
By Maturity											
- Short-term	6.9	6.9	6.9	6.9	6.9	6.9	6.9	6.9	6.1	6.5	6.6
- Long-term	93.1	93.1	93.1	93.1	93.1	93.1	93.1	93.1	82.8	87.2	88.9
Memo items:											
1. Share of Government Debt to Total Debt (%)	76.1	71.8	69.6	66.5	65.1	60.7	55.3	50.2	40.0	44.6	49.7
2. Share of Private Debt to Total Debt (%)	23.9	28.2	30.4	33.5	34.9	39.3	44.7	49.8	60.0	55.4	50.3
3. Share of Total Debt to Real GDP (%)	36.7	43.2	44.6	48.4	51.2	59.1	63.6	62.5	99.4	396.2	n.a.
4. Share of Total Debt to Export (%)	234.5	244.7	225.4	216.0	218.9	240.9	237.4	221.2	252.2	308.9	n.a.

[a]As of August 1999.

Source: Bank Indonesia, *Recent Economic Indicators*, various issues (1989–99).

term debt, coupled with capital flight in 1997–1998, sharply increased risk premiums on loans and drove up interest rates.

Table 2.1 shows that as of March 1999 Indonesia's total external debt amounted to 160 per cent of GDP, or 215 per cent of exports. Debt service ratio was about 33 per cent of the total export value. These figures are relatively high by international standards and could cause transfer and fiscal problems.[1]

THE FRAGILE FINANCIAL SECTOR AND EXCHANGE RATE MANAGEMENT

The Wrong Sequence of Financial Sector Policy Reforms

In terms of total assets and real estate, the banking system is the core of the financial system in Indonesia. The long period of credit ceiling cum selective credit policy with subsidized interest rates, prior to 1983, had encouraged the corporate sector to adopt a high debt-equity-ratio. This policy was reinforced by taxation and regulatory policy that favoured credit financing. The banking system mainly operates on a collateral basis and land and buildings are the main forms of collaterals for an extension of credit.

The rapid financial liberalization was not accompanied by commensurate strengthening of regulation and supervision as well as a clear cut "exit policy". The high percentage of group lending, for example, indicates that the legal lending limits regulations were hardly implemented. Inadequate financial regulation allowed banks to make excessive risky loans without adequate monitoring. One manifestation of this was overbuilding in the non-traded sector of the economy — such as real estate and infrastructural projects — as well as in the traded sector that requires a lot of imported inputs and produces low value added.

To keep financially distressed banks afloat, Bank Indonesia injected liquidity credit to these banks during the period of August 1997 to early 1998. The liquidity was sterilized by issuing SBI — Bank Indonesia's certificate of deposits (see Figure 2.1). The sterilization operation and the shifting of public sector's deposits from commercial banks to the central bank raised interest rates (see Figure 2.2). As if this were not enough, in January 1998, the authorities provided a blanket guarantee for all (domestic and external) liabilities of the commercial banks.

FIGURE 2.1

Share Liquidity Credit to Base Money (BM), Share of Intervention (IR) to Open Market Operation (OMO), and Share of Liquidity Credit to BM and OMO, 1995–99

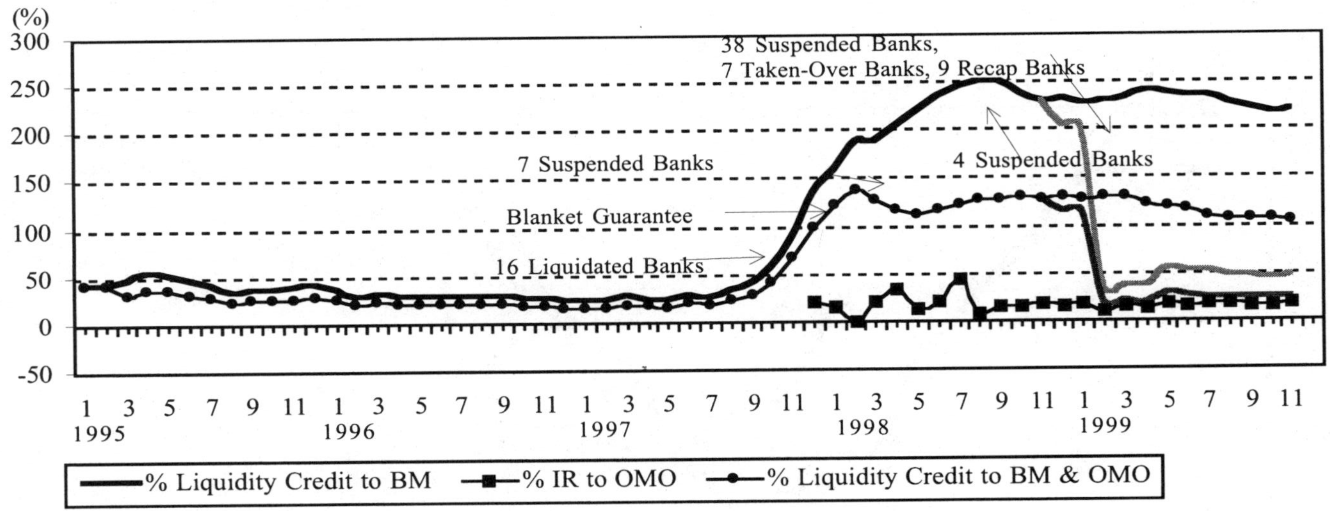

Having been converted into government bonds, comprise of Rp17.2 trillion for Exim Bank (December 1998) and Rp144,5 trillion for 10 Suspended Banks, 4 Taken-Over Banks, 24 Supervised Banks under IBRA and 16 Banks in Liquidation (February 1999).

Chronology: Liquidation of 16 banks, 1 November 1997; Blanket Guarantee, 29 January 1998; The suspension of 7 banks, 4 April 1998; The suspension of 4 banks, 21 August 1998; The suspension of 38 banks, the take-over of 7 banks and the recapitalization of 9 banks, 13 March 1999.

Source: Bank Indonesia.

FIGURE 2.2
Inflation, One Month SBI Rate and Exchange Rate, 1997–99

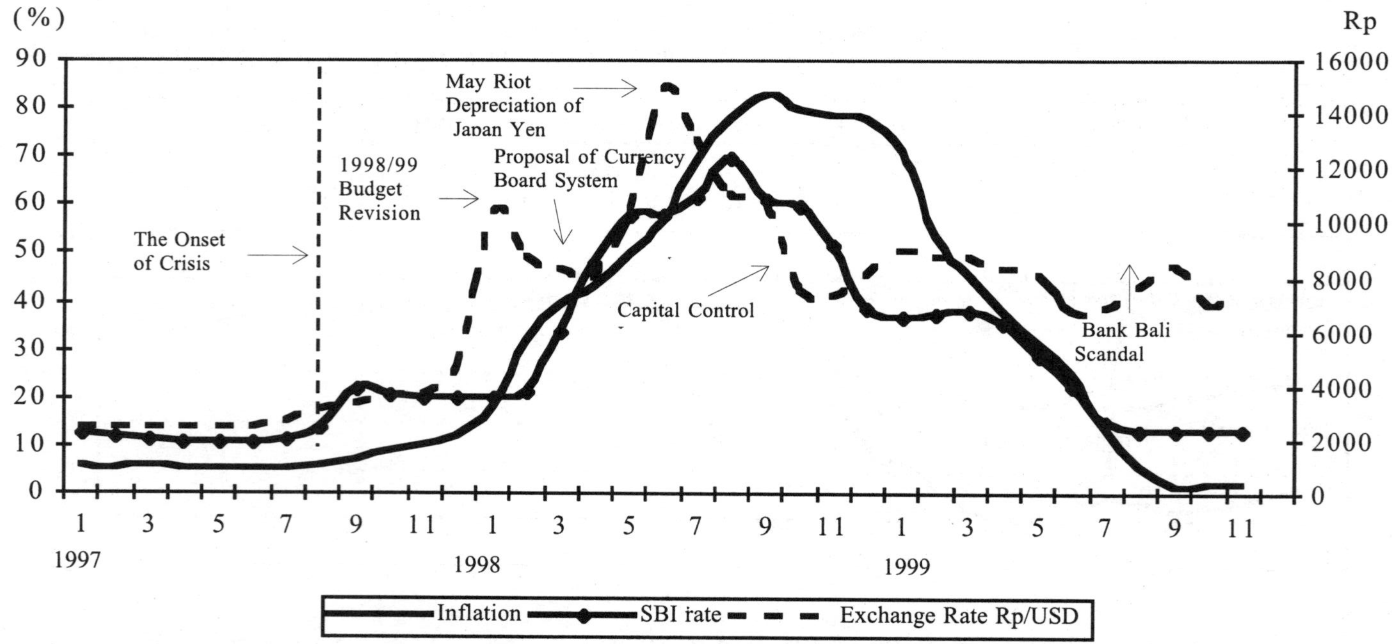

Source: Bank Indonesia.

Fragile Banking System

Table 2.2 shows the indicators of the fragility of the banking sector. The table shows a sharp increase in the non-performing loan (NPL) ratio (see also Figure 2.3) indicates the severe economic slow-down and the series of corporate bankruptcies since 1997. The raising NPL ratio drives up operating costs of the banks. To cover the immediate losses from NPLs, banks are required to accumulate provisions until they can recover part of the credits or to write off from the balance sheet. There is also interest costs for carrying NPLs on the balance sheet. The high NPLs has also caused a negative spread between lending and deposit interest rates.

Banks and their customers are in financial difficulty because of a combination of a number of factors. The sharp devaluation of the rupiah has correspondingly raised (measured in the rupiah) their foreign liabilities. The deposit base of the banks was eroded further due to a combination of capital flight, bank runs, panic buying, extremely high interest rates and the plummet in share prices. The financial conditions of both banks and the corporate sector was also made worse by the tight internal and external liquidity. An "over-stretched" banking system was evidenced by a high loan-to-deposit ratio and the rising difference between loan growth rate minus GDP growth rate. Higher exposure of the banking system to foreign exchange risk is shown by an increasing ratio of foreign liabilities to total liabilities. Part of the short-term external borrowings in foreign currencies has been used to finance medium- and long-term domestic credit in the rupiah. This has caused currency and maturity mismatches.

The franchise value of the banks was actually rising, and getting stronger, as is shown by a relatively low cash ratio or small amount of cash assets, and a relatively high loan to asset ratio. As depicted in Table 2.2, the stronger franchise value should have given greater incentive to banks to monitor and discipline their borrowers to retain liquidity. In reality this did not happen partly because of weak implementation of the rules and regulations governing the banking system and large group lending.

THE EXCHANGE RATE SYSTEM

Indonesia adopted a reverse sequence of what is considered standard economic reform. Liberalization of the capital account was completed in 1971, long before the liberalization of the current account of the balance of payments initiated in the second half of the 1980s. In the past, the foreign exchange system caused no problem for Indonesia simply because there was no reputable company that had access to international financial

TABLE 2.2
Indonesia: Banking Sector Indicators, 1985–99

	1985	1986	1987	1988	1989	1990	1991	1992	1993	1994	1995	1996	1997	1998	1999[d]
Number of Banks	114	110	109	108	145	171	192	208	234	240	240	239	222	222	16
Private Banks	69	65	64	63	88	109	129	144	161	166	165	164	144	130	80
State-owned Banks[a]	5	5	5	5	5	7	7	7	7	7	7	7	7	7	19
Foreign Banks and Joint Venture Banks	11	11	11	11	23	28	29	30	39	40	41	41	44	58	41
Regional Development Banks	29	29	29	29	29	27	27	27	27	27	27	27	27	27	27
Loan to Deposit Ratio (%)	102,9	96,3	101,9	105,7	112,6	118,2	130,7	129,3	132,4	134,9	137,7	131,0	123,7	129,2	80,7
LGR Minus GDPGR (%)	14,7	19,8	8,8	23,1	31,2	48,1	–9,9	7,7	6,9	5,7	4,0	4,7	12,1	45,5	–42,6
LGR Minus IPGR (%)	29,0	20,8	35,9	34,4	44,2	61,4	9,0	25,9	22,4	16,0	23,1	22,5	16,2	45,1	n.a.
NFL to TBL (%)	–20,0	–23,6	–18,2	–14,1	–10,6	0,9	0,7	2,2	4,9	5,8	3,8	2,8	5,2	2,6	6,4
M2 Multiplier[b]	3,4	3,4	3,8	5,0	5,4	6,7	7,7	7,0	7,8	7,4	8,0	7,5	7,6	7,7	8,2
M2/Forex Reserves (%)	414,2	415,4	367,5	481,5	597,2	596,8	539,0	552,6	602,3	643,4	690,3	638,6	419,9	407,5	549,1
Non-performing loan[c]	n.a.	n.a.	n.a.	n.a.	n.a.	n.a.	9,2	n.a.	14,2	12,1	10,4	8,8	14,0	63,3	63,8
of which: Bad Debt	n.a.	n.a.	n.a.	n.a.	n.a.	n.a.	1,7	n.a.	3,3	4,0	3,3	2,9	2,3	23,4	28,5
Cash Assets to Deposit Ratio	15,9	13,3	12,4	14,5	11,1	6,5	13,7	3,2	2,6	2,5	2,6	4,7	5,8	8,2	7,5
Loans to Assets Ratio	n.a.	53,3	58,2	61,5	65,4	73,4	76,2	73,7	75,4	80,3	79,2	77,0	71,9	70,9	66,7

Notes: Loan Growth Rate (LGR), GDP Growth Rate (GDPGR), Industrial Production Growth Rate (IPGR), Net Foreign Liabilities (NFL), Total Bank Liabilities (TBL)

[a] Including the takeover of 12 banks by the Indonesian Banks Restructuring Agency (IBRA), as of June 1999.

[b] Ratio of M2 to Reserve Money.

[c] As percentage of total loan outstanding of Commercial Banks. Non-performing loan data tends to be underestimated. The decline of non-performing loans to 8.8 per cent of total credit in 1996 was mainly due to write-offs of the bad loans at state commercial banks and private "non-foreign exchange" banks. At end of March 1998, bank non-performing loans reached over 70 per cent of total loan for several banks.

[d] Data as of June 1999.

Sources: IMF, *International Financial Statistics*, various issues; Bank Indonesia, *Annual Report*, various issues.

FIGURE 2.3
The Emergence of Non-Performing Loans, 1997–99

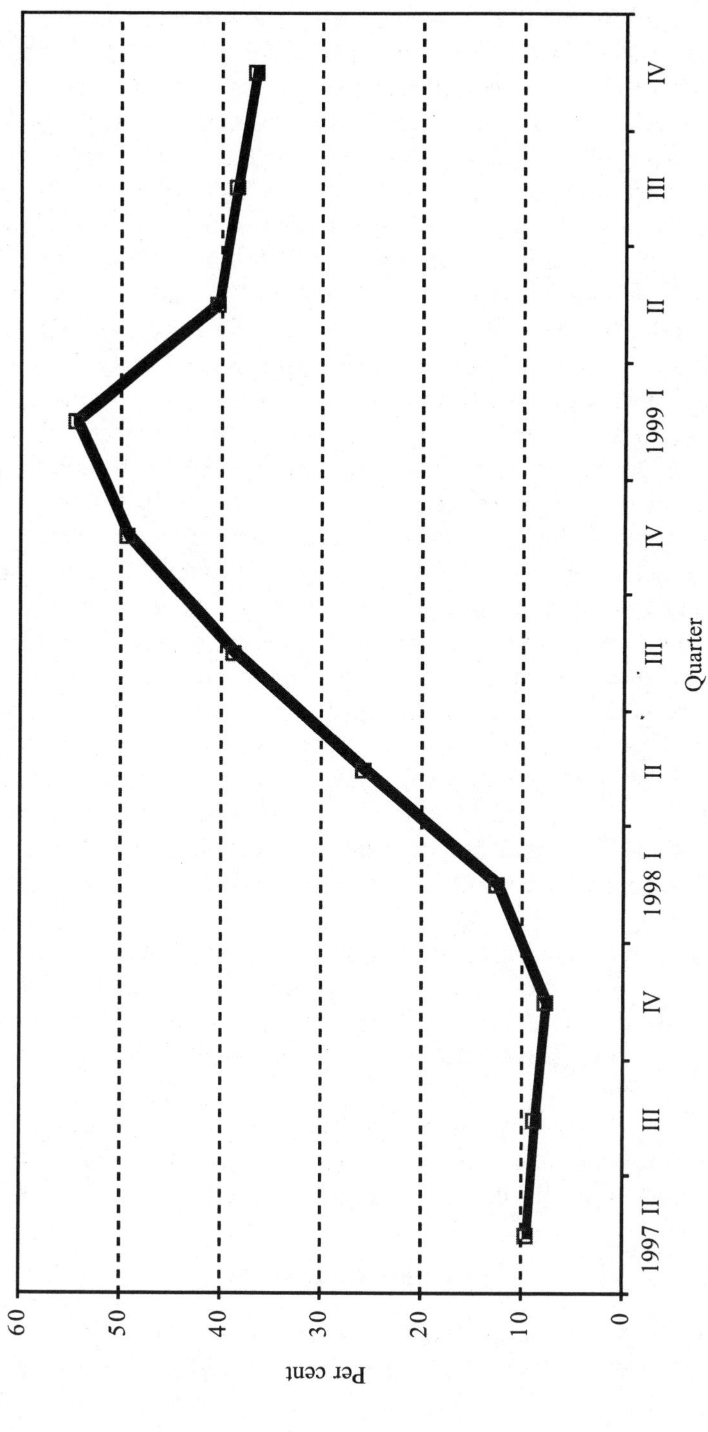

Source: Bank Indonesia.

markets. In the 1990s, however, such a system attracted massive short-term capital inflows to buy shares and other forms of commercial papers floated by Indonesian companies, both in the international and domestic markets. As an illustration, Steady Safe, a taxi and city bus company in Jakarta, was able to receive massive loans from Peregrine, a Hong Kong based investment bank.

In theory, prior to August 1997, Indonesia adopted a managed floating exchange rate system. The central bank intervened in the foreign exchange market by buying and selling the rupiah in "an intervention band" round the central rate. The central rate was pegged to a basket of major currencies whose composition was undisclosed. In reality, however, prior to August 1997, nominal devaluation was predictable, hovering around 5–7 per cent per annum against the U.S. dollar. As the share of the U.S. dollar was relatively dominant in the currency basket, the Real Effective Exchange Rate (REER) was modestly appreciated in the 1990s along with the appreciation of the U.S. dollar against other major currencies, including the Japanese yen. The decline shown in Figure 2.4 demonstrates the depreciation of the rupiah over time. This reduces international competitiveness, squanders savings, and encourages the allocation of resources into the non-traded sector of the economy.

The rapid growth of bank deposits and external borrowing, combined with an increase in both money and credit multipliers, have allowed a rapid growth in both money supply and bank credits. The latter were made possible because of the decline in statutory reserve requirement (from 15 per cent in 1983 to 2 per cent in October 1988) and a decline in the currency-deposit ratio that usually happens following the financial sector reform.

Part of the foreign component of the money base was held in check through a sterilization operation concerning capital inflows. This entails high domestic interest rates thus driving a large wedge between domestic and international interest rates, creating additional incentives for companies to borrow from overseas.

Bank Indonesia bears an expensive interest burden of the sterilization operations as its certificates of deposits (SBIs) were the principal instruments being used in the sterilization operations (see Figure 2.5).

SHORT-TERM IMPACTS

The combination of a sharp rupiah devaluation, a steep rise in interest rates and extremely tight internal and external liquidity has caused a very deep

FIGURE 2.4
Indonesia: Nominal and Real Effective Exchange Rate, 1993–99
(US$/Rp, 1993 = 100)

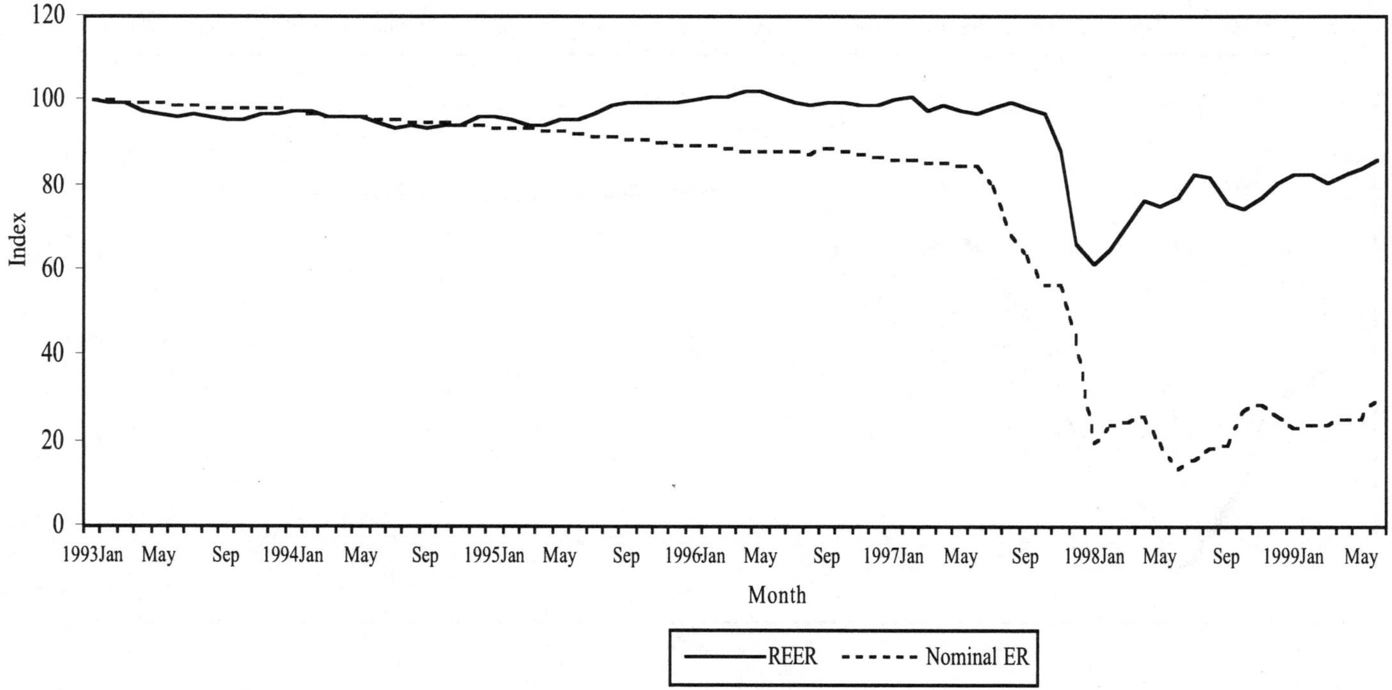

Source: J P Morgan website, *Real Broad Effective Exchange Rate*; Bank Indonesia, *Indonesian Financial Statistics*, various issues.

FIGURE 2.5
Indonesia: Differential between Domestic Deposit Rate and LIBOR, 1995–99

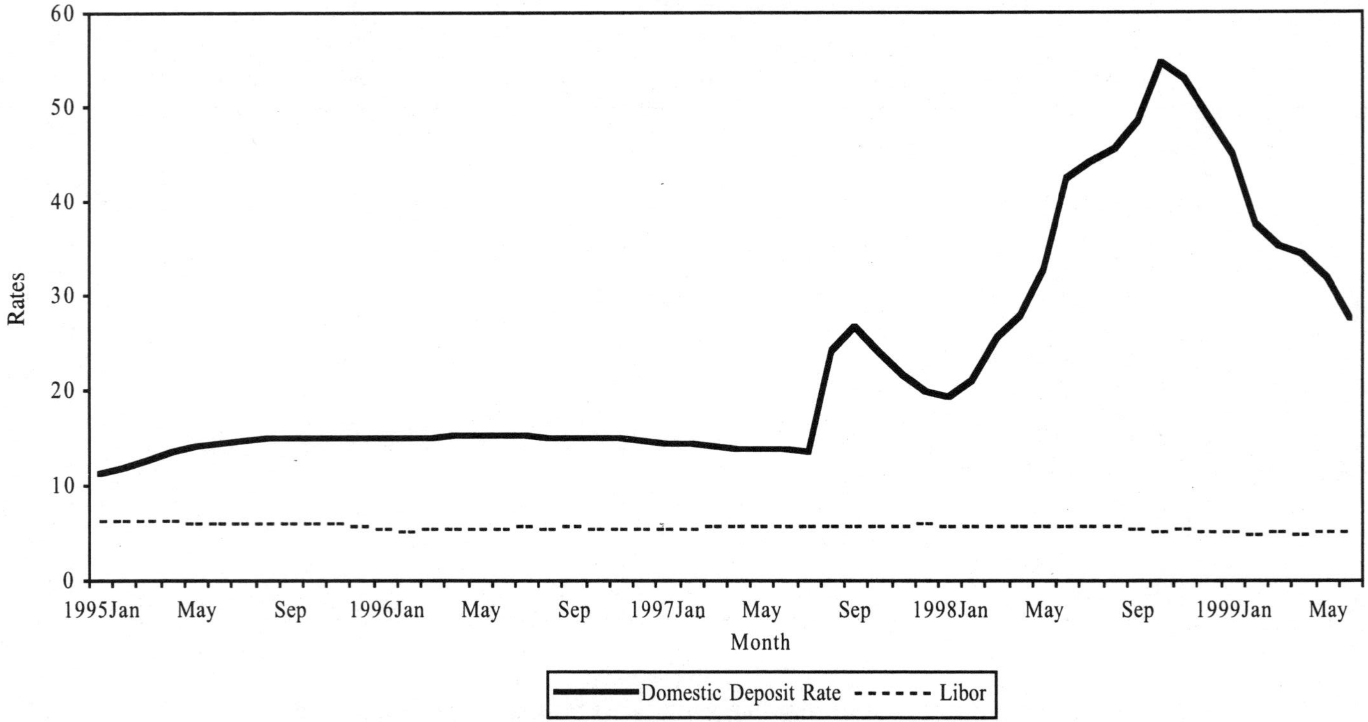

Source: Bank Indonesia, *Indonesian Financial Statistics*, various issues.

domestic economic recession. Fiscal stimulus was absent during the early state of the crisis as the International Monetary Fund (IMF) prescribed a short-run stabilization policy to cut government expenditure and other components of domestic spending. The IMF reversed its policy stance in April 1998, nine months after the crisis, to encourage a fiscal stimulus through social safety net programmes. The economy contracted by 14.7 per cent in 1998, one of the worst rates in modern history.

The crisis has caused economic distress as the fiscal deficit has soared to between 6–7 per cent of annual GDP since fiscal year of 1998/1999. A number of factors have contributed to the fiscal distress. Government revenues dried up due to domestic recession, a slow growth of non-oil exports, a low price for oil, and a high inflation rate. On the other hand, government expenditures soared for external debt repayments, subsidies on prices of state-vended products (now mainly refined oil products sold in the domestic market), recapitalization of the banking system (including Bank Indonesia, also known as the central bank) and subsidies via a preferential exchange rate for servicing of external debt of the corporate sector. The administrative reform, which gives more autonomy and fiscal power to local governments, starting next year, will also affect both the revenue and expenditure sides of the government budget.

The crisis also caused high inflation rates (in 1998 over 70 per cent). The rupiah devaluation raised prices of tradeables, including imports. The rapid growth of money supply, because of panic buying and bank runs, has also contributed to the rising inflation rates.

As indicated earlier, the interaction of a fragile financial system and a macroeconomic crisis has caused an increase in corporate bankruptcies, due to sharply increased liabilities and reduced sales. There are two origins of the rise in liabilities of the corporate sector: (i) the rise in domestic interest rates, and (ii) the rise in the risk premium for the unhedged foreign borrowings. The rise in the prices of imported inputs and the lack availability of working capital have caused negative productivity shock. The economic recession has increased the unemployment rate and number of people below the poverty line. The import compression did have the side effect of improving the current account balance.

POLICY RESPONSES

Prior to President Soeharto's fall from power in May 1998, his regime wasted six months pondering various alternative solutions to the economic crisis. Moreover, the quality of government policy response was eroded with the erosion of the quality of technical competence and integrity of President Soeharto's cabinet ministers, as he relied more and more on his family members and cronies for advice.

In the beginning of the crisis, Indonesia signed a Letter of Intent (LoI) with the IMF in October 1997. The standard IMF programme consists of the following measures: (i) short-term stabilization policy to reduce domestic absorption; (ii) medium-term economy wide reform to remove economic distortions for improving productivity and efficiency; and (iii) measures to strengthen market infrastructure (accounting and legal systems) to improve asymmetry of information and reduce transaction costs.

Unhappy with the severe cuts in their pet projects and the slow results of the IMF programme, in February 1998 some of Soeharto's children and associates brought in Dr Steven Hanke of Johns Hopkins University, to advise the President on the use of a currency board system as the alternative to the IMF programme. The currency board system would have pegged the rupiah to U.S. dollar. The monetary policy would have been constrained in this system, like the old U.S. gold standard, as the money supply is directly linked to the balance of payments developments. In such a system, the central bank stops operating as the lender of last resort.

Another alternative considered was to impose controls on capital account transactions, at least short-term capital inflows and outflows. A number of variants has been looked at under this proposal. The first mechanism is to control capital flows by using market based mechanism. This includes a "Tobin tax", the Chilean method of taxing capital inflows by freezing them for a certain period of time in non-renumerated deposits at the central bank. Other methods include discretionary measures, such as the foreign exchange controls currently adopted by the partially open economy of the People's Republic of China, or controlling certain types capital inflows to affect both the overall size and structure of capital inflows as recently introduced in Malaysia. At least in the short-run, the control cuts the link between interest rates and exchange rates. This gives more freedom for policy makers to pursue domestic policy objectives.

Indonesia, however, simply does not have the administrative capability to implement exchange controls. The country is big in size with more than 17,000 islands, many close to Singapore, the leading financial centre in the region. Moreover, Indonesia does not have adequate legal and accounting system as well as efficient bureaucracy to administer the control. The large size of the country, the significant role of non-traded sector in the economy, inadequate external reserves, the distressed banking system, lax discipline, and weak market infrastructure (particularly the legal and accounting systems), mitigated against Indonesia adopting the currency board system.

STABILIZATION AND ADJUSTMENT PROGRAMME

At the end, the new government signed the fourth IMF programme in June 1998. This secured US$43 billion of IMF funds. The fiscal distress and fragility of the banking system constrained Indonesia from adopting a fully fledged stabilization programme. The IMF programme has specific targets in: (1) monetary aggregates (net domestic credit); (2) fiscal account (public sector borrowing); (3) short-term social safety net; (4) external sector (external indebtedness); (5) bank restructuring; and (6) strengthening market infrastructure.

(1) Monetary Policy

By adopting the flexible exchange rate system on 14 August 1997 the policy objective of the government has shifted to defending its exchange reserve position. This allows interest rates to rise precipitously. Moreover, the monetary policy has also been tightened either by restricting domestic credit of the banking system or by the inability of the financially distressed banking system to extend loans. The relaxation in the prudential rules and regulations governing the banking industry do not have a significant impact on the ability of the banking system to extend new credit.

(2) Fiscal policy

With an existing tight monetary policy, the focus of Indonesia's adjustment programme is fiscal. The economic crisis has caused fiscal distress as government revenues are currently insufficient to meet the rising expenditure to finance soaring costs of overhauling the financial system, funding the social safety net and providing the fiscal stimulus. One of the main objectives of the fiscal policy is to redefine the scope of government. Privatization of state-owned enterprises (SOEs) is part of the process to scale back the role of government in providing goods and services. It is also an instrument for improving the efficiency and productivity of SOEs. The policy also shifts the role of the budget from a tool of resource allocation to a principal instrument of macroeconomic policy and the vehicle for providing public goods.

In the years prior to the crisis, 1968–97, the budget deficit had always been financed by foreign financial assistance, preferably concessionary loans from official sources. Following the crisis, the authorities had to find other sources of revenue to finance the larger unsustainable budget deficit. These include revenues from asset recovery by the Indonesian Bank Restructuring Agency (IBRA), proceeds from privatization of state-owned enterprises and the flotation of government bonds in domestic market.

The authorities have also introduced various measures to raise revenue from taxation. The efforts have a limited success as the tax system in an emerging economy, like Indonesia, is inflexible, inefficient and less progressive. As a result, the expenditure side of the government budget is expected to carry multiple tasks, including stimulating economic growth and pursuing the objective of equity. These objectives can be pursued by increasing the portion of non-debt budget expenditures towards the non-tradable sector of the economy. Such expenditures include public schools, extension and outreach services, public health care programmes and public works programmes in rural areas (see Table 2.3).

(3) Short-term programme to protect the poor from falling primary income

To ease the burden of the poor, the authorities, to some extent, have raised secondary or social income to supplement the fall in the primary income, namely income derived from labour and assets. As Indonesia has no modern social safety net system, the authorities have tried to raise social income by providing food and other basic needs at subsidized prices as well as the creation of labour-intensive public works, requiring high budgetary subsidies. Mainly due to poor administration, in the beginning, the subsidies did not reach the needy. At the same time, the subsidies created a large gap between domestic and international prices of the state-vended products and provided incentives for their illegal exportation (smuggling) to neighbouring countries.

(4) Dealing with the debt overhang

The soaring external debt repayments, in the middle of the economic crisis, required transfers of larger shares of Indonesia's export earnings to foreign sources. To ease the pressures, Indonesia needed temporary debt relief.

TABLE 2.3
Indonesia: Central Government Budget Summary, 1994/95–2000/01
(in Rp billions)

	1994/95	1995/96	1996/97	1997/98	1998/99	1999/2000	2000/01
Revenue and Expenditure							
1. Domestic Revenues	66,418	73,014	84,792	108,814	159,135	149,303	140,804
2. Routine Expenditures[a]	44,069	50,435	61,568	84,606	140,535	171,205	134,556
3. Development Expenditures	30,692	28,781	33,454	46,398	65,750	92,683	83,648
4. Budget Deficit (= 2 + 3 – 1)	8,343	6,202	10,230	22,190	47,150	114,585	77,400
5. Government Saving (= 1 – 2)	22,349	22,579	23,224	24,208	18,600	-21,902	6,248
Borrowing Fund							
6. Programme Aid	0	0	0	0	24,926	74,045	47,400
7. Project Aid	9,838	9,009	11,048	23,817	25,313	40,541	30,000
8. Total Borrowing (= 6 + 7)	9,838	9,009	11,048	23,817	50,239	114,586	77,400
9. Change in balances (= 8 – 4)[b]	1,495	2,807	818	1,627	3,089	1	0
Memorandum Item:							
1. Share of Deficit to Total Expenditure (%)	11.2	7.8	10.8	16.9	22.9	43.4	35.5
2. Share of Government Saving to Domestic Revenues (%)	33.6	30.9	27.4	22.2	11.7	-14.7	4.4
3. Share of Programme Aid to Total Borrowing (%)	0.0	0.0	0.0	0.0	49.6	64.6	61.2
4. Share of Project Aid to Total Borrowing (%)	100.0	100.0	100.0	100.0	50.4	35.4	38.8
5. Share of Balances to Domestic Revenues (%)	2.3	3.8	1.0	1.5	1.9	0.0	0.0
6. Share of Balances to Total Expenditures (%)	2.0	3.5	0.9	1.2	1.5	0.0	0.0
7. Share of Balances to Total Borrowing (%)	15.2	31.2	7.4	6.8	6.1	0.0	0.0

[a] Including debt service payment.
[b] Positive means increasing.
Sources: Ministry of Finance;World Bank, *Indonesia: From Crisis to Opportunity*, 1999.

(i) Public sector debt

It is true that the bulk of the public sector debt is long term in nature. However, the associated principal and interest servicing cost still runs high, at some US$9 billion a year. To be able to repay its external debt, the public sector has to accumulate a budget surplus as well as a surplus in the balance of payments. To ease the pressures on the public budget and the balance of payments, on 23 September 1998 the Paris Club creditor nations agreed to reschedule US$4.2 billion in principal repayments of Indonesia's public external debt.

(ii) Private sector debt

The private sector external debt is relatively more difficult to settle as there is a large number of both foreign lenders and domestic borrowers. Foreign lenders include foreign private banks, institutional investors and other non-bank entities. This debt is to be solved on a voluntary basis based on a combination of Mexico's Ficorca programme and the Korean scheme. The Korean idea would mean taking the short-term and non-trade debts of Indonesian banks and restructuring them into loans with a one to four-year maturity. Interest rates on the new loans will be paid based on Libor (London Inter-Bank Offered Rate) plus margin, ranging between 2.75 and 3.5 per cent.

The non-bank corporate debt is rescheduled and restructured along the lines of the Mexican programme. A trust institution, called Indonesian Debt Restructuring Agency (INDRA), is already established under the central bank which provides exchange rate risk protection and assurances to the availability of foreign exchange to private debtors that agree with their foreign creditors to restructure their external debts for a period of eight years, with three years of grace during which no principal will be payable. So far, the progress of the programme is very slow partly because of a weak bankruptcy law.

(5) Bank Restructuring Programme

The financially distressed banking system cannot lower interest rates and expand credit. A combination of structural weakness in the banking system and the corporate sector also limits the tightness of the monetary policy.

To restructure the banking industry, the government adopted three broad policies. The first element of the bank restructuring programme is to strengthen the capital base of the banks. The risk base capital adequacy ratio (CAR) of the banks was temporary lowered in November 1998 to 4 per cent, which is to be raised back to minimum of 8 per cent by 2003. The second component of the programme is to improve governance of the banking system. For this objective, Indonesia now adopts stricter prudential rules and regulations and accounting standards — on a par with international standards and improves their enforcements and implementations. Each major bank is now required to have a Compliance Director. Moreover, the major shareholders, managers and executive officers of commercial banks are now required to take fit and proper test to continue in the banking industry.

The banking system is now practically nationalized as the major private banks are now controlled by IBRA. Established in early 1998, IBRA assumed the function of lender of last resort. It also assumed the responsibility for financially distressed banks and, together with the banks' shareholders, prepares and implement immediate rehabilitation plans by restructuring or promoting mergers with other banks.

On 26 January 1998, the authorities provided a blanket guarantee to both domestic and foreign depositors and creditors of all banks incorporated in Indonesia. The guarantee scheme was to be effective for at least two years, and its discontinuation will be announced six months in advance and be replaced by a deposit insurance scheme.

The Asset Management Unit (AMU) has been established under IBRA with the only role is to purchase the non-performing loans (NPLs) from banks. This allows the banks to focus on their traditional activities, which are deposit taking and lending. The purchase of NPLs will significantly add to the resources available for banks for lending purposes. To some extent, IBRA has adopted the Swedish model by trying to save both the banks and the borrowers by means of injecting better management methods and fresh capital into the companies.

The bank recapitalization programme was announced on 9 December 1998.[2] The objective of the programme is to increase the banks' capital adequacy ratio (CAR) to 4 per cent, or a half of the 8 per cent minimum standard as set by the Bank for International Settlements (BIS). The programme is only available for national commercial banks which have a CAR between minus 25 per cent and plus 4 per cent. The 40 banks with a CAR below 25 per cent are required to inject fresh capital within 30 days or risk being closed down. The 10 foreign banks and 32 joint venture banks are excluded from the programme.

The government needs to recapitalize Bank Indonesia (the central bank) and 126 national commercial banks at a cost of Rp570 trillion (US$70 billion at exchange rate Rp7,500 per U.S. dollar) or nearly 58 per cent of Indonesia's GDP (see Table 2.4). The would be recapitalized banks include 7 state banks, 49 private banks (including 13 taken over by the government) and 15 provincial development banks. Four of the seven state-owned banks (PT Bapindo, PT Bank Dagang Negara, PT Bank Ekspor Impor Indonesia, and PT Bank Bumi Daya) are to be merged with the newly established PT Bank Mandiri. As shown in Table 2.2, the number of banks has been reduced from 208 in December 1998 to 167 in June 1999. The number of banks under government control (local and central) expanded from 34 in June 1997 to 48 by January 2000 with a combined market share around 73 per cent.

To ease the fiscal costs of the bank restructuring programme, the authorities encourage the participation of foreign investors in the banking Indonesia. This has been done, among other measures, by allowing foreigners to own 100 per cent of domestic banks.

(6) Policy measures to strengthen market infrastructure

A number of policy measures need to be taken to improve governance systems and reduce transaction costs. First, to review and dismantle government contracts of the former Soeharto administration that were offered through a network of corruption, collusion, and nepotism (known by the Indonesian acronym: KKN). Second, to improve the domestic competition policy. Third, to restructure, corporatize and privatize state-owned enterprises. Fourth, to speed up trade and policy reforms. Fifth, to strengthen accounting and legal systems, and to improve both market transparency and contract enforcement. Sixth, to modernize the antiquated bankruptcy code.

RECENT DEVELOPMENTS AND OUTLOOK

The availability of financial assistance from the international community, combined with progress in the implementation of the IMF programme and favourable external factors (such as depreciation of the U.S. dollar against other major currencies and improvement in commodity prices, including oil), has helped strengthen external value of the rupiah (vis-à-vis the U.S. dollar), from above Rp15,000 in June and Rp10,000 in early October 1998 to presently below Rp7,000 (see Figure 2.2).

TABLE 2.4
Indonesia: The Cost of Bank Restructuring (as of November 1999)
(In Rp trillions)

	Total bonds	Per cent of total	Fixed rate bonds			Variable rate bonds	Index rate bonds
			Total	5-year	10-year		
Bonds issued to date	425	75	12	3	9	194	218
Bank Indonesia	218	38	0	0	0	0	218
Recapitalized banks							
State banks	103	18	4	1	3	98	0
Private banks (7 banks)	22	4	3	1	2	19	0
Banks taken over in 1998 (BTO 4)	81	14	5	1	4	76	0
Regional development banks	1	0	0.4	0.1	0.3	0.8	0
Remaining bonds to be issued	145	25	6	2	4	139	0
Banks taken over in 1999 (BTO 8)	12	2	n.a.	n.a.	n.a.	n.a.	n.a.
Private Banks	3	0	n.a.	n.a.	n.a.	n.a.	n.a.
State banks	130	23	n.a.	n.a.	n.a.	n.a.	n.a.
Total	**570**	**100**	**18**	**5**	**13**	**333**	**218**

Source: Bank Indonesia.

Appreciation of the rupiah, along with the progress of the restructuring of the banking system, reduces both the inflation rate and the interest rate. The inflation rate dropped from around the extremely high 70 per cent mark in 1988 to just over 2 per cent in 1999. The average SBI rates steadily dropped from 69 per cent in August 1998 to 38 per cent in the December of the same year to between 10 and 12 per cent in 1999. Despite the reduction in interest rates, however, access of the corporate sector to bank credit remains very limited. The credit crunch limits the capacity of corporate sector to increase capacity utilization, production and non-oil exports.

If the country can manage to solve the political problems and rebuild its social system, Indonesia will have stronger fundamentals and therefore can more easily resume economic growth. The crisis does not seriously affect the conditions which supported the long-term growth potential of the Indonesian economy: human and physical capital stock. The high savings and investment emphasis on improvement in human resources are still intact. Deregulation and economic reform that further integrate the economy to international markets will eliminate economic distortions and enhance productivity and efficiency. Improvements in market infrastructure and economic institutions will further enhance productivity with the reduction of transaction costs. This enables the country to exploit its comparative advantage in labour intensive sectors and natural resource based industries. At the same time, it allows Indonesia to use its ample domestic market — with a population of 220 million — as the new engine of growth.

The combination of marked progress in stabilizing the inflation rate, interest rate and exchange rate at low levels (see Figure 2.2) and significant progress in bank restructuring has provided Indonesia a good start to move forward. Bank Indonesia's projection for 2000 is presented in Table 2.5. The interest rate (one month SBI) is expected to remain stable at between 10 and 12 per cent per annum. There is pressure to raise interest rates as the recapitalized banks, beginning 1 February 2000, are allowed to sell 10 per cent of their holding of government bonds in the secondary market. On the other hand, the improvements in bank productivity, due to significant progress in the bank recapitalization programme, tend to reduce interest rates.

The inflation rate is expected to hover between 3 to 5 per cent per annum. The planned across-the-board 20 per cent rise in the salaries and wages of civil servants this year, and the upward adjustment in prices of state-vended products, will increase the annual inflation rate in the year of

TABLE 2.5
Indonesian Economic Projection
Year 2000

Targets and Projections (In per cent, unless otherwise stated)	
Targets	
Inflation[a]	3–5
Growth of base money[b]	8.3
Projections	
Real GDP Growth	3–4
Aggregate Demand	
Consumption	
Private consumption	3–4
Government consumption	5–6
Investment	
Private investment	1–2
Government investment	2–3
Export and import	
Export of goods and services	1–2
Import of goods and services	11–12
Share of current account surplus to GDP	2.1
SBI One-Month Rate (p.a.)	10–12
Exchange Rate (Rp/U.S. dollar, average)	Rp7,000

[a]Excluded the effect of price increases caused by government policies.
[b]Calculated from the Base Money Target in December 1999.
Source: Bank Indonesia.

2000 by about 2 per cent. The combination of a conservative stabilization policy and a rebound in exports and capital inflows will help stabilize the external value of the rupiah at present rate (Rp7,000 per U.S. dollar). The economy in real terms is expected to grow at around the 3 to 4 per cent level in the 2000 financial year (see Table 2.5).

LESSONS

In conclusion, there are a number of important lessons that need to be taken from the crisis that has beset Indonesia since late 1997.

- Short-run stabilization measures and medium and long-run economic reform require a politically credible and a technically competent government.

- Sound macroeconomic management and a robust banking system are the two main pillars of macroeconomic stability. This underwrites the structure of economic growth and exports and the subsidy cost of low inflation rates.
- Micro-economic weaknesses, such as high debt/equity ratio and an over-dependence on unhedged short-term external borrowings, can undermine macroeconomic strengths.
- An important warning sign of financial fragility occurs when banks and the corporate sector borrow more in foreign currency and compound this problem by investing in the unproductive economic sector.
- Careful analysis must be made of the magnitude and structure of private capital inflows.
- Less distortive prudential measures to discourage destabilizing short-term capital inflows need to be imposed.
- The Real Effective Exchange Rate (REER) must receive attention. REER may be the most powerful transmission mechanism in an emerging economy as it affects: (a) external competitiveness in the international market; and (b) allocation of resources between traded sector and non-traded sector in domestic economy.
- Indonesia desperately needs a breathing space from the international community, particularly from the IMF, the World Bank, and the Asian Development Bank (ADB) to allow for necessary adjustment without deep economic recession or adverse effects on the low income group.
- Banking policies of "free entry" and "no exit" are an explosive combination.
- Deregulation of the financial sector should be accompanied by improvements in bank supervision and in implementation of rules and regulations.
- To reduce the burden of the recapitalization programme, liquidate the non-viable banks immediately, but give support to the viable ones.

Notes

1. The World Bank considers a debt to GNP ratio of less than 48 per cent as low risk, 40 to 80 per cent as a medium risk and over 80 per cent as high risk. In terms of the ratio of total debt service to exports, the World Bank considers 18 per cent as the "warning" threshold.
2. *Jakarta Post,* 10 December 1998.

3

Economic Policy
Key Issues

Boediono

INTRODUCTION

In Indonesia events are continuing to unfold rapidly. No longer being in the "hot seat" of government office is a mixed blessing. On the one hand I have a bit more time to be reflective, and even be sympathetic to my colleagues working to gain control of the situation. On the other hand I feel less well placed to comment on recent developments in economic policy as compared to my ministerial colleagues. From this viewpoint, which is to stand back from the crisis management job, this chapter will focus on recent economic developments and the challenge Indonesia faces. This contribution will focus on three areas: the general climate of economic policy; the evolution of the recovery; and key policy issues.

THE CLIMATE

There is little doubt that the overall climate for economic recovery has improved substantially with the new Wahid government. Given the degree of social and economic dislocation, change was inevitable and, with the new government, the issue of legitimacy has largely been taken care of. While the risk of social unrest remains, it appears to be greatly reduced in the main population centres. Conflicts, stemming from ethnic and religious animosity and unresolved human rights problems, most particularly in Maluku and Aceh, continue to pose problems for overall stability but these are increasingly isolated.

With these developments the government is gaining increasing support from the international community and Indonesia is beginning to experience some reversal in capital flows. There is rising interest on the part of long-term foreign direct investors. However, many private sector investors will probably need more time and more convincing, including a clearer resolution of contentious issues in the power sector and elsewhere, before Indonesia sees their return in full force.

Wahid's cabinet composed of many new faces and inevitably with little previous government experience. In itself, this is not a major problem. Any transition involves a period of learning and the speed and dramatic nature of the transition in Indonesia would imply a longer period than usual. However, there are risks when the learning process drags on, especially when expectations are high and the problems are many.

Forging a policy consensus within the government itself, let alone with parliament, needs time, effort, will and vision. However, with the government on a learning curve, the administration is in limbo. In particular departmental reorganizations are incomplete, and the operational format for decentralization unsettled. Under these circumstances the bureaucracy is less able to maintain the continuity of government processes as the political transition evolves. If these organizational matters are not resolved, implementation problems will rise, morale will fall, government service delivery will suffer and legitimacy will again be an issue. Having said that, this writer is optimistic that the government will get over these "teething problems" before too long.

Empowered by the election, the parliament has been more active in responding to issues of public concern, and this is a healthy development. But the parliament in a democratic state must be more than a sounding board for public opinion. It must also be the government's critical, yet reliable, partner in making the hard policy choices required to hasten the recovery and put the economy on a sustainable long-term track.

Finally, we also have to come to terms with the injustices and grievances we have inherited from the past. Given their pervasive nature this is very difficult issue. On the one hand, there are scarce resources for both the time and attention of key policy makers and there is a trade-off between energy spent righting past wrongs and the energy required to take on the formidable challenges of the present. On the other hand, we must be clear about the consequences for unacceptable behaviour to set incentives correctly as we move forward. These are difficult choices and the government will have to find a compromise that will probably not satisfy either those who want to punish wrong doing or those who want to move on with the current problems.

In sum, this is truly a crucial time for Indonesians to put aside narrow self-interest, and make the "larger system" work. No one else can or will make it work for us. Indonesians have to tap all the statesmanship and forbearance and unite to attain the common cause.

THE ECONOMY

As an economy comes out of a crisis it stabilizes, and only then does the real sector recover. Stabilization has been achieved in Indonesia and recovery is in process. The exchange rate has been much less volatile for over a year, and most recently has been stable in the general range of Rp7,000 to the U.S. dollar. Inflation, in spite of a small uptick in December, is still under control at 1.6 per cent for 1999 and interest rates have begun to decline again with the one month SBI auction rates falling to the 12 per cent range from 13 per cent where they had persisted since August 1999. These drops have led to declines in deposit rates, and lending rates with various lags with the state banks, unfortunately, acting as a drag, probably because of delays in their recapitalization. Finally, much to everyone's delight and relief the Y2K concerns have been laid to rest and the stock market appears to be off to a good start in the new year.

With these indicators stabilizing or even improving, the "real" economy, while not yet robust, is beginning to show significantly more strength. The most recent GDP figures are the preliminary third quarter estimates which posted growth of 1.5 per cent for the third straight quarter of positive growth. Supporting evidence for a strengthening economy also comes from retail sales which were growing at over 5 per cent in real terms at the end of the year, and PLN (Perusahaan Listrik Negara) electricity sales, which have now surpassed pre-crisis levels. Even cement, heavily used by the construction sector, and thus a lagging indicator in times of hardship, showed some pick-up at the end of 1999. While the fourth quarter GDP estimate is not in, it appears, from the evidence available, that growth has continued, if not strengthened further. In particular there is anecdotal evidence of increasing activity based on rising consumer demand. In fact, newspapers are even beginning to run stories on the lack of new cars to be had due to higher demand.

The early stages of the recovery are almost always consumer-led, and this is true for Indonesia, but there are now signs of a pick-up in some of the other elements of aggregate demand. In October and November 1999 non-oil exports finally began to show some growth, posting a 17 per cent increase over the admittedly low numbers last year, but providing some indication that exports will contribute more of a stimulus in the year ahead than they did last year. Imports of capital goods, an indicator of manufacturing investment, however, remain weak. This may not be a problem currently, with excess capacity in this sector, but will be a constraint to growth if the trend continues for the next year or so.

Forecasts for next year's growth seem to be growing more optimistic. In January, as part of a larger story on East Asian recovery a forecast on CNN indicated that Indonesia's GDP growth for the coming financial year is expected to be 5.5 per cent.[1] Foreign observers appear to believe that Indonesia is following the same path as South Korea and Thailand with a lag, and are generally more optimistic than domestic observers. One of the lowest forecasts for next year is that of BPS (Biro Pusat Statistik or Central Bureau of Statistics), which estimates growth to be in the 2 per cent range. The central bank and the Planning Agency (Bappenas) have higher estimates around the 4 per cent range. Even the lowest of these estimates reflects a significant boost over the levels seen in the last couple of years. This year should bring with it a good news effect that should have a positive impact on both confidence, and more importantly the ability and resolve to address corporate and bank restructuring.

With monetary policy gradually relaxing, and fiscal policy tightening as the recovery takes hold, the exchange rate should remain in the current range or strengthen to its longer-run equilibrium probably in the 6,000 to 7,000 range (as compared to the U.S. dollar). Inflation is more problematic given the likely impact of rising fuel and electricity prices as well as underlying trends. This year's inflation of 1.6 per cent reflects a significant drop in food prices, but tariffs are very likely to be applied that will prevent key rice and sugar prices from falling further. While food prices have declined, virtually every other price item in the Consumer Price Index (CPI) has risen between 3 and 5 per cent. With any substantial increase in administered prices, recalling that transport prices will have to be hiked in line with fuel increases, it seems unlikely that inflation can remain at its current low. That is unless food prices are allowed to drop or the exchange rate strengthens significantly. These difficult issues will need to be considered for the upcoming budget, which is another key issue facing the government.

However, there is one issue related to the recovery and ultimately the budget that needs to be addressed. As indicated earlier Indonesian commentators are generally more pessimistic than foreign observers and have even raised the possibility of a "W-shaped" recovery. In this scenario the government fails to pull together adequately, bank and corporate restructuring are insufficient and the economy suffers a second downturn. This commentator does not believe that this is likely, or at least not in the time-frame predicted, but the underlying analysis should still be a warning. People, and particularly the political and business elite, may find that growth of 3 or 4 per cent is adequate to alleviate some of the worst problems of recent years without taking the painful steps required to improve government and private institutions. However, complacency about growth in the 3 to 4 per cent range would be a disaster as the economy would not create employment, reduce poverty and raise taxes at the level required to be socially or fiscally sustainable. Thus even if the news this year is good, in keeping with the highest levels currently predicted, the government cannot afford to be complacent. In subsequent future years Indonesia must continuously achieve growth of significantly more than 4 per cent if it is to grow out of the crisis.

OUTSTANDING POLICY ISSUES

To summarize the main policy issues that need to be tackled in the immediate future, the government needs to do the following.

First, Indonesia must maintain the right climate. As mentioned earlier, Indonesia is off to a good start, but needs to strengthen the favourable trends. We need to forge the idea that it takes all of us in government, and out of it, pulling together to make the larger system work effectively. In addition, the government needs to get over its "teething problems" soon. It is also crucial that Indonesia comes to terms with its past while allocating sufficient time and energy to deal with the challenges of the present.

The government must also get the policy framework right. The most immediate task is to get the next budget on a sound footing. This will be the new government's first major policy initiative. It will be carefully examined by a range of observers and it is important that it be well accepted by the market. At this time it would seem that the draft budget for the year 2000 is quite realistic. However, given the uncertainties, the range of predictions, and the need to restore relatively high growth, a bigger fiscal stimulus is needed, even if it means slightly higher foreign borrowings for this year. In addition, fiscal decentralization initiatives being planned for are critical to national stability. The government needs to make these initiatives much more specific, and public. This should minimize the risk of wasteful spending or, an equally bad prospect, that essential services are not delivered. Finally, while supportive of a larger stimulus one must acknowledge the debt problem the government faces, therefore a mechanism is needed to assure that the aggregate national deficit remains under control, whatever the pressures from the political process.

A complete policy framework includes not only the budget, but also the entire economic recovery action plan. The Letter of Intent (LoI) that the government prepared for the IMF board meeting in January 2000 is such a comprehensive framework. This author's general assessment of the current LoI is that it is a good framework for these discussions. The format is rather detailed, but in the current situation it may help focus the government on the implementation of programmes. In fact it is just the government's capacity to implement programmes that is now being assessed by the market and more broadly. Given the implementation problems and the need to assure that there is no break in funding, parliament should act to endorse the budget and the LoI without much delay. Constructive criticism is to be welcomed, but there is not the time or ability to achieve perfection. The passing of the budget and the LoI are key tests of whether the government and the parliament can work together to lead the country out of the crisis.

Given the concerns about the longer-term sustainability it is important to have a credible medium-term policy framework. For this, there must be a solid 5-year plan. Currently, the plan is being developed by Bappenas (Badan Perencanaan Nasional) in combination with the line departments. To be effective, and credible to the market, the plan must set out priorities clearly without being burdened by excessive rhetoric or unrealistic objectives.

The basic elements of the short-term and the medium-term frameworks are well established by now. The macroeconomic framework is designed to ensure the maintenance of low inflation and fiscal sustainability. Within this framework the policy mix should evolve over time from a combination of tight monetary policy-cum-fiscal stimulus (deficit) to a more accommodating monetary policy and an "approximately" balanced budget toward the end of the plan period. The recovery has been led by increased consumer and government spending. This pattern is natural in the early stages of a recovery but is ultimately not sustainable. The next stage of the recovery must rely increasingly on exports and investment. It is imperative, therefore, to free these two sectors from any impediments to their early revival.

The most crucial and urgent agenda is in the twin-restructuring programme, namely the banking and corporate sector restructuring. To maintain the momentum of recovery the implementation of these programmes must be accelerated. However, there is also a vital need to undertake broader institutional reform for regional governments, the civil service and the legal system, as these are the foundation for sustainable long-term growth. There is also the need to provide an improved safety net for the poor during recovery, while, transforming these programmes into more sustainable, that is, well-targeted and cost-effective, anti-poverty programmes in the longer-run. There is a need to eliminate the remaining obstacles to the free flow of goods and resources among sectors and regions, a condition vital to speeding up recovery and maintaining growth in the longer run especially as Indonesia moves to increased regional autonomy. Indonesia needs to continue its progress in establishing healthy competitive markets to take advantage of the global economy.

In conclusion, it is crucial to maintain the impetus of the recovery. The new government of President Abdurrahman Wahid is off to a relatively good start and the recovery is taking hold, but a lot needs to be done if the good beginning is not to falter. Broad political consensus on implementing the basic elements of the national recovery programme must be forged without delay. These basic elements are well established; what is needed is agreement on the details and fine tuning. Once agreed, the focus of the government and the parliament should be on timely implementation. The international community can also do much to assist Indonesia manage this transition in the critical months and years ahead.

Notes

1. CNN Asia Edition, 11 January 2000.

SECTION II
Monetary-Banking, Inflation, and Exchange Rate Policy

4

Indonesia's Economic Policy under the Wahid Administration

Bambang Kusumanto

This chapter will discuss the current economic policy of the government of Indonesia, together with macroeconomic issues and stabilization policies. Indonesia's new government inherited an enormous economic challenge. To illustrate the dimension of the challenge Indonesian policy makers faced in stabilizing the economy a brief description of the economic crisis is necessary. Following the float of the rupiah in August 1997, the exchange rate initially depreciated in line with other currencies that were hit by the regional crisis. However, things changed towards the end of 1997 when investors became aware of the fragility of the Indonesian banking system and when concerns about President Soeharto's health and the problems associated with a potential transition of leadership in Indonesia fuelled an overall feeling of uncertainty and anxiety. The period that followed can only be described as traumatic. In terms of economic developments, this period was characterized by bank runs, capital flight, rapidly increasing money supply, currency depreciation, and accelerating inflation. By June 1998, the rupiah was trading at approximately Rp14,000 per U.S. dollar, reflecting a staggering 84 per cent loss in value when compared to the pre-crisis average. Aggregate production declined by almost 14 per cent in 1998 and year-on-year inflation as measured by changes in the consumer price index reached 82 per cent in September 1998. These figures give an indication of the magnitude of the crisis and the huge task policy makers faced in stabilizing the economy.

Nonetheless, the economic policies that have been in place since mid-1998 have yielded significant success over the past year and a half. Economic growth has now been positive for three consecutive quarters. Current estimates place the aggregate economic expansion in 1999 at 1 per cent. It is generally predicted that the Indonesian economy will grow by approximately 5 per cent in 2000. While this is still far from Indonesia's growth experience of the previous three decades and below the economic expansion of many other regional economies, it reflects a significant turnaround. Recall that Indonesia's economy contracted by almost 14 per cent in 1998 causing the most severe economic contraction in the region. The most significant success of Indonesia's stabilization policy, however, was in the fight against inflation. Inflation, which threatened to develop into hyperinflation in 1998 was contained at 2 per cent in 1999 and is expected to remain a single digit number in 2000. Exports, which declined significantly in dollar and volume terms, following the 1998 civil unrest, have been improving in recent months. At the same time that domestic economic policy yields successes, the international economic environment appears to improve. In particular, prices for internationally traded commodities are showing signs of recovery, possibly leading to an improvement of Indonesia's terms of trade in the near term.

What have been the main elements of Indonesia's stabilization policy? At a first glance the stabilization policy appears to be rather conventional. After an initial period of severe monetary turbulence, broadly speaking, the stabilization policy was a mix of monetary constraint and expansionary fiscal policy. Monetary constraint brought money growth and domestic price developments under control and strengthened the exchange rate. Expansionary fiscal policy was aimed at supporting aggregate demand. However, Indonesia's stabilization policy went beyond changes in macroeconomic policies since we also initiated a significant programme of structural and organizational reforms. Two of those structural changes were the adoption of a flexible exchange rate regime and the establishment of an independent central bank. In August 1997 the system of a crawling exchange rate band was abandoned and in May 1999, Bank Indonesia became an independent institution. Bank Indonesia's method of conducting open market operations has also been changed in order to increase the efficiency of the monetary transmission mechanism in the economy. Open market operations now use a quantity-based auction system for short-term securities, allowing for the efficient control of base money.

The implementation of the auction system allowed interest rates to adjust and to counteract the downward pressure on the exchange rate and helped correct the overshooting of the exchange rate that far exceeded the degree of real exchange rate adjustment warranted in light of the underlying economic fundamentals. Unfortunately, interest rates had to rise to a very high level in mid-1998, with the average yield on Bank Indonesia's securities peaking at 71 per cent in September 1998, to stabilize money growth, the exchange rate, and inflation. This policy was successful. The rupiah began to recover, moving from a range of Rp14,000–15,000 per U.S. dollar between mid-June and mid-July 1998 to Rp13,000 per U.S. dollar by mid-August and Rp11,000 per U.S. dollar by early September 1998. Finally, with a lag of one to two months, inflation vanished. By October 1998, Indonesia was actually experiencing deflation. Through the efficient control of the money supply, Bank Indonesia now provides a stable price environment that is one of the most important prerequisites for effective and efficient resource mobilization and allocation through the financial sector.

The freely floating exchange rate, the implementation of a new central bank law and the improvement of monetary policy instruments, however, are only three aspects of the changes in the monetary and financial sector of the economy. Indonesia experienced a severe banking crisis which forced the government to intervene strongly. The banking panic forced Bank Indonesia to act as a lender of last resort. In hindsight there were shortcomings in how liquidity support to commercial banks was handled but there is no doubt that Bank Indonesia had to provide funds to banks suffering from liquidity problems caused by a flight of deposits. As a consequence of its intervention, the government had to issue large amounts of recapitalization bonds and assumed ownership of almost the entire banking system. The total amount of recapitalization bonds is likely to exceed half of Indonesia's GDP and servicing these bonds will heavily burden the central government's budget for years.

The amount of issued bonds raises the question of how weak the Indonesian banking system was. However, the cost of financial sector restructuring is not simply a reflection of the poor condition of the banking sector; it also reflects a very specific approach to the restructuring programme. Without going into the details of the programme, it is important to understand the basic principle. Commercial banks that qualified for the programme received government bonds. At the same time non-performing assets have been transferred to the Indonesian Bank Restructuring Agency (IBRA), thus restoring the banks' balance sheets. This basically means that the fiscal cost of restructuring the banking sector is realized immediately and paid up-front.

What does this all mean for the fiscal authorities? Broadly speaking, there are two consequences. The most striking consequences of the economic crisis and the subsequent stabilization policy has been the increased role that the government plays in the economy. This changed role is reflected in the newly acquired ownership of previously privately owned assets through the bank recapitalization process. Thus the crisis resulted in the government taking on more financial and more managerial responsibility. The situation is indeed very different from the pre-crisis period in which the government was pursuing a policy of gradual privatization of state-owned assets. The second consequence is the burden on the state budget. Just prior to the crisis, the fiscal surplus amounted to approximately 2.3 per cent of GDP, standing in stark contrast to a deficit of approximately 5 per cent during the current fiscal year. It is obvious that this is temporary. Nonetheless, the Ministry of Finance recognizes that fiscal stimulus to promote economic growth must not be withdrawn too early.

Much of the burden of the stabilization policy has now shifted to the fiscal authority, creating a challenge to the new administration and imposing difficult fiscal choices. It is obvious that the deficit, the debt burden, as well as the government's role as an owner of productive assets, will all have to be reduced. However, reducing the deficit is not an easy task since there are currently few opportunities for either increasing revenue or reducing expenditure that would not threaten the current economic recovery and social stability. Disposing of assets must also be done in a careful, albeit expeditious, manner. To illustrate the fiscal challenges the administration faces at the moment some indicative figures will show the enormity of the task. The bank recapitalization programme alone requires gross interest payments of between 4 to 5 per cent of GDP, absorbing more than 10 per cent of the central government's budget in the fiscal year 2000. Civil servant wages will have to be increased as an initial step towards creating a more professional public sector thus adding to the government's wage bill. Depreciation of the rupiah and higher crude oil prices have led to an enormous domestic energy subsidy, requiring price adjustments. Despite encouraging signs of economic recovery, a major increase in domestic non-oil revenue cannot be expected.

At the same time that public finances turned from a budget surplus into a budget deficit, public debt has strongly risen. Measured as a percentage value of GDP, sovereign debt rose from less than 25 per cent just prior to the crisis to around 100 per cent, raising the question of fiscal sustainability. Most of this increase has been due to growing domestic debt arising from the issuance of recapitalization bonds. Nonetheless, net external public obligations have also risen strongly, almost doubling during the crisis. Reducing the public debt-to-GDP ratio in the medium term has therefore been declared as one of the goals of the new government. This will be done by limiting expenditure growth and by strengthening our ability to mobilize revenue domestically. Until government finances are balanced, however, revenue shortfalls will be financed through foreign borrowings. While this runs counter to the objective of reducing the stock of outstanding foreign debt, we recognize that relying on foreign borrowing for the time being conveys significant advantages. There is strong reason to believe that domestically issued sovereign debt at market interest rates would be more expensive than concessionary foreign debt. Moreover, foreign borrowing is less likely to crowd out domestic investment. Furthermore, it must be remembered that foreign borrowing serves not only as a way to finance the budget deficit but also supports the balance of payments, thereby helping to strengthen the exchange rate.

In the medium term our revenue mobilization efforts will depend heavily on receipts from asset disposals. As mentioned previously, the government has ended up owning much of the country's financial sector and sizeable real sector assets, but this is a temporary condition. The government does not intend to maintain control or ownership of these assets. We fully recognize the importance of private ownership of productive assets in the economy. Moreover, most recent experience indicates that the government is not necessarily a competent business manager. For example, as a banker, the performance of the government has been weak. While state banks accounted for only one third of banking assets prior to the crisis, they account for more than half of the cost to restructure the entire banking sector. Given this poor record, the privatization of state banks and banks that have been taken over by the government is a prerequisite to create a healthy and vibrant banking sector. We expect to begin this privatization process during the first quarter of 2000 with an initial public offering (IPO) of Bank Central Asia (BCA). Following this IPO we will proceed by privatizing key state banks and banks that have been taken over by the government.

Besides re-privatizing these assets related to the bank restructuring programme, the new government has also prepared a privatization programme of genuine state-owned enterprises. This programme will comprise enterprises which operate in competitive markets and for which there is no reason for public ownership. Moreover, we will move swiftly in restructuring and, if necessary, in resolving unprofitable and heavily debt-burdened public enterprises.

This brief overview should provide the reader with an idea of what the essentials of our stabilization policy are and how we intend to proceed with our economic policy. As emphasized in this short chapter, the most significant consequence of the economic crisis and our subsequent stabilization policy has been the increased role the government plays in the economy. One of the challenges will be to restore the relative roles of the government and the private sector in the economy.

5

Restarting Economic Growth in Indonesia[1]

Anthony S. Chan

There are many new players in the Indonesian economic decision-making process but there has not yet seen a clear commitment to a new policy direction. One might say that they are still in the process of aggregating preferences and seeking common ground which highlights the differences and difficulties of policy-making. Those problems are not often discussed or even acknowledged in discussions of economic crises in general and of Indonesia in particular. This is not a novel thought but it is important to highlight the need for an outside force to act upon the new "policy committees" to bring about a change in direction or rather to begin a vigorous process of implementation.

The notable success of the commitment to, and implementation of, prudent monetary policy has not been sufficient for restarting robust growth in Indonesia. Given the state of the financial and corporate sectors one can hardly expect that it will. Bear in mind that the ultimate purpose for advocating a resolution of the banking and corporate sector debt problems is to facilitate the reflow of credit and by extension growth in the economy.

To follow the logic behind that statement it is important to ask what else is needed to restart this flow. The resolution of the problems in the financial sector is only a necessary first step. But what else is needed? A significant obstacle to solving the debt problems is caused by an inadequate legal system and the institutions needed to enforce and to adjudicate disputes. There must also be improvements in corporate governance. Other challenges lie with the implementation of a competition regime, decentralization, and modernizing the administrative systems of government. There is also a general perception of a lack of accountability by both private as well as public officials.

What is needed is a parallel processing approach to solving these problems and implementing policy change — namely, the problems need to be addressed simultaneously. Until now my impression is that the approach has been closer to a sequential one. This chapter will point out that the connection between the need for the solutions to the macro problems and the implications of the cost of delays for the nation's poorest has been lacking in the debates. While a more vigorous start to the new administration would have been desirable it is not too late to begin.

MONETARY POLICY

First of all, it is important to note the tremendous success in conducting monetary policy by Bank Indonesia. In January 1999 inter-bank interest rates averaged 37.70 per cent and by the end of the year it had come down to just over 12 per cent. More importantly the range at the beginning of the year was 28–80 per cent and by the second week in November 1999 was 10–13.63 per cent. Cumulative inflation for 1999 is about 2 per cent. There has clearly been a commitment to disciplined monetary policy and it has paid off. The exchange rate benefited as well — from about Rp9,000 in December 1998 to Rp7,100 at the present time. By some calculations, this amounts to about a 32 per cent depreciation of the real exchange rate from July 1997. One might expect that exports would do well as a consequence. Anecdotal reports suggest that in fact areas strong on non-traditional exports have been doing well but at the same time export data still show a year-on-year decrease which must give pause.

Thus the current economic situation suggests something of a puzzle. Nevertheless the economy seems to have been stabilized and now is the time to think about how to return to a sustainable growth path.

CREDIT AND GROWTH

Credit is important for working capital and is often a substitute for long-term financing in countries where there is a lack of infrastructure for long-term financing. In Indonesia the correlation between GDP and credit is .98 and, as with many countries, the stock of credit tends to move in the same direction as the flow of goods and services in the economy. But there is very little new credit activity. In the third quarter the outstanding stock of credit for foreign and joint venture banks increased by about Rp9.4 billion (a 4.7 per cent increase). Self-finance through retained earnings is not a viable alternative for a rapid recovery. Therefore the question of what else needs to be done must be asked.

One way of thinking about this problem is to look at the supply-side of the loanable funds and ask at what rate given present circumstances in the Indonesian economy will loans be available. The answer must be a high rate, although not as high as it might have been three to six months ago. Intuitively one can think of the usual variables which determine the lending rate — marginal productivity of capital, inflation, expected depreciation, and a risk premium to capture all the other unspecified factors. The outlook for the first three factors is brighter than it has been for sometime but the risk premium remains high. The risk premium may still be too high to encourage new lending and hence new investment because largely institutional factors remain to be addressed. It is two and a half years into the crisis and at some point physical capital will need to be replaced if growth is to continue.

THE RISK PREMIUM

At the heart of every loan contract is the assumption that a binding framework exists to resolve disputes which might arise. The usual one is non-payment and prudence dictates the use of collateral. Both the borrower and the lender know that there is recourse to the courts which will adjudicate the dispute on the basis of a set of laws in an impartial way. Hence, the lender is able to price the risk at a level well within reach of the borrower. Given recent experience in Indonesia this is clearly not the case. Even in cases where there were a priori agreements to use arbitration in a mutually acceptable jurisdiction, the decisions cannot be enforced. When repayment breaks down there is no viable way to pressure the offending side to negotiate. Thus it is difficult to see even if the current financial and corporate problems are resolved how new lending/new investment activity can take place with a risk premium that is within the ability of the parties to tolerate.

CORPORATE GOVERNANCE

A similar situation applies in the case of cash flow lending. Audited statements must be credible if the risk premium is to be reasonable. However even in this case there must be an alternative when disputes arise. In the formal economics literature, the class problems related to behaviour between stockholders and corporate management is known as principal-agent problems. The problems of effective bank supervision, credit supervision, and transparency in publicly held corporations all fall under this category. The point is that this is a broad area that is much in need of attention. Information on banks and businesses need to regain credibility if the risk premium associated with lending to these businesses is to go down.

OTHER FACTORS AFFECTING THE RISK PREMIUM

Decentralization and the implementation of the competition regime are sources of potential concern. One such concern is whether there will be a national free trade area — an integrated national market. The related issues of the organization of government administration and compensation will have to be addressed.

CONCLUSION: A COMPREHENSIVE APPROACH

None of these issues are new and none of the proposed solutions are original. But to relate back to the quotation at the beginning — the key question is from where will the new force come in order to change the direction of the old ways of policy-making. If one firmly believes that it is the economy that matters most, then the challenge is for the new technocrats to find a way to form a consensus on how these problems are to be addressed. Policy solutions can be guided by rigorous analysis but someone or some group must emerge to take the lead in getting the consensus necessary to go forward.

In this context a key issue has been missing from the public debates. That is, how the failure to properly supervise the financial sector and the costs of resuscitating this sector will impact on the social progress of society as a whole. It is not difficult to see that a cost of 30–60 per cent of GDP to revive this sector will severely impact discretionary spending. The clear goal should be to minimize the probability of such a financial meltdown reoccurring. It is the recommendation of this writer that teams be formed to address all these issues in a comprehensive manner and that the leaders be given a free hand.

Note

1. The views expressed in this paper are the personal opinions of the author and should not be interpreted in anyway as representing the official views of USAID.

6

Inflation and the Central Bank[1]

Joshua Felman

While preparing this chapter, I was very busy negotiating the Letter of Intent (LoI) with many of the people also participating in this volume. This chapter is designed to address the problem of inflation and the exchange rate policy. This poses a difficulty because it was not clear what should be presented on this topic. A year ago things would have been very different, as everyone in Indonesia wanted to talk about monetary policy, especially perhaps those who understood it the least. But now, monetary policy never seems to come up in casual conversations, and this is the ultimate tribute that anyone can pay to a central bank (Bank Indonesia) that it does its job so well and so unintrusively that no one seems to notice its activities any more. Yet it is precisely for this reason that it is worth recalling Bank Indonesia's accomplishments over the past year and a half. Inflation, which in mid-1998 was running at 5–10 per cent per month, has been brought down to 2 per cent per year. The exchange rate has been brought back from Rp15,000 per U.S. dollar to around Rp7,000 per U.S. dollar, and interest rates had been cut from 70 per cent to around 11 per cent. These are truly impressive achievements and they beg some important questions: How were these achievements really achieved? And are they likely to prove durable? Or is Indonesia likely to suffer a relapse?

This chapter endeavours to answer these questions even if it does require some use of the crystal ball. In order to accomplish this, first it is important to explain Indonesia's monetary framework which is highly misunderstood since it is so unusual in the region. Then it is necessary to outline how Bank Indonesia's determined implementation of this framework succeeded in stabilizing the macroeconomy. And finally, this author will explain whether or not this stability is likely to continue. In this "age of transparency", from the outset, my conclusion is that I expect this stability will continue, barring some nasty political surprises.

Starting with the monetary policy framework, in Indonesia the central bank implements what is known as a "base money policy", which means that it tries to achieve its target of low inflation by controlling an intermediate target, namely base money. Base money can be defined as the amount of cash in circulation plus the amount of reserves that the commercial banks deposit with the central bank. Why would any central bank want to target something so arcane as base money? Why not just peg the exchange rate or set interest rates? Answering these questions is not easy in one short chapter as they are the subjects not just of a paper, but books, and volumes of books. But some sort of answer is necessary.

Take the option of pegging the exchange rate. In the case of Indonesia there is a very fundamental problem with this strategy. Pegging means that monetary policy cannot focus on domestic objectives, as they must be subordinated to external constraints. In other words, the priority must be given to maintaining the exchange rate peg. For example, if the political problems that have flared up in Ambon made foreign investors uneasy and they begin to shift their funds out of Indonesia, this would weaken the exchange rate and if it was pegged, domestic interest rates would have to go up to defend the currency. But raising interest rates is the last thing Bank Indonesia wants to do because it would further depress the domestic economy at the time when it is already highly depressed. Of course Indonesia could have tried to get around this problem by imposing capital controls, as is the case in Malaysia. However, this is never really considered since it would have been like locking the proverbial barn door after the horse had bolted. In Indonesia the issue was not preventing capital outflow because the capital had already fled. What was needed was to get capital back and the only way to do this was to maintain an open capital account, thus pegging was not appropriate.

That leads to another possible strategy. Why not just control interest rates? After all this would achieve the objective of allowing the central bank to focus on the needs of the domestic economy. The problem with this strategy was that the outbreak of the crisis had shattered the banking system and in circumstances such as this, interest rates can be a very poor guide to monetary policy. For example, in December 1997 the central bank raised money market rates to around 30 per cent at a time when inflation was only around 5 per cent. Since real interest rates were apparently quite high, Bank Indonesia thought it was pursuing a very tight monetary policy, however it was wrong about this as the policy was not tight. Those apparently high real interest rates were woefully insufficient to convince depositors to leave their money in banks that were unsound. So the general public took the money out and converted it into either cash or U.S. dollars, causing inflation to skyrocket and the exchange rate to collapse. This is something of a simplification of what was a very complex period but the point remains, interest rates are very unreliable guide to monetary policy-making during the crisis. In fact, base money is much better.

When base money is rising by more than a normal trend amount, this is a clear sign that trouble is brewing ahead, since it means people are withdrawing money from banks. When base money is relatively stable, it is a good sign that the situation is under control. So Bank Indonesia adopted base money targetting as its prime method to determine monetary policy. To show its commitment to this new framework, the central bank began to publish, in mid-1998, its monetary targets as well as the out-turns each week so that the public could see whether or not it was adhering to its commitments. Then under this framework interest rates are determined by the market in weekly auctions of central bank certificates (SBI) and the exchange rate is allowed to float freely. This is the monetary framework, but how then did the central bank use this framework to conquer inflation? The answer was relatively simple. From May 1998 to December 1998, base money was kept completely flat, which is to say that no money was printed at all, even though inflation was still exceptionally high and it was eating away at the value of the real money in circulation. It was this tough policy that stopped inflation in its tracks.

On this last point there seems to be considerable confusion. There are many who seemed to believe the causation was entirely different. According to them all the improvement was due to an IMF bailout. In this version of events, the IMF gave Indonesia an instalment of around US$10 billion, and the central bank spent this money intervening on the foreign exchange market, which then appreciated the exchange rate and brought down prices. This is a tempting story, and not least of all because a lot of people want to give credit to the IMF, but in all good conscience one must give credit where credit is due. Bank Indonesia must take the credit for controlling inflation. Unfortunately this cannot be demonstrated by providing the actual figures on Bank Indonesia's foreign exchange intervention because they are confidential. But suffice it to say that the central bank did not spend the IMF money, as these funds went into reserve. Indonesia's case was both something very different from the policies of other Asian economies affected by the economic crisis and something straight out of economic textbooks. To summarize, Bank Indonesia stopped the money printing press, and that was what stopped inflation.

But can the stability be maintained? After all there are serious potential threats to this new found stability. There are three threats that have been mentioned.

First, there is the administering price in wage adjustments. Fuel and electricity prices are highly subsidized and all government wages are well below market levels. The new government is planning to correct the situation, and it has already adopted a multi-year programme to do this, starting with the fiscal year 2000 budget. As this programme is implemented, the adjustments would certainly boost the overall price level. The only question is by how much. No one really knows for sure since much depends on whether private sector wages will follow public sector wage increases. The best guess though is that they will not raise wages that much, partly because firms are not in the position to pay, and partly because workers are facing large-scale unemployment. Accordingly, the central bank believes that the inflationary impact will be modest and they expect to limit core-underlying inflation to around 3 to 5 per cent this year. The administrative adjustments would add only about 2 per cent on top. The IMF concurs with these figures. In sum, the administrative adjustments are of concern, but they are not a real threat to price stability. Much more serious threats come from the existence of a large domestic government debt mentioned elsewhere in the volume. Total government debt is likely to amount to around 90 per cent of GDP by the end of the current 1999/2000 fiscal year. This amount, around more than 50 per cent of GDP, would be domestic debt. These are very substantial sums and the resulting debts put a very significant burden on the budget, with around 6.5 per cent of the GDP in interest costs alone during the coming fiscal year 2000 budget. Clearly there is a risk here as the government does not have the funds to pay for this debt service and it starts to borrow from the central bank. The whole monetary framework would be undermined. In this scenario, base money will spiral again, while inflation will inevitably follow.

There are several reasons to believe this will not happen. First, the new Central Bank Law prohibits the government from borrowing from Bank Indonesia. Moreover the international community, led by Japan, the World Bank, and the Asian Development Bank (ADB), is determined to tide the government over until its tax revenues recover by giving it budgetary support and arranging for rescheduling of its official debt. Second, the government itself is committed to keeping the public finances in order, even if this requires a cut in government spending. This determination was exemplified in 1998/99 when the economy suffered the greatest collapse in Asia since World War II. The government deficit of that year was a modest 2 per cent of GDP, one of the smallest deficits in the region. Given the situation, there are good grounds for confidence in believing that the fiscal policy will not threaten price stability. Third, a new threat has apparently arisen. According to newspaper reports in January 2000, an audit into Bank Indonesia has revealed that the central bank is bankrupt, which means it would be unable to operate effectively. However, the audit did not actually say Bank Indonesia is bankrupt. There are very good reasons to believe the bank is perfectly sound, but the authorities have shown caution by commissioning further studies to obtain a definitive view. If it turns out that recapitalization is required, the Minister of Finance has stated publicly that he will stand behind Bank Indonesia and provide the needed funds. It is also worth noting the potential insolvency of a central bank is not like that of a commercial bank. The key difference is that the central bank can always meet its domestic obligations because it literally has the licence to print money. Furthermore, this ability allows it to borrow in the market to cover any incurred deficits. Thus an insolvent central bank can actually continue for some time honouring its obligations and running an effective monetary policy. In fact the Philippines' central bank did exactly that for a full decade.

There is no doubt that many tough monetary problems lie ahead for Indonesia. Price stability, after all, is like a person's reputation, which can never be established once and for all, and can only be earned everyday through hard and unceasing work. It is impossible to predict with absolute certainty what is going to happen, but from the available evidence there are strong and reasonable grounds for optimism.

Note

1. The views expressed in this chapter are mine, and do not necessarily reflect the views of the IMF.

SECTION III
Fiscal Policy, Decentralization, and Good Governance

7

Fiscal Issues and Decentralization

Sri Mulyani Indrawati

This chapter will investigate fiscal issues, decentralization and good governance, although it is difficult to cover all three at once. It is important to understand the fiscal issues facing the Indonesian economy at this time. Of course according to many documents, and especially the Ministry of Finance's budget plan for 2000 released in January, it is very clear that the government still wants to use the fiscal policy as a stimulus or "pump-priming" effect on the economy. There are many challenges involved in using the government budget to create fiscal or economic stimulation. The first question that relates to this: is it the correct policy course to use fiscal policy to stimulate the economy? It is important to question the correct use of the fiscal policy, especially when the real machinery of the economy, the banking sector and the corporations, are still collapsing and have not fully submitted themselves to a proper restructuring programme. The stimulation is based on the assumption that if the aggregate demand collapses, the government expenditure will substitute for it. However looking back over the previous two years of the economic crisis, the government failed to undertake the stimulation of the economy through fiscal deficit, for example, in 1998/99 the deficit only turned out to be only slightly above 2 per cent, but this year will be an improvement as a stimulus, at around 6.8 per cent of the GDP. But this raises the important question of the constraint facing the budget as a fiscal instrument to stimulate the economy. This is the serious problem of solvability and sustainability of the budget.

There are still a lot of challenges that will be faced by the government budget. The difficulty is to define the right level of deficit that will be adequate to stimulate the economy while not jeopardizing the sustainability of the budget itself. Also, what is the right level to create the necessary growth for recovery that will not, at the same time, create inflationary pressures for the economy? What is the most appropriate level? Is it 8.5 per cent, 6.8 per cent or even 5 per cent? The level of 5 per cent deficit is usually prompted as the "right level", but this is never tested nor demonstrated. There is a further complication in defining and even classifying what the real measurement of the deficit is, as the government budget, Anggaran Pengeluaran dan Belanja Negara (APBN) does not comprise the entire government account, as there are "off-budget accounts" which mean the official figures do not indicate the real deficit.

A further question remains on how to allocate this level of deficit, which is a question for the expenditure policy side. Is it necessary to preserve the consumption orientation spending? Increasing government spending and maintaining the current subsidy levels (with perhaps some reduction) creates a limited budget deficit. This will maintain the capital situation and create a new capacity in the economy. There is one consensus on this issue that the government at least should not use this deficit to increase the consumption expenditure, but use it for the maintenance of the capital condition and investment conditions in Indonesia through the maintenance of the current capital, both human and physical. A number of articles have recently appeared in Indonesian publications mentioning that even in Jakarta the roads have deteriorated by between 30 to 70 per cent. The obvious point here is that if Indonesia delays maintenance of the road system, budget allocation will be needed to build new roads after four years, which will cost far more than the initial maintenance spending. So the choices for the government, on the expenditure side, are very critical at this time. However, the government has a very limited degree of freedom because, at the same time, the expenditure policy is constrained by the fact that the government must service its foreign and domestic debt through interest payments which are now becoming an enormous burden for the government. So it seems that the stimulation objective has become the residual policy, while the priority goes to debt repayments.

An important issue for Indonesia is the institutional challenge. The institutional challenges can be divided into three levels. First is the issue of dealing with the debt problem. Currently the government faces a very large public debt to GDP ratio, both domestic and foreign (the domestic debt forms the majority). There needs to be institutional preparation and development from the government through a debt management office. This should be the first priority of the Ministry of Finance to establish, as debt management continues through the same old system of compartmentalization. Institutional development to manage this debt is necessary on the projection and planning of the repayment of public debt. Unfortunately, going on the past two years experience in Indonesia, the domestic public debt was driven not by the needs of the government to create, or to design the right stimulation in the economy, but more because the government cannot avoid it due to the cost of bank restructuring. Equally unfortunate is that the state-owned banks are the most uncertain source of domestic debt for Indonesia, for which the IMF, *inter alia*, must take the blame. If the Indonesian Government was consistent with their own plans at that time for the C-bank category, which was to close them, then all the state-owned banks also in this category should have been rationalized without too much cost. Of course the IMF, the World Bank, and the Bank Indonesia stated at that time that the cost of closing banks was too expensive. However, after two years, it is apparent that these banks are a greater drain on public funds than it was first imagined.

From a macro-management point of view, the government should have a flexible plan for the budget deficit target and how to use this deficit to stimulate the economy. The government, especially the Ministry of Finance, has become like a "garbage can" with regards to this programme as they have merely become the recipients of the cost of the programme. The fiscal policy challenge is not how to manage the optimal fiscal deficit but to minimize the cost of the existing domestic debt, which is the result of banking restructuring. This has also occurred because the government still has a blanket guarantee over the one source of the ever-growing domestic debt in this case.

The second element of domestic debt management is the preparation and development of the right instruments. The government is currently only issuing Treasury Bonds, but soon they may need to issue Treasury Notes, or T-bills. What is the level of interest and how should it be managed? Will it substitute the SBI as the money market instrument? These are questions that the Ministry of Finance needs to address. The third area of prudent debt management is to develop the market infrastructure for this instrument, which is currently dominated by the central bank, when it should be in the hands of the Ministry of Finance.

Another element of the institutional challenge is the relationship between the central and local government, or the decentralization issue. There are many crucial issues in this local and central government relationship. Methodologically, it is necessary to differentiate the challenge of this local–central government relationship into three levels. The first is the conceptual level, the second one is the institutional level, and the third is the individual level.

On the conceptual level, there is currently a huge gap between the local government, and the central government. The IMF, the World Bank, and USAID, as multilateral and bilateral institutions, always insist that the evolution of decentralization should begin by clearly defining the function and responsibility between the central and local government, particularly with regard to funding and resource issues. However the local government, and the local people, are not necessarily concerned about the overall function and responsibility of Indonesia, but they are interested in gaining the money first, and ignoring the concerns of the central government. Some has said, "it's your problem, it's not my problem". So we have a very serious gap between reality and expectations in which the local authorities want to have more money and, at the same time they, do not want to share the burden.

On the institutional level there are a lot of challenges and problems. The first is related to the technical capabilities of implementation, although the preparation of so-called "local autonomy" began in the early 1980s when the government established the local government planning agency. Stemming from this, a lot of training has been done although the volume and the speed of the training have never met the demand at the local level. So there is a serious technical capability issue at the local level about whether the devolved authorities can assume such a huge responsibility. Indonesia will give priority to at least the four most important, most resource-rich provinces, namely, Aceh, Riau, Eastern Kalimantan and West Papua. They will get quite a significant amount of funding starting next year from the 2000 budget. The question is whether they can manage this properly or simply use this limited fund for personal enrichment. People will posit the argument that the money will create the necessary human resource quality but this remains to be seen.

The second problem concerns the existence of institutional processes of check and balances on the local government and, in particular, whether the local parliament will properly monitor the local administrations. There is a tendency for both local parliaments and local governments to use allocated funds on consumption-orientated policies rather than on the investment side. One can easily imagine a scenario of local government salary increases and a wide array of lavish projects, such as gymnasiums, sport centres or statutes of local heroes. This increase in consumption by local government may conflict with the central government's anti-inflationary policies.

The third issue of institutional challenge concerns the issue of governance. This relates to the extremely high levels of corruption in the Soeharto administration. There is currently a proposed scenario that by significantly increasing the salary of the higher level officers it will reduce significantly the degree of KKN (corruption, collusion and nepotism) in Indonesia. But the prevalence of KKN will not necessarily be completely undermined by this salary increase, as lucrative "extra payments" from the business community will continue to be attractive. The additional legal income will not necessarily "weed out" KKN from the system. So some serious questions remain over how to implement more effective bureaucratic reforms.

The final issue that needs to be addressed is whether Indonesia needs a fiscal adjustment programme. Indonesia certainly needs a fiscal adjustment programme in which the government should make an effort to shift the fiscal deficit to a more reasonable deficit and then gradually move to the surplus. If the Indonesian Government fails to revive the economy to a quite significant level of growth, it will have a serious problem in maintaining the solvency and sustainability of the fiscal policy. As long as economic growth is larger than the real interest rate, then Indonesia is still quite safe in using additional debt to finance the deficit. But over time there is certainly a need to adjust the fiscal stand both in the form of revenue (every source of additional and potential revenue should be collected) and controlling expenditure.

The question is whether the government has enough political will to make this fiscal adjustment. In my experience there is a commitment to this from Abdurrahman Wahid (or Gus Dur) and his leading cabinet ministers, who have responsibility for the economy, to take this step. The Ministry of Finance is always saying that it wants to reduce the debt. Generally they mention "foreign debt" to the public without citing the need to reduce overall total public debt, which should be managed carefully because the outstanding debt is quite critical for the sustainability of the fiscal policy.

A sense of urgency to create a fiscal adjustment programme is lacking, perhaps because the IMF and the World Bank is always in the background and the government can always count on them to provide additional money. It is easy enough to hold the multilateral institutions hostage by saying, "if you do not give us additional money, then the programme of the recovery will collapse". This kind of statement is generally useful in urging support.

There is some urgency over the course of action that should be undertaken by the Ministry of Finance. The room for manoeuvre is becoming very limited because more and more money needs to be allocated to service the debt. The government needs a greater sense of urgency over its fiscal adjustment programme.

8

Good Governance and the Indonesian Economy[1]

Howard Dick

A key demand of the reform movement that brought about the downfall of Soeharto was the abolition of "corruption, collusion and nepotism" (KKN). The key word in this debate was "abolition". No compromise was envisaged. However, no strategy was put forward to achieve this. Corruption was seen as a moral issue. The rotten old (New) Order should be swept away and a new government formed of right-minded people with the task of cleansing the nation — or so it was imagined. Such Utopian thinking is part of the revolutionary experience but can do no more than set very broad guidelines for the practical and very messy business of establishing a new government and regime. The essence of the problem is that not just with the New Order officials, but the whole society. Individuals such as former President Soeharto and his family could be identified and perhaps prosecuted but modes of behaviour and institutions could not readily be transformed. Even under a saintly president it would be a difficult process of evolution — the making of history in real time.

As a matter of practical politics, the issue breaks down into goals, strategy and tactics. Goals are quite difficult. If a "zero-KKN" option is not feasible, and the base level of corruption cannot be assessed, how is a target level and rate of adjustment to be determined? How is progress to be measured? An intuitively simple goal thus refracts into a set of partial objectives that soon lose their articulation with each other. This problem is compounded by the nature of cabinet. All ministers are obliged to tackle corruption as part of their portfolio but "doing things" tends to get higher priority, so that in practice the anti-corruption drive becomes part of specific portfolios such as justice and the office of attorney-general. A programme lacking clear objectives and with fragmented responsibility is guaranteed to lead to problems of implementation.

Strategy is about choices and processes. One choice is the extent to which an anti-corruption drive pursues charges against members of the former regime, as opposed to setting in place processes to improve the quality of the new one. Of course it is possible, and to some extent necessary, to do both. If no charges are laid against highly corrupt members of the former regime, the public record shows that corruption does pay. Even if one is found out, one keeps the winnings. This is a perverse incentive. At the very least there need to be investigations and public reporting, but how many resources should be devoted to laborious investigation of money trails and their international ramifications in order to generate legally conclusive evidence of wrongdoing? How many Bank Bali type cases can be investigated in the year 2000? Equating the problem with past malpractices, instead of ongoing processes, may sidetrack an effective anti-corruption drive. A further complication is that a long series of commercial exposes, as in regard to bank loans, may weaken the recovery of business confidence. Is there a case for legal amnesty in return for full disclosure and co-operation in debt rescheduling? Here policy choices must be made.

This chapter will focus on improving processes and outcomes from a strategic perspective. Goals cannot be resolved here and tactics are a matter for politicians to decide. In view of constraints of space and time, I take the literature as read. Nor will this contributor provide a list of policy recommendations, since the problem of "good governance" is far more intractable than piecemeal social re-engineering. Thus legal reform is desirable, because good laws are better than bad laws, but it will be a long time yet before Indonesian society functions according to Rule of Law. An analogy can be made of water gushing out of a leaking pipe. The immediate problem appears to be to patch the leak. The more effective response may be to reduce the water pressure at the source, then deal with the leak. I will therefore apply lateral thinking to try to identify some underlying dynamics of KKN, economic, social and political, and suggest how a better understanding of them in the Indonesian case may inform policy priorities and responses, including in respect to decentralization.

DEMAND AND SUPPLY: THREE DYNAMICS

The moral calculus is that corruption occurs because "bad people" abuse their power. Hence, identify and root out the bad people and the problem is solved. Economists would be more inclined to think in terms of demand and supply of scarce resources in imperfect markets. Very crudely, they may distinguish between (economic) demand and social and political supply of public sector services. (Economic) demand is simply the willingness of individual, groups and firms to pay a premium for formal or informal services in a situation of artificial scarcity. Social supply recognizes that the supply price of civil servants and supplementation strategies, including KKN, derives from attempts by officials to maintain or improve their family's standard of living. Political supply allows that the needs of the immediate *group* of department, agency or military unit, or of an affiliated organization or political party, may influence the supply price. This classification is not a standard one from the literature but for the purposes of this exposition helps to distinguish between economic, social and political dynamics which are fundamental to the phenomenon of corruption. Applying Harry G. Johnson's principle that distortions should be tackled at their source,[2] the focus of the discussion should be on these three dynamics.

i) Economic dynamics

Given artificial bottlenecks in supply, individuals, groups and firms are prepared to pay bureaucratic gatekeepers (gamekeepers?) a premium for faster or better service. They may also seek to pay a premium or unofficial rent to secure a competitive advantage over others. The first is fairly legitimate and suggests that government departments and agencies should be encouraged as part of the transparency process to formulate charters that set out service standards, charges and complaints procedures. In general, public sector charges are too low in relation to ability to pay, provided concessions are allowed for those who are disadvantaged.

The second mode of behaviour, equivalent to rent-seeking, is clearly an abuse of power. On this topic there is already a large literature. Transparency is obviously desirable in the allocation of public resources, especially contracts. More fundamentally, it is desirable through deregulation to eliminate bureaucratic requirements such as restricted licences and permits that serve as choke points for informal levies and rents and become bases for competitive advantage. A government's ability to do so, however, depends very much upon social and political dynamics.

A particularly awkward problem is the contested role of the Indonesian Chinese in the private sector. Simply put, dominance of ethnic Chinese — and foreign — capital in the medium- to large-scale sector is tolerated in return for a flow of levies and rents back to bureaucratic powerholders, the military and politicians. This has been the case since the 1950s and is a pattern which can be traced back to colonial, indeed even pre-colonial, times. It is not amenable to quick reform. Even if a better legal system and a more efficient public sector could be conjured up, rent-seeking patterns of behaviour — or is it Robin Hood behaviour? — will persist as long as the private sector is perceived as having no independent legitimacy. The disposal of IBRA's (Indonesian Bank Restructuring Agency) massive portfolio cannot avoid this fundamental problem, which at root is actually social and political: Indonesians of Chinese descent are still subject to alienation. In fact, they have to go on paying what amounts to subscriptions for the right to be second-class citizens.

ii) Social dynamics

Social supply recognizes that *individual* public servants as members of households seek to attain or maintain a comfortable and socially reputable standard of living. To the extent that this cannot be provided from the formal salary package, it may be supplemented in other ways. The New Order saw a trend of rising expectations among the middle class, to which all but lower-ranking civil servants may be judged to belong. Not only a self-contained house and garden but also a car, a wide range of other consumer durables, and a tertiary education for one's children are very expensive expectations that have increased the supply price of civil servants.

On top of this, Indonesia is generally regarded as having too many civil servants. The public sector burgeoned in the period of Guided Democracy (1959–66) and despite rationalization in the early years of the New Order, remains large. Nevertheless, this does not show up in comparative figures of central government revenue and expenditure (see Table 8.1).

Comparatively, the Indonesian central government appears to have a modest footprint. Taxation effort and expenditure are both relatively low as a percentage of GDP and until the crisis were trending downwards in response to rapid economic growth. In 1999/2000 revenues will still be only around 16 per cent of GDP, with expenditures rising through deficit-financing to 21 per cent.

The complication is that the actual footprint is larger than official revenues and expenditures. Additional funds are raised by way of informal levies on government services and rents extracted by virtue of public

TABLE 8.1
Central Government Revenue and Expenditure as Percentage of GDP (1997)

	Revenue	Expenditure	Govt Consumption (1998)	Military Exp.
Indonesia	16.0	14.7	7	1.8
Thailand	18.0	18.7	10	2.5
Philippines	19.0	18.5	13	1.5
Malaysia	23.6	20.1	11	3.0

Source: World Bank, *World Development Report 1999/2000*.

sector leverage. By their nature, neither can readily be quantified. As yet, there is no authoritative estimate. The problem can be traced back to Guided Democracy, when the civil service real remuneration was eroded by inflation. At that time the solution was for civil servants to work two or more jobs. For academic staff at state universities, this solution still applies and according to social norms is not regarded as KKN. The New Order raised civil servants' salaries, drastically pruned numbers and required more or less full-time attendance of those who remained. Together with rising consumer expectations, this increased efforts to supplement incomes. The main legal way was to acquire projects through the development budget. Additional supplementation could be gained by siphoning off funds (leakages) by over-invoicing or under-delivery. Construction projects were the classic case. Similar techniques could be applied to requisitions under the routine budget.

The new government has sought to deal with the problem in a mix of strategic and ad hoc ways. The departments of Information and Social Affairs have been closed, which does not immediately reduce the number of civil servants but eliminates two redundant bastions. To what extent the functions of the rest of the bureaucracy will be reviewed and, wherever possible, streamlined or eliminated is not yet clear. The very act of appointing new ministers unavoidably perpetuates bureaucratic vested interests. As yet uncertain is the impact of the new decentralization laws, which are expected to reallocate tasks from central and provincial to district governments. Unless there are *dis*economies of scale, overall numbers of officials with discretionary powers are likely to increase rather than decrease.

The government has committed itself to raising civil service salaries to realistic levels, initially for ministers and top officials (echelon II). This is clearly essential to good governance and logically should be extended to lower decision-making levels. For the time being, however, lower ranks will have to be satisfied with two 10 per cent "catch-up" increments as further compensation for crisis inflation. To the extent that higher salaries substitute for informal and illegal salary supplementation there is actually no net cost and logically a net economic gain through higher productivity and elimination of distortions. The difficulty is to set in place a set of incentives to ensure that substitution does in fact occur. How is compliance to be monitored? What are the rewards and penalties? Should senior civil servants be placed on contract?

None of this, however, tackles the fundamental dynamic, namely the expectation of high and rising middle class living standards. In a globalizing world it is natural that Indonesia's educated elite will seek parity with western colleagues. The other side of the coin, however, and a real political issue, is equity *vis-à-vis* the Indonesian people (*rakyat*). Perhaps the worst legacy of the New Order was to entrench as normal and acceptable an ethic of conspicuous consumption. "If you have it, spend it — if you don't have it, get it and flaunt it." Compared with the early 1970s, extraordinarily luxurious standards of housing and vehicle ownership now pass as normal, at least in Jakarta. There is no longer any sense of embarrassment associated with this consumption (*tidak tahu malu*).

A suggestion that the new government might launch a campaign of modest living will seem naive. In the mid-1980s there was a short-lived campaign for modest lifestyles (*pola hidup sederhana*), which was regarded very cynically and had no obvious effect. Economists and historians also tend to be sceptical as to the efficacy of sumptuary legislation. It never achieves the aim. Nevertheless, it may have a stabilizing effect. The other day I read somewhere the sensible comment: "Don't try and keep up with the Joneses (Santosos?). Drag them down to your level. It's cheaper!" This new government and new regime, with a popular mandate and support from religious parties, would gain political points by a campaign which set out some criteria for what is excessive (*terlalu*) for government officials in terms of publicly visible housing and vehicle ownership. It might also be emphasized that civil servants found guilty of embezzlement will have their ill-gotten gains returned to the state. This would go further than the new obligation to declare the family assets of senior officials and politicians. Both Herb Feith and Emil Salim mentioned in the 1950s that there were still ministers for whom it was a point of honour to live modestly. Indonesia now has a credibly non-materialist president. Surely there are opportunities here to break the consumerist cycle at a time when the nation is facing great hardship. This would also help to lay more solid foundations for decentralization.

iii) Political dynamics

In the authoritarian New Order "slush funds" flowed upwards to the Soeharto family through Pertamina, Bulog (Badan Urusan Logistik Nasional), state banks, the Department of Forestry and various other agencies and *yayasan* (foundations). In the new political system, competition between parties will be fought out in terms of a) ideology and policy, b) funds, and c) rewards. This is inevitable and it is no surprise to find evidence that it is already happening. Before the old KKN can be brought under control, new KKN seems to be emerging, as Faisal Basri has recently claimed.[3]

No country has satisfactorily resolved the issue of political funding (note: Germany, U.S., Britain, France, Italy are cases in point). That does not mean, however, that efforts should not be made. Where there are no checks, the outcome is likely to be a competitive spiral. The fact that the long-term party strength is still uncertain, and the cost of campaigning across a country as populous and vast as Indonesia, makes the issue particularly intractable.

Based upon international experience, some suggestions can be made:

1. Parties and parliamentarians need funds and they will get them one way or another. Party membership will not generate large revenues. Parliament should therefore try to hammer out a workable political funding law that embodies a set of norms and institutions as a basic political consensus. The principle that party accounts should be audited is a good one and public funding in proportion to votes and declared expenditure is a good incentive. As under the new Thai constitution, vote buying should be illegal, under sanction of returns being declared null-and-void.
2. Parliamentarians should be paid well from the public purse, including the maintenance of offices and support staff. Such payment is often begrudged but this vital institution must work effectively. Failure to do so merely shifts the burden to less desirable unofficial sources.

3. Ministers should be liable for dismissal if they are found to have seriously abused their office for party benefit. In that event, in a coalition government a ministry should be allocated to another party. Faisal Basri has recently suggested that some parties and ministries are already contending.

DECENTRALIZATION

From the viewpoint of good governance, decentralization will be a tremendous transitional problem. Although some institutional capacity already exists through regional councils and planning agencies, it is stronger at the provincial than at the district level and very uneven across the archipelago. The training requirements are enormous. At the same time, the principle of local accountability is sound and does meet local aspirations. The requirement that *bupati* (mayor) be elected instead of appointed by the central government is a fundamental democratic reform to an institution that traces back via the colonial *binnenlands bestuur* or *pangreh praja* (bureaucratic class) to the Dutch East India Company (VOC) and pre-colonial era. It may be hoped that the abuses that were highlighted by Douwes Dekker's *Max Havelaar* may at last be eliminated, along with *dwi fungsi* (the military's dual function).

However, the experience of the Philippines and Thailand, America and Japan, is that local government may fall into the hands not of the "good guys" but of local bosses, an alliance of vested interests, comprising well-connected bureaucrats, local businessmen and even criminal gangs who are prepared to buy votes ruthlessly and intimidate opponents. It may be in the interests of some political parties to ally with such people if they can deliver votes. Will citizens, journalists or politicians be brave enough to speak out against corrupt real estate deals and vote-buying? Will inter-party competition and provincial and central government supervision be sufficient protection? Perhaps. The advantage over the Philippines is that there are not yet in Indonesia such powerful local families controlling economic resources. There is more pluralism. The Thai case, however, suggests that local military or ex-military personnel may underwrite alliances that protect their local interests. Such local power struggles may mirror and even interact with national-level struggles. Hard politics may be a more important influence on the outcome than problems of funding and human resources.

A practical matter is the central co-ordination of regional projects. At present projects in the regions must gain approvals from Bappenas (Badan

Perencanaan Nasional), Sekretarit Negara (Sekneg) and the Ministry of Finance, as well as line departments such as public works, and transport and communication. Such overlapping responsibility with all its opportunities for multiple siphoning of project funds is something that can be fixed quite readily by a reallocation of responsibilities. Do Bappenas and Sekneg need to maintain financial supervision of projects as well as the Ministry of Finance? Then again, who should audit the Ministry of Finance?

CONCLUSION

The key governance issue for Indonesia is not KKN, which are symptoms, but the long-run size and functions of the public sector. Recent trends towards deregulation and privatization have so far brought about change only on the margin. Decentralization reforms may be more far-reaching. Nevertheless, the public sector as an interlocking set of institutions, cannot be re-engineered at will over a short period. The *status quo* reflects fundamental accommodations in Indonesian society and politics.

For example, the modern *priyayi* (aristocratic) class, now Indonesian rather than Javanese, still sees its role as governing the country and holding in check the economic power of the ethnic Chinese and foreigners. And there is a very large military establishment that believes that its mission is not just to defend the country but to help govern and develop it. The size and functions of the public sector cannot be transformed without change in the aspirations of these social groups. *Dwi fungsi* is now under challenge, to some extent even within the military. But will the children of the *priyayi* aspire to compete in business with the ethnic Chinese rather than to seek careers in government, education or the professions? If not, the size of the public sector is likely to remain supply-driven.

The political transformation is already influencing appointments to top positions in the public sector and bringing about some redistribution of power within that structure. The rhetoric of reform continues to prevail but the actual reform process may lose momentum unless goals and strategies can be more clearly stated and followed up by sound political tactics. A leaner, more transparently funded and more efficient public sector would unquestionably boost Indonesia's economic growth. Whether a political consensus can be maintained to achieve it is an open question. If the committed reformers become outnumbered in cabinet by administrators and political fixers, the reform process will be vulnerable.

Notes

1. This chapter derives from work into good governance being carried out in conjunction with Anggito Abimanyu and under the auspices of the Australian Centre for International Business. I am grateful to Mudrajad Kuncoro and Wihana Kirana Jaya for comments and assistance.
2. See Harry G. Johnson, *On Economic and Society: Selected Essays* (Chicago: University of Chicago Press, 1982).
3. *Jakarta Post*, 5 January 2000.

9

Five Crucial Issues for the Economy

Mark Baird

Much comment has already been made about the Indonesian economy. In the opinion of this author five topics will form the leading issues of the budget for 2001, namely: (1) the fiscal deficit; (2) civil service salaries; (3) subsidies; (4) decentralization; and (5) the development programme. Much of this is covered in other contributions that may or may not agree with my own conclusions.

First, on the fiscal deficit, as mentioned by Sri Mulyani Indrawati in this volume: Is 5 per cent too much or too little? And why is there so much comfort that this is about the right level? It stems from the fact that this is a year of transition where the government is trying to balance this concern for stimulus with its concern for sustainability. Compare a 5 per cent deficit to the outcome for 2000, and one can see that it does provide a modest degree of stimulus. If one compares it to the budget for 2000, it is certainly a plan to move the budget in the direction of a lower deficit. It is the continuation of that trend that will determine whether or not this is going to be sustainable and whether or not it is going to be credible. But as a target for a transition period, 5 per cent sounds about right. In practice, the Indonesian Government has rarely been able to reach the deficit targets, as they have been originally perceived, and that is not such a bad thing. If the money cannot be well spent, if there are genuine concerns about governance, as we have had for instance in 2000 in social safety net programmes, the money should not be spent and there will be a fall short in the target.

On the other hand if the Indonesian Government can get its act together the 5 per cent target provides the right signal of balancing stimulus and sustainability. If that is reduced in subsequent years, World Bank projections suggest that Indonesia could reduce the government debt to GDP ratio from the current level of about 100 per cent to close to 60 per cent in five years, and 40 per cent in ten years. For 2001, a target of 5 per cent can be financed relatively easily, with half of it from asset sales and privatization, and the other half from external financing. Indonesia has available a considerable amount of budget support that was not dispersed in 2000 because of the Bank Bali scandal. That money can be carried over to cover some of the 2001 deficit. It is my understanding that the government does plan to go to the Paris Club, which will help with the rescheduling of official bilateral aid. There will be a very small residual requirement for new commitments from the consolidated group and that can be met from the major donors including Japan, the World Bank, and the ADB. So in terms of feasibility it is possible from a financing point of view and it is appropriate from a fiscal stimulus point of view.

Sri Mulyani also raises the good question about what should really be the fiscal strategy to improve the economy. The World Bank simply follows the indications given by the government, in the form of state policy guidelines, that they would like to reduce the deficit, reduce external debt, and reduce dependence on external borrowings. That means the World Bank would probably be lending less in the future, and possibly also shift lending back towards projects and away from balance of payments and budget support. If the Indonesian Government were to revisit those assumptions, the donor community would also be very willing to enter into that debate and see what is feasible. However the instinct to try to lower the current debt burden is correct. The key question is how fast and how soon can Indonesia do that while protecting public services and the delivery of public services.

Second, on civil service salaries, discussed in this volume by both Sri Mulyani and Howard Dick, nobody would question the need to raise salaries. It is very difficult to tell civil servants to "do a good job" but then not provide a living wage. It provides the excuse for entering into corrupt practices, but as other commentators warn us, raising salaries by itself does not remove the temptation. It is disappointing that there has not been more discussion around the issue of how civil servants will be held accountable for their performance. Salary increases should be phased in as accountability is strengthened. And equally the increases should probably start at the top, then work their way down. It is certainly more affordable but of course it will put a lot of pressure on the overall civil service salary structure to rise. If there is no complementary action to rationalize salaries, and perhaps to cut the size of the civil service, this is quickly going to create an additional fiscal problem. This remains an area that is not a one-year programme but a multi-year programme. Furthermore, these changes must go hand-in-hand with changes in the judicial reform. Judicial reform is not a matter of enacting new laws. It is a matter of ensuring laws can be implemented, and any effort to hold civil servants accountable is not going to be effective unless the judiciary can be strengthened. There is hope in this area, as there is clear commitment from the president for judicial change. There are also indications that there will be changes in the Supreme Court. There is already a very active and credible Attorney-General, Marzuki Darusman, but there is not yet a complete and coherent judicial reform programme. All of this have to be part of the multi-year programme and deserves a lot more attention.

Third, there is a commitment by the Wahid government to reduce subsidies, but politically that is never easy or popular. In the case of Indonesia, it is clearly the time to start. This is not a problem created by this current government. It is a problem left over by the previous Soeharto regime, and it is not going to be solved in the short term, but Indonesia must make a credible start in 2000 or it will risk greater difficulties in the future. The key areas where this is important are energy and agriculture. In energy, or the provision of power, there is a clear case for significant tariff increases. This has nothing to do with the cost of energy projects. It is simply the fact that tariffs have not kept up with the exchange rate adjustments during the crisis in the operating costs of PLN (Perusahaan Listrik Negara). It is easy to separate out small domestic consumers, and maintain their tariffs at the same level, and so the social arguments against price changes are rather weak.

In petroleum, which is more problematic, there is agreement that petroleum prices should be raised, and there is also agreement that there needs to be some system of subsidies to protect the poor, particularly in the cases of kerosene use among low income families, and for public transport. There is still debate over the question of relative price distortions within petroleum products. The World Bank and ADB believe that if kerosene prices do not increase significantly, the incentive for ineffective substitution will continue and this is not beneficial to the economy or the energy sector. Of course the higher kerosene prices are raised, the more the government needs to ensure it protects the poor. Whether there can be effective mechanisms put in place is an open question to which the government is now giving a lot of attention.

In agriculture where rice is the most important commodity, the government has made the decision to introduce a 30 per cent tariff on foreign imports of rice. The reasons for these are well known — world prices are now significantly below the purchase price in Indonesia. The government chose to largely bridge that gap through a tariff. The tariff is, however, too high, as there was scope for reducing the purchase price and sharing the benefits of lower world prices between farmers and the poor. Analysis shows clearly that the poor in Indonesia are large consumers of rice. Consumers, landless labourers, and self-sufficient farmers do not benefit from the market price increase, so this cannot really be described as a pro-poor policy. The World Bank is obligated to point out whether or not policies are consistent with the objective of alleviating poverty. However, the government, in all fairness, has indicated that the import monopoly of the state-run Bulog (Badan Urusan Logistik Nasional, or National Logistics Board) will be removed and that the rice tariff will be reviewed at the end of this current crop season. Therefore, it is a political compromise that is understandable but which misses an opportunity to pass more of the benefits of lower world prices onto the poor of Indonesia.

Credit programmes, particularly Kredit Usaha Tani (KUT), or farmers' credit scheme, have not been very successful in the past despite huge subsidies, both explicit and implicit. It is time to shift these programmes in large part back to the banking sector with the government providing a degree of subsidy on the interest but no longer guaranteeing or making up shortfalls on repayment.

Fourth, decentralization will be a crucial issue for the future. It is probably not entirely correct, as is sometimes claimed, to say the World Bank has pushed for decentralization. However, it always sounds like a good idea so many support it in principle. In Indonesia it is simply a political reality and the two necessary laws, number 22 and 25, are already on the books. It is up to Indonesia to hold a legitimate political debate on the issue, but the role of the major donors involved is to ensure that what is on the books can be implemented effectively. One cannot escape the conclusion that this whole proposal entails major risk for Indonesia and probably one of the major risks to the restructuring programme.

Others have highlighted the fiscal risks, which is to say that if expenditures are not devolved quickly enough, there will be a negative impact on the fiscal deficit of the central government, and a very serious risk that fiscal discipline will be undermined. Equally there should be concern about implementation of public sector projects. The law, as is currently designed, gives primary responsibility to the district level, and bypasses the provincial level. There are good political reasons for this, but it is simply not the case that all development programmes can be effectively implemented at the district and sub-district level. There are many programmes that need a broader range of coverage. For example, could a nationwide immunization programme for children be achieved on a district basis? Or can environmental programmes be solved on a district basis? It simply will not work for many issues. Hopefully, in implementation, there will be a degree of pragmatism about how these laws would be implemented on a sector by sector, and issue by issue, basis.

There is also an important issue of what role the central government will have in the future, as there is some risk that this will end up with duplication of tasks. As the central government holds on to some functions which have effectively been given to lower levels of government, central ministries will have to redefine their roles very quickly and encourage development of local capacity rather than prevent it.

Optimism about "local capacity" does not extend to optimism on local government capacity, although there is a lot of capable administration in some areas of Indonesia. The issue really revolves around how to use strengthened local decision-making, and that has as much to do with the role of civil society as it does have to do about the role of local government. The World Bank has found through its projects, such as the village improvement programme, and the urban poverty programme, that there really are methods of involving people more effectively in local decision-making that: (1) lead to better decisions; and (2) reduce opportunities for corruption. It is a tremendous check and balance, and an added input to the capacity of local government. Discussion about "governance" should not exclusively refer to just "government", but wider civil society as a much more effective participant in decision-making.

Finally, the development programme is almost certainly going to have to be trimmed in 2001. As a representative of an agency that is responsible for supporting development programmes, this is somewhat concerning. But given implementation capacity in Indonesia, it is, perhaps, not overly alarming. The focus should continue to be on using resources that are available effectively, and that means maintaining some of the social safety net programmes that have worked well. This is going to be important with the import tariff on rice. Education scholarships have been an effective way of keeping children in school, and some of the health and medical programmes have produced great outcomes. There is also a scope for extending some of the new style poverty programmes, which are really not crisis programmes, but attempts that bring local decision-making into poverty-solving schemes.

There is a desperate need to expand operations and maintenance. A lot of the past investments into education, health, irrigation, roads, and so on are at the risk of completely falling apart due to inadequate expenditure.

The scope that is required is quite dramatic and the donor community would be very receptive to ensuring that this support is targetted in these areas. However, it is doubtful that the government will have a lot of leeway to start large new infrastructure projects. There is also a lot of excess capacity in Indonesia right now, but I think this is the time for Bappenas (the National Development Planning Board) to start planning the future of development or needs of Indonesia and to start reorganizing the donor programmes around those priorities. While many would resist the idea of a Jakarta subway, the issue of urban transport in Jakarta is a real problem and unless real solutions are found, there will be ad hoc projects which are aimed at the objective but may not be the most effective way of achieving it. The crucial role for Bappenas, in such instances, would be to provide co-ordination across the ministries, and provide valuable advice to the president in order to support the future development of Indonesia.

SECTION IV
Social Issues, Employment, and Poverty Alleviation

10

The Socio-Economic Impact of the Crisis

Anggito Abimanyu

INTRODUCTION

The economic crisis in Indonesia has had a deep impact on employment, household income, and consumption, making it difficult for millions of individuals and households to meet basic needs. The impact was particularly severe because of the coincidence of massive exchange rate depreciation and its effect on tradeable goods prices on the one hand, and the drought and food price increases on the other. Understanding the extent and depth of the impact of the crisis on household income and the labour market is critical for devising short- and medium-term policy strategies. It is also essential for the targetting of social expenditures and the Social Safety Nets programme. The main objective of this chapter is to describe and estimate the socio-economic impact of the crisis and provides its alternative of solutions.

SOCIO-ECONOMIC IMPACT

The monetary crisis started to strike Indonesia in the middle of 1997, after having hit several countries in Asia first. Starting from the fall of the rupiah as measured against the U.S. dollar and the subsidence of the financial sector, which was originally thought to be a temporary financial disturbance, turned out to carry on and shake the real sector even more and finally widened as a full-blown economic crisis.

There are several channels through which its impacts are felt by households. These can be traced to the different sources of household income — wages, salaries, and self-employment incomes; returns on physical assets; and the receipt of public transfers — and to the prices households face when purchasing goods and services. There are also effects at the level of the broader community, which affects individual welfare.

Employment Impact

The decrease in Indonesian 1998 GDP, which was caused by a decrease in the Indonesian economic output sectors, also created huge unemployment. In 1997 the quantity of the labour force that was absorbed by several sectors is estimated to be as much as 87 million workers (see Table 10.1). Meanwhile, in 1998 the figure declined to 80.6 million workers with the decrease in the Indonesian economic accomplishment. This numeric comparison shows that the 1998 economic crisis caused the massive lay-off of Indonesian workers, which amounts to around 6.4 million workers out of work. The results of the economic crisis were different in terms of massive lay-offs of workers across each economic sector. Sectors that experienced a decrease in the absorption of the quantity of workers were manufacturing, construction, commerce, hotels and restaurants, transportation and communication, financial, rent and company service, as well as other services. Sectors that experienced an increase were agriculture, animal husbandry, forestry, fishery, electricity, gas, and drinking water. Some workers managed to be absorbed by the agricultural sector, which saw an increase from 35.8 million workers in 1997 to 36.3 million workers in 1998. The electricity, gas and water sectors increased from 233,240 workers in 1997 to 239,780 workers in 1998. In summary, the agricultural sector is a stepping stone for many in society, and can employ workers who are laid off but can readily transfer to the informal agricultural sector.

Household Expenditure and Income Distribution

Average expenditure by class of population in total was improving since early 1999 due to low inflation and an early economic recovery. From December 1998 to August 1999, the average expenditure increased by 7.4 per cent, but there are distribution problems that occur within the class of population and household location (rural and urban). The 20 per cent highest income group, mainly in urban areas, enjoyed most of the benefits of this early recovery (see Table 10.2).

Looking at households, the economic crisis has caused a more unbalanced income distribution amongst household groups in Indonesia.

TABLE 10.1
Employment Impact of Social-Employment Crisis, 1997 and 1998

	Aug 1997	Dec 1998	Absolute Change	% Rate of Change
A. Formal Sector:				
Total	27,130.0	25,630.4	–1,499.6	–5.5
Employee in Non-Agri	25,518.0	23,691.2	–1,826.8	–7.2
Prof. Self-Employed[a]	145.6	598.9	453.3	311.3
Employer	1,466.4	1,340.3	126.1	-8.6
Formal as % of Employed	31.8	29.6		
B. Informal Sector:				
Total	58,275.5	61,079.3	2,803.8	4.8
Employee in Agri	4,759.8	7,054.6	2,294.8	48.2
Non-Prof. Self-Employed[a]	37,701.9	37,396.6	–305.3	–0.8
Employer	15,813.8	16,628.2	814.4	5.1
Informal as % of Employed	68.2	70.4		
C. Profile of Informal Sector				
Sex:				
Male	19,197.9	18,135	–1,062.6	–5.5
Female	7,932.1	7,495.1	–437	–5.5
Residence:				
Urban	16,298.0	16,436	138.8	0.9
Rural	10,832.0	9,193	–1,638.4	–15.1
D. Profile of Informal Sector				
Sex:				
Male	33,807.6	35,855.9	2,048.3	6.1
Female	24,467.9	25,223.4	755.5	3.1
Residence:				
Urban	13,055.8	15,043.5	1,987.7	15.2
Rural	45,219.7	46,035.7	816	1.8

[a] Self-employed is defined as self-employed working alone and self-employed assisted by unpaid workers (excluding employers).
Source: SAKERNAS 1997 and 1998.

According to a breakdown of ten household groups (Social Accounting Matrix or SAM data), the discrepancy of income amongst household groups is provided in an estimated scale of per capita disposable income. It is perceived that the households with the lowest per capita income in 1998 were the households of agricultural workers, and households with the highest per capita income in the 1975–95 period were non-agricultural households.

The disparity of income amongst households, over 1975–98, has tended to widen over time. The disparity of income amongst household

TABLE 10.2
Average Expenditure (Rp/Capita/Month) Due to the Group Population 1996, 1998 and 1999

Class of Population	Average Expenditure (rupiah/capita/month)				% Changes		
	1996	Dec 98	Feb 99	Aug 99	Dec 98 – Feb 99	Feb 99 – Aug 99	Dec 98 – Aug 99
Urban:							
40% Lowest	46,918	92,790	91,484	97,369	–1.4	6.4	4.9
40% Medium	91,576	168,249	165,874	184,030	–1.4	10.9	9.4
20% Highest	226,633	387,463	376,773	430,960	–2.8	14.4	11.2
Total	100,639	181,809	178,291	198,701	–1.9	11.4	9.3
Rural:							
40% Lowest	30,552	65,970	65,286	67,379	–1.0	3.2	2.1
40% Medium	50,809	109,394	109,394	112,801	–1.2	4.4	3.1
20% Highest	100,920	202,463	202,463	217,919	1.1	6.5	7.6
Total	52,696	110,601	110,601	115,603	–0.3	4.9	4.5
Urban and Rural:							
40% Lowest	36,449	76,492	75,608	79,365	–1.2	5.0	3.8
40% Medium	65,493	132,505	130,855	141,262	–1.2	8.0	6.6
20% Highest	146,214	275,026	272,514	303,138	–0.9	11.2	10.2
Total	69,968	138,547	137,062	148,817	–1.1	8.2	7.4

Source: SUSENAS (Indonesia Socio-Economic Survey).

groups that is widening over the years 1975–98 is also shown by comparing household per capita income with the lowest income over the years 1975–98 against households with the highest income over the same years (see Figure 10.1). The income ratio of these two household groups over the years 1975–98 tended to decline and started to climb over the years 1990–98. The household income of the upper class increased faster (16.6 per cent per year) compared with the household income of agricultural workers (14.7 per cent per year). The difference in the rapidness of income expansion between the two household groups, and the significant difference in nominal value or per capita income between these two household groups, indicate the widening of income disparity amongst household groups in Indonesia over 1975–98.

Poverty

The impact of the economic crisis, which doubled the number of unemployed and widened the income disparity gap in Indonesia, surely brought consequences on the increase in the poverty figure of Indonesia, particularly during the worst of the crisis, 1997–98. The latest figure of August 1999 has shown that the number of poor households has declined compared to the crisis period of 1997–98 due to economic measures,

FIGURE 10.1
Ratio Between the Rich (Non-Agriculture Rich Urban Group) and the Poor (Landless Group) Within the Ten Household Groups

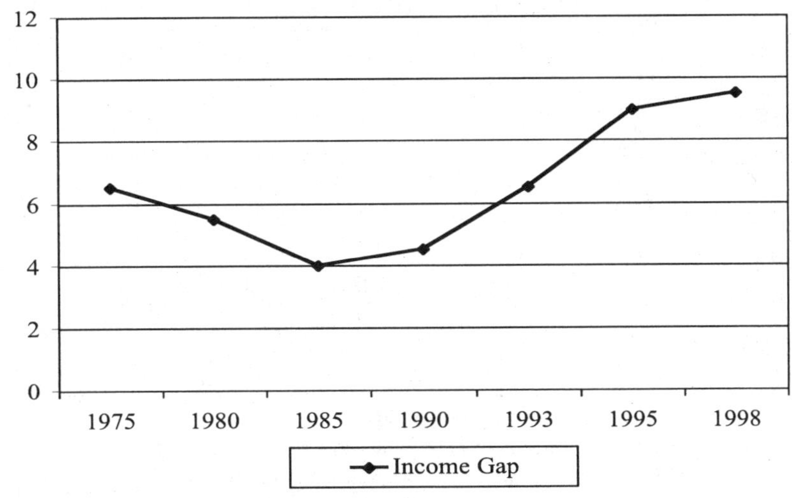

particularly price stabilization and stimulus package programmes. This poverty figure is calculated based on the 1999 poverty line assumption that was made by Biro Pusat Statistik (BPS or Central Bureau of Statistics), as much as Rp91,558 for cities and Rp69,317 for rural areas. Methodology that is used is based on minimum food and non-food needs for the near-poor inhabitants, with a consumption standard of 2,100 calories per capita per day for food, and typical basic needs for non-food items. By using this method, the poverty figure of August 1999 is determined to be as high as 38 million people, or around 18.4 per cent of the population (see Table 10.3). Using the same poverty line as 1996, it is concluded that during the period of December 1998 to August 1999, there has been a 5.8 per cent decline in poor households.

Regional Impact

The discussion about the differences in regional economic structures due to the crisis in general seems to have reached conclusion. General observation shows that Java was hit by the crisis harder than areas outside

TABLE 10.3
Number and Percentage of Poor, With Different Methods in the Rural and Urban Areas, 1996–99

	Number of Poor (in millions)			Percentage of Poor		
Period	Urban	Rural	Urban + Rural	Urban	Rural	Urban + Rural
1996	7.2	15.3	22.5	9.7	12.30	11.3
1996a	11.5	26.5	38.0	15.6	21.3	19.2
Dec 98	12.3	21.9	34.2	15.4	17.6	16.7
Dec 98a	17.6	31.9	49.5	21.9	25.3	24.2
Feb 99	14.3	27.3	41.6	17.8	22.0	20.3
Feb 99a	19.3	36.8	56.1	23.9	29.6	27.4
Aug 99	7.5	15.8	23.3	9.1	12.8	11.3
Aug 99a	13.1	24.9	38.0	15.9	20.1	18.4
Changes Dec 98 – Aug 99	–4.5	–7.0	–11.5	–6.06	–5.16	–5.82

Note: 1996, Dec 98, Feb 98 and Aug 99 used the same poverty line as in 1996; 1996a, Dec 96a, Feb 96a, and Aug 99a used the renewable poverty line.
Source: SUSENAS (Indonesia Socio-Economic Survey), 1996–99.

Java. Another observation is that the urban areas were hit more than the rural areas. These two observations show that the more modernized areas (represented by Java and urban areas) were hit more by the crisis than the less modernized or agricultural-dominated areas (represented by outside Java and rural areas). It was enhanced by the fact that many farmers outside Java enjoyed an economic boom during the crisis, due to an increasing comparative advantage produced by the weakening Indonesia rupiah.

Community Environment Effects

Communities have also felt the impact of macroeconomic crises, as traditional ties and networks and other forms of social capital are disrupted because of economic hardship, migration, and the emergence of fault lines between different ethnic, religious, or racial groups. There is evidence from several countries that "social capital" is damaged during crises. Recent tensions and riots in Indonesia are but one example. In a different context, there is evidence from participatory poverty assessment that economic hardship has severely eroded family and community ties in the countries of the former Soviet Union.

As incomes drop and poverty and unemployment rise, crime and other types of violence — including domestic violence — tend to be more pervasive.[1] Similarly cuts in public expenditure on sanitation, garbage collection and other services can lead to a deterioration in hygiene and public health conditions in poor neighbourhoods. A number of cholera outbreaks in Latin America in the 1980s were widely linked to worsening public health conditions in the wake of stringent budgetary austerity.

CONCLUSION

The objective of this paper has been to understand the socio-economic impact of the crisis and explore ways of overcoming the impact in both short run and long run as a part of policy for poverty alleviation in Indonesia. The early doomsday predictions of the effects of the crisis on household did not fully materialize. In making this observation, one should understand the difference between the phenomena of a short-run "transient poverty", as opposed to a long-run "chronic poverty". "Transient poverty" best refers to a sudden increase in the number of the poor owing to the impact of a fast fluctuation in prices of basic needs and in income levels. In contrast, "chronic poverty" indicates economic inability to fulfil fundamental needs, due to structural factors such as limited financial resources, less economic opportunities, less access to public service and social welfare, as well as low quality of human development. Mitigating the incidence of "transient poverty" is usually easy, such as by controlling basic commodities. Therefore, any policy for poverty alleviation and human development improvements should be directed to those suffering from chronic poverty as the primary target area.

The overarching priority for policy makers must be to take steps to avoid irreversible welfare losses to the poor that occur when, for example, children are taken out of school and often never return, higher infant malnutrition leads to cognitive delays, or crisis-induced violence becomes a permanent fixture. Distributional concerns must also be considered in the design of policy responses including both the basic elements of a stabilization programme, and the micro-level interventions of the reform programme.

An agenda to combat a negative socio-economic impact of the crisis should include the following actions. First, choose stabilization policies that achieve their macroeconomic objective at the least cost to the most vulnerable (economic growth is necessary, inflation targetting, fiscal stimulus, budget deficit, social safety net, and so on). Second, ensure that fiscal adjustment protects the items of spending which are most important for the poor. For example the effect of government transfer to rural poverty is large. From a policy perspective, the introduction of a broad-based agricultural strategy will have a substantial impact as shown by the large (absolute) number of marginal additive transfers. This suggests that improving rural infrastructure should have an additional impact on poverty reduction and form a precondition for a broad-based agricultural strategy.

Third, set up reinforced social safety nets capable of providing effective insurance before a crisis and assistance once a crisis hits. On the current SSN-programme, the general picture, however, points to the need for a large improvement in the programme implementations, in particular in targetting the beneficiaries of a particular programme and raising coverage within the target groups. Considering the importance of the programmes in mitigating the social impact of the crisis, it is necessary that programme implementation be improved to better target those most in need. This can be done through, amongst other actions, extensive information dissemination campaign and intensive monitoring.

Fourth, set up mechanisms to provide information for monitoring the impact of the crisis and evaluating responses. Adequate information on the impact of the crisis on various groups helps design appropriate policy responses, and provides feedback on the impact of the policies of which allows corrections if the desired impact does not materialize. At a national level, it is important to support well-informed debate on issues, impacts and alternatives. At a local level, providing public information on intended public action — and the rights of potential beneficiaries — can help reduce corruption.

Five, use selective interventions that help preserve the social fabric of societies in crisis and build social capital. There is evidence that at least some of the negative impacts of crisis — rising social tension and the breakdown in family and community ties — may persist after the end of the crisis. This is also evidence that the cost if this higher level of violence, both in direct human terms and in terms of displaced or discouraged economic activity, can be quite high. It is important not to neglect this policy area, where the results may be achieved through partnerships with local NGOs and civil society organizations in general.

Note

1. Pablo Fajnzylber, Daniel Leaderman, and Norman Loyaza, *What Causes Violent Crime?* (Washington, D.C.: World Bank, March 1998). See also <www.worldbank.org/poverty/inequal/abstract/violence.html#fajnzylber98>.

11

An Update on Poverty and Social Issues

Mohamad Ikhsan

The social impact of the crisis was not quite as bad as was expected. Even though real per capita income and wage contracted by 15.1 per cent and 31 per cent respectively, educational indicators are relatively fairly stable. Net primary enrolment went up slightly from 94 per cent to 95 per cent in 1998/99, secondary enrolment dropped slightly from 54.4 per cent to 53.2 per cent. Similarly, health outcomes do not show a rise in stunted development amongst children.

The series expenditure surveys conducted by the Biro Pusat Statistik (BPS, or Central Bureau of Statistics) demonstrate that the real household expenditure rose significantly since February 1999 to August 1999. Table 11.1 depicts the development of per capita real mean expenditures from February 1996 to August 1999. Among those groups, the poorest 40 per cent experienced the highest growth rates, while the upper 20 per cent, who were hit hard by the crisis, have also regained their income. The adjustment process after the crisis also revealed that the rural households gained more than their counterparts in the urban sector. During the first eight months of 1999, rural households recorded about a 14.4 per cent growth rate in their real expenditure while urban residents' expenditure grew at 8.5 per cent in real terms. Deflating the per capita household expenditures by the BPS poverty line, one witnesses that the mean real expenditures in August 1999 are not far from the pre-crisis level. These figures are consistent across the expenditure groups and sectors. The improvement of real expenditure for the middle and upper classes is also reflected in an increase in income tax revenues.

With a combination of an improvement in real expenditure, the stabilization policies, which has produced a steady decline in general prices, and a controversial social safety net programme, the poverty incidence has declined significantly during that period (see Table 11.2).

TABLE 11.1
Indonesia: Household's Real Income per Person
(Rupiah per month)

	Average Real Expenditure				Percentage Real Growth (%)		
	1996	Dec 98	Feb 99	Aug 99	Dec 98 – Feb 99	Feb 99 – Aug 99	Dec 98 – Aug 99
Urban							
40%lowest	46,918	40,686	39,287	46,592	–3.44	18.59	14.52
40%middle	91,576	84,700	80,086	91,992	–5.45	14.87	8.61
20% highest	226,633	195,058	181,910	215,426	–6.74	18.42	10.44
Total	100,639	91,527	86,081	99,326	–5.95	15.39	8.52
Rural							
40% lowest	30,552	27,693	26,145	30,056	–5.59	14.96	8.54
40% middle	50,209	55,071	52,158	56,386	–5.29	8.11	2.39
20% highest	10o,920	101,925	98,769	108,932	–3.07	10.26	6.88
Total	52,696	55,679	53,217	57,787	–4.42	8.59	3.79
Urban+Rural							
40% lowest	36,449	32,626	31,129	36,403	–4.59	16.94	11.58
40% middle	65,493	66,706	63,178	70,613	–5.29	11.77	5.86
20% highest	146,241	138,454	131,573	151,531	–4.97	15.17	9.44
Total	69,968	69,748	66,175	74,390	–5.12	12.41	6.66

Source: LPEM Staff estimates based on BPS data.

TABLE 11.2
Indonesia: Number and Percentage of the Poverty Population Using Different Measures, 1996–99

	Number of People (in millions)			Percentage of Poor People		
Period	Urban	Rural	Urban + Rural	Urban	Rural	Urban + Rural
1996	7.2	1.3	22.5	9.71	12.3	11.34
1996a	11.5	26.5	38.0	15.63	21.27	19.23
Dec 1998	17.6	31.9	49.5	21.92	25.27	24.23
Dec 1998a	12.3	21.9	34.2	15.35	17.64	16.74
Feb 1999	19.3	36.8	56.1	23.88	29.63	27.36
Feb 1999a	14.3	27.3	41.6	17.75	21.97	20.31
Aug 1999	12.4	25.1	37.5	15.09	20.22	18.17
Aug 1999a	7.5	15.8	23.3	9.13	12.76	11.31

Indeed, the headcount index has reached the pre-crisis level. However, one should be aware that those improvements are caused by the government transfers through Operasi Pasar Khusus (Special Market Operation) on rice prices and other social safety net programmes. With a subsidized rice price, the poor or the vulnerable groups can maintain their welfare levels.

The crisis is heterogeneous and has more strongly impacted on Java and urban areas. Java was hit much harder than the outlying islands. The impact of the crisis in rural areas was intensified by the El Nino weather pattern which caused a drought. But when the agricultural production process resumed, the corrections on agricultural prices during 1998–99

TABLE 11.3
Indonesia: Monthly Real Wages by Sector
(In Rp thousands)

Sector	1997	1998	% Change
Electricity, Gas, Water	626.76	381.56	–39.1
Manufacturing	347.56	216.66	–37.7
Construction	369.34	238.90	–35.3
Services	429.24	285.36	–33.5
Trade	355.24	238.82	–32.8
Transportation, etc.	444.24	306.07	–31.1
Finance & Insurance	647.54	446.85	–31.0
Agriculture	180.82	132.79	–26.6
Mining	510.55	401.11	–21.4
All sectors	366.49	241.42	–34.1

have produced a recovery to farmer profit and rural wages. Nominal wages has increased even though in real terms they are still negative.

The social impact was not translated in an increase in unemployment, which has been claimed by others, but more as a decline in real wages (see Table 11.3). Indeed during August 1997–98 there were a million new jobs created, mostly from the informal sector. Employment in the formal sectors was reduced by roughly the same number in this period (see Table 11.4).

However, the long-term impact should be taken into account seriously, given the development in the intensity of poverty, labour market problems,

TABLE 11.4
Indonesia: Employment Changes, 1997–98

	1997		1998		Change	
	Number in millions	% of TE[a]	Number in millions	% of TE	Number in millions	% of TE
Urban:						
Total Employment	29.4	100.0	30.3	100.0	0.9	3.2
Formal	16.8	57.2	16.5	54.3	–0.4	–2.1
Employer with permanent employee	0.7	2.3	0.7	2.4	0.0	5.9
Employee	16.1	54.9	15.7	51.9	–0.4	–2.4
Informal	12.6	42.8	13.9	45.7	1.3	10.3
Self-employed with no employee	6.8	23.0	7.5	24.6	0.7	10.4
Self-employed with temporary or family worker	3.4	11.6	3.7	12.1	0.3	7.3
Family worker	2.4	8.1	2.7	9.0	0.3	14.2
Rural:						
Total Employment	56.1	100.0	57.4	100.0	1.3	2.4
Formal	15.0	26.7	13.9	24.2	–1.1	–7.2
Employer with permanent employee	0.8	1.4	0.8	1.4	0.0	2.6
Employee	14.2	25.3	13.1	22.8	–1.1	–7.7
Informal	41.1	73.3	43.5	75.8	2.4	5.8
Self-employed with no employee	13.1	23.4	13.1	22.8	0.0	–0.3
Self-employed with temporary or family worker	14.6	26.0	16.0	27.9	1.5	9.9
Family worker	13.4	24.0	14.4	25.1	1.0	7.2

[a] TE = Total employment.
Source: PBS, Sakernas, 1997–98.

declining health condition, and the poor educational condition of children across Indonesia. Even thought there was a reduction in poverty incidences in several areas, there were significant increases in both the poverty gap and the squared poverty gap. This indicates that the poor become poorer during the crisis, including in the areas where poverty incidence decreases. This has serious policy implications. Transfer per capita needed to alleviate poverty should be increased significantly. Also, the poverty strategy should be changed from a "crisis type strategy" to a long-term strategy to help the "old poor" to cope with the macroeconomic shocks.

TABLE 11.5
Indonesia: The Distribution of Working Hours, 1997–98

	1997		1998		Change	
	Number in millions	% of TE	Number in millions	% of TE	Number in millions	% of TE
Total Employment	85.4	100.0	87.7	100.0	2.3	2.7
less than 15 hrs	8.2	9.6	9.2	10.8	1.0	12.5
less than 35 hrs	30.6	35.8	34.3	40.2	3.7	12.2
more than 35 hrs	54.8	64.2	53.4	62.5	–1.5	–2.7
Men						
Total	53.0	100.0	53.9	100.0	0.9	1.7
less than 15 hrs	3.0	5.7	3.4	6.4	0.4	13.3
less than 35 hrs	14.0	26.5	15.9	30.1	1.9	13.6
more than 35 hrs	39.0	73.5	38.0	71.6	–1.0	–2.6
Women						
Total	32.4	100.0	33.8	100.0	1.4	4.2
less than 15 hrs	5.2	16.0	5.8	17.1	0.6	12.0
less than 35 hrs	16.5	51.0	18.4	54.4	1.8	11.1
more than 35 hrs	15.9	51.0	15.4	45.6	–0.5	–2.9
Urban						
Total	29.4	100.0	30.3	100.0	0.9	3.2
less than 15 hrs	1.7	5.37	1.9	6.4	0.9	15.6
less than 35 hrs	6.1	20.9	7.3	24.1	1.2	19.4
more than 35 hrs	23.2	79.1	23.0	75.9	–0.2	–1.0
Rural						
Total	56.1	100.0	57.6	100.0	1.5	2.7
less than 15 hrs	6.5	11.6	7.3	12.6	0.8	11.7
less than 35 hrs	24.4	43.6	27.0	46.9	2.6	10.4
more than 35 hrs	31.6	56.4	30.6	53.1	–1.0	–3.3

Source: PBS, Sakernas, 1997–98.

The increase in the intensity of poverty also emerges from the labour market figures (see Table 11.5). First, real wage declined significantly, and workers were only able to work lesser hours. Second, most households, with the family head working in the informal sector, are poor. The expansion in the informal sector will increase the poverty gap. Many poor households either failed to achieve the minimum food requirement, or changed their food composition towards less expensive food items with less protein. As a result, there are some indications of malnutrition in several regions.

Another finding from the 1998 Labour Survey is that more experienced workers became unemployed during the crisis (see Table 11.6). This implies that when the economy recovers, those experienced workers will have the first opportunity to enter the labour (formal) markets, leaving the new entrants and least educated workers to wait until the economy returns to the six or seven percentile growth rate. The new entrants, especially from poor households, will flood the informal sector. This, in turn, will push informal wages down and as a result the intensity of poverty will increase.

TABLE 11.6
Indonesia: Percentage of Experienced Unemployed Workers

	Men		Women	
	1997	1998	1997	1998
Urban	20.51	42.88	13.14	38.86
Rural	21.88	42.24	17.21	30.13
Total	21.02	42.64	14.86	32.64

Source: PBS, Sakernas, 1997 and 1998.

In summary, in order to deal with poverty a number of important policy issues need to be addressed. First, there is the need for better-targeted social safety net programmes. Second, the Government should refocus and reorientate expenditure for maximizing the multiplier effect and hence domestic demand. The expansion of the economy is the best remedy for poverty reduction. Third, trade protectionism is not a correct instrument to alleviate poverty. Indeed, a current plan to increase rice protection would inflict more harm on the poor, as consumers, rather than help them. Fourth, there is no indication on how equity issues will be handled by this Government. Changes in land policy, particularly with regards to agriculture and housing, should be addressed quickly and correctly.

12

Policies for Sustainable Economic Development in Indonesia[1]

Aris Ananta

Only its collapse convinced them to try something different. Old ideas were overtaken and overwhelmed. It has happened before — and could again. (Samuelson 1993)[2]

"CRISIS" AND "RECOVERY"

Booming prosperity before the end of 1997 had created a joyful expectation for the future in Indonesia. In a sudden and dramatic crash, all was lost in such a short time. Indonesia was woefully unprepared for this event. Many Indonesians who talked about poverty, but had not really experienced poverty itself, were then forced into relative deprivation. They had not fallen under the poverty line, and, indeed, they may still be in a much better economic situation than that, but their prospects became very bleak. It was like the feeling of riding a roller coaster, but without knowing the end of the fast descending ride. They were, to mention a few, the academics, politicians, bureaucrats, business people, people in NGOs and journalists. Some held political power, and more than a few were involved in decision making to "help" the poor people. The current crisis that hit Indonesia had not been anticipated by most people. The crisis has certainly shocked policy makers enough to want to make major reforms. However, the important question remains: Will changes go far enough or will they be minimal without undertaking reform that will undermine the changes for another meltdown?

Hilton Root has argued that social chaos, war, and sometimes revolution have preceded rapid growth in East Asia.[3] The Cold War has brought East Asia into an atmosphere of political uncertainty. The governments had to work within highly acute political risk; and right decisions were needed simply to survive. This is consistent with the gloomy lesson from the Great Depression, as concluded by Kim Hill, that the Great Depression came to an end only with the onset of World War II.[4] There had been many large drastic domestic and international changes, but the depression continued throughout the 1930s. Countries that had quickly recovered still suffered some of the impact until the onset of World War II.

Certainly, a war is not the recommended policy for Indonesia. Neither is social chaos. But, Indonesia has been driven into crisis and near chaos. Therefore, innovative approaches should be applied before the economy nosedives again. Without innovative recommendations, the economy continues on a series of booms and busts in the long term.

Further, the current "recovery" may not provide real improvement in the economy. As Paul Krugman argues, "recovery" may occur despite the absence of improvement in the fundamentals.[5] So it is for Indonesia. What Indonesia needs is not simply for the economy to return to the pre-crisis level. If it does, then potentially Indonesian stands to lose so much once again. The opportunity cost of two or three years during the recession is very high. Indonesia should take from the crisis much better fundamentals than before the crisis began. The crisis must be seen as an opportunity for more sound economic development — in particular one that is centred on its people. This chapter is an on-going exercise to contribute some innovative ideas for reforms in the Indonesian economy. The recommendations presented here are not necessarily new, some are actually repetitions of old ideas, but a fresh look at them may be beneficial to work towards long-run, sustainable economic development — development which will not simply fall into another crisis once the economy starts recovering.

The recommendations are long-term objectives. What is needed is sustainable economic development, not simply economic growth. There are so many aspects of policy recommendation for sustainable economic development, but this paper focuses to three factors: namely, people-centred development, economic institutions, and "integration" with the world economy. These three factors are fundamental in contributing to sustainable economic development. In more technical terminology, these three factors are the necessary conditions, while others are supplementary to them. It does not mean that others are not important, but these three aspects should be given more attention in producing economic policies in the long run to achieve sustainable economic development.

The existing textbooks on development economics and macroeconomic theories do not seem to be able to explain (let alone prescribe the medicine) the Indonesian, and Asian crises. When the "four tigers" promoted an export promotion strategy in the 1960s, the literature on economic development was dominated by import-substitution strategy; yet, the ASEAN economies of the time followed their own appropriate course. Something innovative, in that magnitude, is urgently needed. It is not impossible that something like Keynes' "economics revolution" of the 1930s can be pursued at this point in time.

Therefore, decades from now the teaching of economics, especially in development economics and macroeconomics, will be greatly influenced by the experience of hindsight into the Asian financial crisis. But furthermore, the current crisis can be converted into an opportunity to produce a much better, sustainable, development paradigm.

PEOPLE-CENTRED DEVELOPMENT

The Concept

Long before the current economic crisis, some economists had argued for alternatives to a sole concentration on GNP measured growth. Income per capita and national income growth rate had been the preoccupation of most policy makers. Discussions on economic success had hinged on the measurement of income per capita and income growth. Until July 1997 the orientation seemed plausible. East Asian and Southeast Asian economies remained strong. Income per capita had measurably been growing fast.

During the crisis, questions have arisen: Can and will the economies of East and Southeast Asia return to the pre-crisis growth rates? When will they achieve the same growth of national income again? After that, will they grow faster? Will they return to so-called "miracle" economic growth? If growth is strong enough to warrant the epithet "miracle", will this be long-term? In other words, will Asia then have a sustainable growth, without once again tumbling into a similar crisis in the future?

How about an alternative? Rather than placing national income as the sole criterion, true progress can only be measured with a combination of other criteria, such as health, education and other measures of living standards. The United Nations Development Programme (UNDP, 1992) started this practice in the early 1990s, and founded the Human Development Index (HDI).[6] There may be some weaknesses in this index, but the UNDP's initiative to use HDI as an alternative measure should have been followed by much more concrete steps in formulating and developing economic policies in many countries even before the onset of the crisis. This has implications for the criteria that should be used to measure "recovery".

Though policies pursuing a more holistic progress, such as that measured by HDI, may result in a relatively slower economic growth rate, the policies promise a more sustainable growth. In terms of the current crisis, such policies — engaging in people-centred development — will help avoid the risk of falling into the same crisis once the country has successfully overcome it. It should be noted, though, that the people-centred development is not an anti-growth concept. Indeed, long-term and sustainable growth is the objective of the people-centred development. And certainly, economic growth is needed to pursue people-centred development.

This section is not necessarily to propose the complete use of HDI, but the introduction of HDI-type measurements to guide policy implementation should be seen as a challenge to the conventional national income-orientated growth, especially during such a crisis. There is a need to reorientate the development in Indonesia. HDI is an illustration of criteria to measure true development. Of course, more precise criteria must then be developed by modifying or even changing the HDI to suit Indonesia's unique circumstances. A faster improvement in the index, with slower GNP growth, may be much better than faster growth of GNP with lower improvement (or even, deterioration) of the index indicators.

The new Wahid government, established on 20 October 1999, should explicitly orientate development to the people. The New Order, with its new economic policies, beginning in 1966, started with much attention to the investment in human capital, reflected for example in the intensive programmes on education, health, and family planning. The New Order has recorded success in reduction of poverty, and vast improvements in the areas of health and education.

Yet, it had not explicitly stated that development should be people-centred. Worse, in the last ten years of the New Order, development no longer benefited the majority of Indonesians. Preoccupation with the achievement of "leading" macroeconomic indicators had been a feature of Indonesian economic policies during the decade before the crisis.

The measurement of economic development still hinge too much on the conventional macroeconomic indicators, such as the GDP levels, the inflation rate, the interest rate, and the current account balance. Development should not ignore those macroeconomic indicators; but the point is that macroeconomic indicators should be supplements to indicators which measure monetarily unquantifiable progress in living standards. In other words, measurement of economic development must be changed so that income is only one indicator of development. The success of the recovery should not be viewed from the resumption of economic growth and macroeconomic indicators only.

A focus on people-centred development should see human capital as the crucial fundamental of the economy. It should also emphasize the importance of the welfare of the population, who act as vital consumers of products and services. In the economic jargon, focus must be on maximizing the utility of the people, rather than simply maximizing income, because the later is an imprecise mechanism to measure well-being. The large Indonesian population is a great potential domestic market, which should be targeted more than foreign markets. This emphasis will be crucial in order to reduce the risk from international economic fluctuations.

Monetary, Production, and Human Capital Reforms

Because of the crisis, countries, especially those worst hit by the crisis, soon realized the need for drastic reform of their monetary sector. The crisis, including Indonesia's meltdown, was often seen as a financial crisis. However, to date, the financial sector has not been successfully reformed.

In addition to the financial and banking sector, the Government of Indonesia has also worked on the real (or the productive) sector, though it seems that the attention given to the productive sector is not as large as to the emphasis in the banking sector. Some believe that the monetary crisis has caused the crisis in the productive sector and that once the monetary crisis is overcome, the productive sector will automatically return to the so-called boom era. Others, however, maintain that the crisis in the productive sector may be independent of the financial crisis, though the crisis may have triggered the appearance of the crisis in the productive sector.

Equally serious attention must be given to the reform of the productive sector, including cost-cutting efforts such as the elimination of "informal" fees, the elimination of special privileges, and the reduction of bureaucratic red tape. A success in monetary reform will not bring back Indonesia's "miracle" economy unless the productive sector is also drastically reformed.

Unfortunately, a much more fundamental reform has not been seriously dealt with in Indonesian economic policies. Human capital is often outside the scope of economic policies. Yet, it may not be an exaggeration to say that human capital reform is the most fundamental reform Indonesia needs at this present time. It does not mean that Indonesia should neglect its financial and real sector reforms; rather, the reform on human capital development must be given equal, if not more, weight in economic policy making.

Human Capital Development

Human capital is, admittedly, a very general concept. However, there are three essential elements of human capital: the freedom from fear, health, and education.[7] Perhaps, they are all equally important.

The government needs to make sure that crime rates decrease; that it is safe for people to travel and to do business; that it is safe for people to do business without fear of being illegally taxed by corrupt officials; and that there is an end to rioting, lootings, and intimidations. If people have freedom from fear, they do not need to hire their own "security guards" or "backing" from powerful individuals. Freedom from fear should be counted as a public good, which can be enjoyed by all, including the poor, rather than just those who have money. Indonesia should strive toward a "freedom-from-fear"-based economy.

With the creativity that most Indonesians have, this freedom from fear will allow the Indonesians to be more productive and more creative in all levels of business — the small, medium, and large. Freedom from fear is the most fundamental need of the Indonesian people, especially the poor. Financial assistance is not such an important thing for small- and medium-sized enterprises. Unfortunately, the notion of personal security has never been seen as an integral part of economic policies, including the social safety net programmes.

The next crucial human capital investment is in the area of health. The policies should not be focused on curative action, but more on preventive and promotive action. The monetary-orientated development will describe as "progress" if one person gets sick and money is spent on a cure, simply because the expenditure has increased and the GDP has risen. Growth in the pharmaceutical industry, because of the growing numbers of sick people, is an indication of rising economy from a conventional monetary-orientated approach. On the other hand, in people-centred development, being healthy is more a measure of development, without necessarily having to be able to convert the healthiness into economic growth rates. Getting sick should be viewed as a "minus" in terms of living standards.

Although being healthy is an end by itself, it is also the case that being healthy means a more productive labour force and less expenditure for medication and traditional curative health services. This can be called a "health-based economy", or one that is based on a healthy labour force. Therefore, all health related programmes should be prioritized on preventive and promotive, rather than just curative, efforts.

The last component of human capital investment, the most often mentioned by economic policy makers, is education. This is the basis of the frequently discussed "knowledge-based economy". The education should not be limited to formal education, but is geared to the achievement of well-informed society. The members of the society will be best served with those knowledgeable and adaptable to many aspects of life. Further, with this knowledge, the freedom from fear and an excellent health status, Indonesia can achieve sustainable material benefits; though monetary benefit is not the main objective of holistic development.

DOMESTIC MARKET-LED DEVELOPMENT

In the 1960s and 1970s policies on import substitution had been dominant in many developing countries. The idea was, essentially, to block imports so as to develop domestic industries. The idea was that a country should aim for self-sufficiency. Governments often designed policies to protect "infant" industries. Domestic production and consumption was promoted and often portrayed as patriotic fervour. This policy was supposed to reduce, or even eliminate, the dependency on the international market and its fluctuations.

This strategy was the principal route towards industrialization for almost 200 years after the emergence of Britain as the hegemonic industrial power. When the United States was newly independent, President Jefferson followed a mercantilist strategy to compete with industrialized Britain. He essentially embargoed British imports. Germany also created protective tariffs to boost its industrialization in the mid-nineteenth century. Further, all the leading continental European powers and Japan had followed a similar strategy as they realized that military strength was underpinned by industrial strength.

However, the import substitution strategy and the accompanying infant industry policies, as applied in developing countries, resulted in much inefficiency in the second half of the twentieth century. Domestic prices became artificially high. Consumers suffered and the poor could not afford the high cost of this strategy. Therefore, during the 1980s many developing countries turned to the export promotion strategy, which had already been successfully implemented by Taiwan, South Korea, Hong Kong, and Singapore — the four emerging "dragon economies". These four countries were successful because of their export-orientated strategy, which surpassed import substitution.

Under the export promotion strategy, importation was considered acceptable as long as the domestic market could also export. The most important thing is the ability to export greater volumes of products and services in which a country had a competitive or comparative advantage. With foreign exchange reserves, the domestic market can obtain foreign goods not locally produced. With this policy, a competitive environment will be created and efficiencies will emerge in the global market place.

This outward looking strategy has been actually as old as the publication of Adam Smith's influential tome, *The Wealth of Nations* (1776). He argued that home markets had to export their products in order to achieve the economies of scale. By extension it is often said that a large country like Indonesia must also promote and depend on exports because its population, though large in number, is still poor. The Soeharto administration unsuccessfully attempted to gain a competitive advantage by exporting "expensive" and "prestigious" hi-tech goods, such as airplanes.

During the current Indonesian crisis, the dependence on the international market might have contributed to the severity of the crisis. Indeed, the crisis was triggered by an international situation. As the Indonesian currency plummeted many domestic prices had risen because many of them had imported components. Indonesia came to a painful realization of just how dependent they were on imported materials.

Indeed, studies have shown that there was strong negative relationship between population size and the extent of international trade. Small countries (in terms of number of people) were highly specialized and depended mostly on international trade. It is also worth noting that the policies that ended the worst of the Great Depression in the 1930s were not based on export promotion, but on raising domestic aggregate demand. This is especially true with respect to the United States, which had a very large population suffering from the prolonged depression.

Chowdhury and Islam have noted that there is inconclusive evidence on export-led growth.[8] They admit that exports have played a significant role in the growth of East Asian Newly Industrialized Economies (NIEs), yet they argue that this does not necessarily mean that growth depended on the international economy. Rather, the high growth rates were attributable to both their ability to exploit the world market and their domestic capacity to increase the supply for exports. Internal factors might have been a significant factor.

Luckily, more than a few leaders have started to realize the danger of too much dependence on exports as a means to recovery and even to achieve sustainable economic development. Gerald Tan mentions several risks associated with the export promotion strategy.[9] He finds that countries with a large exposure to the international economy had been very sensitive to abrupt, unpredictable, changes in international economic fluctuation, which are beyond the control of the individual countries. The second risk is that the country will eventually lose its initial comparative advantage. Success in exports will make its currency very strong. The *Far Eastern Economic Review*, on 10 June 1999, produced a cover story challenging the paradigm on export-led growth. It argued that Asia needed a new engine of growth. Asia does not have to crowd the world market with their exports; they could turn instead to the markets in their own countries.

The question is now whether Indonesia has to depend so much on the international market. Indonesia has a large population; one estimate puts it at 208 million in the year 2000. People from the lowest 40 per cent income bracket have the most potential, and this constitutes 83 million people. Income and price elasticities are low, which means that a decline in income and a rise in price will not much reduce the quantity demanded.

Indonesia should first prioritize the development of the domestic market, though the goods and services demanded are not those with high prices. Yet, they are the products needed by the society. On the other hand, the most profitable businesses are not necessarily those with a high price, which usually needs a long period of investment. In other words, with its large population, the government should encourage businesses which produce goods and services for low- and middle-income groups. Such businesses could be very lucrative.

Recently, Thailand has been very innovative is utilizing its large market. They invented instant rice to capture the huge Asian market, as most Asians (including middle and lower income people) eat rice everyday. The market will become more attractive if, because of the very large-scale production, instant rice is cheaper than traditional strains.

During the crisis, people lowered their consumption pattern. Those who used to spend their holidays abroad, now travel within Indonesia and choose to go shorter distances. Those who used to go by planes now prefer to use cars or trains. Those who used to go to five star restaurants or hotels now choose cheaper ones. Those who used to visit cheap restaurants now decide to eat more at home and to bring their own food to work. This phenomenon has created new, emerging, profitable business opportunities inside Indonesia.

People learn to reduce luxury items and "gimmicks". It may not be easy to change lifestyles because the Indonesian people have become accustomed to enjoying the "good life". However, the Indonesians have to learn to adjust to unfavourable economic conditions. Private companies can help the Indonesian economy through an innovative campaign to sell more basic commodities.

The people can also concentrate on businesses that revolve around the "simple" goods and services needed by almost all people. It is not difficult to produce, and there is high demand, especially at the time of crisis. Indonesian businesses should learn from the small Vietnamese businesses which emerged after Doi Moi (Vietnam's policy of economic renovation).

The concentration on simple business — such as provision of food, simple clothes and a basic means of transportation — will provide the people with additional income to survive during the crisis. At the same time, it improves the availability of goods and services for daily needs. The price of these goods and services will decline. It is a source of earnings and at the same time it helps the people, especially the lower income group, to better satisfy their daily needs.

The most important, and also profitable, business in Indonesia right now is doing "simple" business in an environment that could be better fostered by health, education, and freedom from fear. Furthermore during the crisis, most people needed these services. In addition, with the large population, this business can be very promising in Indonesia. Indeed, it may be interesting to note what Clarence Enzler observed during the 1930s Great Depression:

> But it sometimes happened that individuals and families who had lived with phantom happiness amid the days before the depression benefited by a *return to simplicity*. Women began to do their own work, gave up parties, hairdressers, shampoos, manicures, or at least became their own beauty technicians.

> They were sometimes able to develop vocational talents and thus fill the hours with worthwhile activities. The sense of values in both men and women sometimes grew into closer attune with truth. Happiness in the simpler things, in group games, neighbourly visits and socials, a return to activities which bind people close in friendship and sincere hospitality were a part of the quest for quieter, less blatant pleasures which the pinch of the economic shoe sometimes occasioned.[10]

Domestic market-led development also stresses the importance of strengthening food production. Historically, agriculture has been the big source of funding, from which industrialization was financed. Agriculture was also the place of the consumers of the industrial output. Without a strong agricultural sector, industrialization must depend on foreign resources and the international market. Without skilled labour, Indonesia would have to import skilled labour. Without sufficient markets, Indonesia will have to export the output. The policy of industrialization seems, therefore, to be hand in hand with the policy of export orientation, which depends much on international resources and market.

However, because food is the most important commodity for the people, it has become a politically sensitive commodity. Industrialization should not occur at the expense of agricultural development. The recommendation here is to return to the domestic market. The domestic market needs the availability of high quality food in sufficient quantity, which is both accessible, and at low prices. The agricultural sector will also create markets for low prices goods and services, which will promote industrialization aimed at fulfilling the needs of lower income people, including those in agriculture sector. With this orientation, Indonesia does not have to depend on foreign resources and markets.

Yet, Indonesia does not have to protect the domestic producers. Foreign investors should also be allowed to produce goods and services for this market to low-income people, including those in the agriculture sector. Let them compete with international producers and allow them to go into the international market if they want.

The fact that Indonesia is largely surrounded by water hints that aquaculture may also be developed. There is the potential to cultivate fish farming and seaweed crops under the water (and they may be very healthy too). Agri- and aqua-business can be seen as promising investments for domestic market-led development.

In short, priority to the domestic market is also in line with promoting a people-centred development strategy. Not only will this policy help the domestic producers to grow, but will also provide goods and services needed by the majority of the population. It is the consumers, rather than the producers, who drive the economy; therefore the nationalist motto "*Aku Cinta Produksi Indonesia*" ("I love Indonesian products") should more appropriately be "*Aku Cinta Konsumen Indonesia*" ("I love Indonesian consumers").

A policy to prioritize the domestic market does not mean that exports and imports should be discouraged or regulated. There must still be free trade. Indonesia should let the market decide whether and how much to export and import. Indonesia must not return to import substitution policies. But, production for the domestic market, rather than for the international market, can be used as the leading policy in sustainable economic development.

It should be mentioned here that domestic market-led development is not necessarily against big business. Big business is not an evil, though priority should be given to small- and medium-sized enterprises. If large enterprises are regarded as an evil and subdued, the small- and medium-sized business will not have the opportunity for expansion.

ECONOMIC INSTITUTIONS

Economic progress does not proceed in a vacuum. Economic and institutional factors do interact and one affects another. In other words, the endogeneity of institutions is crucial in economic policy. The inertia of institutions relative to economic variables is one important aspect of this endogeneity. It is analogous to the rules of game in competitive sport. Institutions differ if, for example, transactions are carried out in Indonesia or in the United States. It may be formal (rules that human beings devise) and informal (such as established conventions and codes of behaviour). Institutions affect the economic activities through their impact on the cost of exchange and the cost of production.

The existence of institutions reduces uncertainty because the actors in the economy know the "rules of the game" and can anticipate to some extent what others will do. Unstable and unclear economic institutions result in high uncertainty, and this results in a high-cost economy. Strong economic institutions, that are conducive to efficient economic activities, are clearly very important to build a sustainable economic development.

In the absence of strong economic institutions uncertainty looms; speculative and unproductive businesses will boom. Though the economy, measured with monetary-orientated indicators, may be growing, it may be a fragile economic base. Indeed, Douglas North observes that institutions play a fundamental role in the long-run economic performance and, therefore, developing countries remained poor because the institutions do not encourage productive activities.[11]

Worse still, development of strong economic institutions cannot be done overnight. The written rules can be changed quickly, but the implementation may take much longer. In this regard, it is interesting to note what Lawrence Summers, the U.S. Deputy Secretary of the Treasury, said on 14 October 1998 that the crisis problems had been enhanced by the deep institutional and political problems in countries such as Indonesia and Russia. The economic success turned out to have outpaced their institutional capacity to carry out core functions (such as tax collection and proper bank regulation) and to implement important reforms. Summers also said the problem was even more severe because it had been spread with unprecedented speed and force by new information technologies and financial instruments.

Good governance is one important issue currently raised with regard to enhancing institutional capacity. Root finds that countries in Southeast and East Asia, which practice good governance, were more likely to have higher per capita private sector investment.[12] The lessons from Southeast and East Asia, he reveals, emphasize that good governance makes a country well integrated to the world economy as well as no longer dependent on international aid.

This writer would define good governance as having three elements: rule of law, transparency, and accountability. The main purpose of good governance is to build confidence and trust in the government, with the community, the business sector, and the investors. It is then not surprising that good governance is a very important element in economic recovery and even for the achievement of long-run sustainable growth. Michael Beckman observed that the severity of the crisis was positively correlated with the degree of cronyism, corruption, poor legal structure, poor corporate accountability, and weak general ethics.[13] Indonesia is the hardest hit and it has one of the highest levels of corruption in Asia.

Root writes that one important key of the success of the "East Asian" miracle was the existence of the ability to make changes, including the ability to understand when the changes should be made.[14] The success of these countries depended so much on the transformation of key institutions, which formulated and implemented development policies. Unfortunately, the ability to introduce new organizations, new rules, and new procedures, has not been incorporated in the calculation of total productivity growth. Therefore, he argues that institutional change has been systematically underestimated in economics literature.

A knowledge-based economy assists the creation of transparency, accountability, and the rule of law. The role of the government in providing information for its citizens is crucial in the improvement of equity in development. Public finance policies in the area of information creation and dissemination are thus becoming very important in enhancing economic institutions.

It is clear, therefore, that bad governance, as evidenced by the absence of strong institutions to support the pre-1997 booming economy, produced a high-cost economy which undid much of its economic gains. Therefore, strong institutions must be created to be able to support the economic reforms. New information technology, a new phenomenon which has unavoidably penetrated the Indonesian economy and made the crisis worse, must be seen as an asset which can help the Indonesian economy overcome the crisis and follow a path of sustainable development.

Further, economic policies must be made by giving enough consideration to the existing economic institutions. Macroeconomic modelling draws conclusions depending on several scenarios of institutional development. The macroeconomic analysis should also take into account how the traditional macroeconomic policies affect, and are affected by, institutional factors.

It may be interesting to consider in some detail the highly relevant and crucially important institutional reforms suggested by Beckman for Asian countries.[15] First is a liveable wage for public servants. He argues that the salary should not be seen as a recurrent expenditure, but as a capital expenditure. The "user pays" mechanism (namely, those who use the service must pay) must be eradicated, and be replaced with a contract involving an attractive salary. If he or she breaks the contract, the contract can be cancelled or not renewed. Those who are not capable or corrupt should not get a contract. Along with the knowledge-based economy, all the rules and procedures must be made clear and transparent. There is no reason why customers, for example, cannot read public service information on hard copy or through the Internet.

The enforcement of bankruptcy laws is part of accountability.[16] If a business fails it must be allowed to go bankrupt. The nature of the market will decide whether one fails. The government should let those unsuccessful firms go bankrupt. However, in Indonesia, bankruptcy has been avoided through illegal cash payments and other gifts.

Separation of bank ownership is necessary according to Beckman.[17] The structure of the ownership of Asia's banks is not conducive to sustainable growth. He stresses that though Asia may overcome the current crisis, it may soon return, possibly worse than before, if there is no restructuring of bank ownership. Currently, owners of banks are also the shareholders of many linked businesses, which creates a substantial conflict of interest. Thus, reform is necessary to prohibit owners of banks from being shareholders or even managing other businesses.

Another argument Beckman posits is to standardize the accounting standard throughout Asia.[18] This reform will reduce, and hopefully eliminate, abuses of accounting practices. With this reform, minority shareholders would also be protected because genuinely independent directors are still relatively few in Asia. Preventing retiring bureaucrats from taking lucrative jobs in the private sector may also be important. These former bureaucrats are in demand because of their connections with the existing bureaucrats. The practice is a type of corruption, whereby civil servants expect to enjoy ill-gotten rewards upon retirement. The United States, for example, prohibits its senior officials from working in sectors that are related to their former responsibility in the bureaucracy.

Beckman's last recommendation concerns reform on mass media.[19] Censorship of the mass media may not come only from the government, but also from the owners. Reporting in the media may create a conflict of interest with the other businesses of the owners. This imperfection of local media has contributed to the current crisis. A separation of ownership must be considered, or some sort of limitations should be placed on the owners of mass media on having shares in other businesses. The independence of local business media must go hand in hand with a better salary for journalists. Some journalists in China, Thailand, and Indonesia are willing to accept "envelopes" (containing money) not to report the negative stories of firms. Better salaries, coupled with possibility of being fired if bribes are received, will reduce the temptation to receive the "envelopes".

INTEGRATION WITH THE WORLD ECONOMY

Is Integration Unavoidable?

The 1990s have been witness to an increasingly rapid trend of globalization. Many products can be found almost everywhere in the world. The rising flow of goods, capital, and labour has come to influence most of the world. The buzzwords "globalization" and "integration" characterize the world economy. Yet, abruptly, the Asian (and Indonesian) economies were hit by the crisis. Suddenly, people ask the legitimate question of whether this trend of globalization and integration of the world economy is in fact a positive timing. It may seem that countries further integrated are the worst hit by the crisis. Indonesia is more integrated into the world economy than the Philippines, and clearly Indonesia had more to lose during the crisis.

Globalization can be defined as the integration of the national economy into the regional and the global economy. Full integration would include the integration of all tradeable goods and services, as well as the factors of production. Accordingly all goods are freely traded among nations and factors of production (especially capital and labour) moving to the optimum location. The issue of integration within the world economy cannot be separated from questions on domestic regional economic integration, in particular during a time of rising demands for either full autonomy within a federal state or independence.

Enhancement of domestic regional development

> Archipelagic in geography, eclectic in civilization and heterogeneous in culture, Indonesia flourishes when it accepts and capitalizes on its diversity and disintegrates when it denies and suppresses it … .[20]

Jamie Mackie mentioned that with the diversity of its regions, Indonesia had been able to integrate its economy because of its strong development-orientated government, oil and capital inflow, as well as its huge investment in both the physical and social infrastructure.[21] The regional price variation has declined, indicating an emerging national integrated network, an inter-regional commerce, and a wide inter-regional labour mobility. This economic integration has also been accompanied with the force of political integration, mainly through the centralization of army authority.

Hal Hill and Anna Weidemann, though, show that some problems remain in the regional development in Indonesia.[22] In time of an abundance of revenue, the problem issues might be submerged. Yet, limitations on the central government budget may induce their appearance to the surface. Hill and Weidemann recommended in 1989 that Jakarta should come to the regions for ideas, money, and initiative. They wrote:

> The "unity" of the last twenty years of strong central government has to be complemented more effectively by the "diversity" which flows from a greater emphasis on regional initiative and self-finance.[23]

The recommendation has as much relevance today as it did in 1989. The current crisis affecting Indonesia, and the fall of Soeharto have loosened previous ties that formed "unity". Aspiration to have more autonomy in determining their own destinies is now emerging.

This decentralization of power — whether in the name of full autonomy, federation, or independence — will speed up local decision making and the local use of regional resources. The local people know more about what they need than bureaucrats in Jakarta do. In line with the recommendation on greater use of market mechanisms, it is important to recommend that regional development should be encouraged by allowing them to decide their own development agenda. Because each economy has different comparative advantages and stages of economic development, the pattern of production will also vary. Regions can best focus on their own specialization. This will include a large amount of exchanges in goods, capital, and labour. They should engage in the free trade of goods with other economies (regional or otherwise) without having to consult with the administration in Jakarta. The integration of these economies would benefit each economy as well as Indonesia as whole.

In the future, each regional economy may use the rupiah as the currency, but this may not prohibit the use of other currencies in their own economies. To a large extent the market would determine which currency is used — possibly a mixture. Free trade and tourism will see the free flow of foreign exchange and presumably foreign currencies will be heavily used although it is hard to see them surpassing the rupiah completely.

Following existing patterns, increasing regional disparity may initially result. Some resource-rich economies (Aceh, Irian Jaya, Riau, Jambi, and East Kalimantan) may become very affluent if they are well managed, and some isolated resource-poor economies (for example, East and West Nusatenggara) may take a long time to emerge from poverty. Yet, with the free flow of goods, capital, and labour, to the more fortunate provinces, the isolated economies may no longer be isolated. With a successful implementation of a knowledge-based economy, namely that the society gains education and access to information, a small economy, with relatively advanced technology, may find that a poor location does not matter as much. The people who shift to Jakarta, for example, would only be those who are really needed to be physically present in Jakarta. Further, the rising power of each economy to determine development commitments reducing thereby the motivation to migrate to other economies.

With this sort of regional development, capital will not concentrate solely in Jakarta. Most likely investment will be more widespread and population mobility will also rise. The centre of economic gravity will not be limited in the densely populated provinces in Java and Bali. Improvement and proper attention in regional development, with more interactions in both goods, services and the factors of production among regions, will also reduce the dependence of the Indonesian economy on international economic fluctuations.

Reform on International Economic Integration

The Asian Development Bank (ADB) argued in 1999 that the liberalization of capital flows, which will benefit the industrialized countries more than the developing countries, should be accompanied by the liberalization of labour movement.[24] This would be of assistance to the developing countries. Further, it was ironic that industrial countries had pressed developing countries to allow more, if not free, capital inflow to developing countries, while they were at the same time busy with policies to protect their jobs and industries. The ADB concludes that recovery from the current crisis, and sustainable economic development, ought to depend on an open global environment — a universal and consistent liberalization in trade, capital flow and labour movement.

For the benefit of Indonesia and other countries, liberalization should be continued, but on a consistent and fair basis. The free movement of goods (free trade), the free movement of capital, and the free movement of labour should be performed simultaneously rather than partially. This consistent liberalization requires the understanding of advanced countries and persistent negotiations from the developing countries. If industrialized countries are reluctant to engage in consistent liberalization, Indonesia would be justified in also rejecting this approach. Indonesia may recommend a limited inflow of capital and labour. Otherwise, Indonesia may fall into the same, or worse, type of crisis, which is neither beneficial to Indonesia or the industrialized countries.

Before the crisis, the large inflow of foreign capital and skilled labours to Indonesia might have made capital and skilled labour relatively cheap compared the existing structure of capital and labour market in Indonesia. Coupled with the pressure to raise minimum wages, Indonesian unskilled workers could have become relatively too expensive. Foreign and domestic firms were then likely to move away from unskilled workers, shifting their capital to industries employing skilled labours. The unskilled workers suffered and, worse, there was no chance to work abroad because of resistance from industrialized countries.

What is meant here by consistent liberalization is that there should be no effort to restrict the purchase of goods, services, and factors of production, be it capital or labour. There should be no restriction simply because the goods, services and the factors production are moving between countries. Restrictions can of course be applied if the goods, for example, are dangerous to social stability. In other words, restrictions should not be applied simply because the goods, services, capital, and labour are from other countries.

It should be noted here that the free flow continues as long as supply and demand exist. The governments of industrialized countries stem the inflow of unskilled labourers. If the government does not want foreign unskilled workers, they should change the structure of the economy such that it reduces the need for foreign unskilled labour. For example, the unskilled workers of a national can be used by the government in its initiation of advanced technology.

If the industrialized countries are reluctant to perform consistent liberalization, there is no reason for Indonesia to apply partial liberalization. Indonesia does not have to depend on international capital and skilled labour. Indonesia can utilize its large domestic market: the low- and middle-income consumers can be satisfied without the inflow of high technology and capital from abroad.

With consistent liberalization, Indonesia and the world would pay the same price for the same goods and services, regardless of which country produces it. For instance, after the adjustment of the transportation cost, the price paid for rice produced by foreign farmers must be allowed to be the same as the price paid for the rice produced by Indonesian farmers. The domestic price should be allowed to rise close to that of imported rice. The rising domestic price will induce a better distribution of rice and more widespread planting of rice. On the other hand, people can also be educated, through a knowledge-based and health-based economy, about healthy and cheaper alternatives to rice consumption.

The same quality of skilled labour working in Indonesia must be paid equally, regardless whether or not he/she is Indonesian. Currently, an expatriate working in Indonesia is paid in U.S. dollar, but Indonesians working in Indonesia is paid in rupiah. An international worker has a higher rate (and paid in U.S. dollar) than an equivalent domestic worker (paid in rupiah) though they may be technically "at the same level". It is in fact more rational that the domestic expert, who knows more about the country, be paid higher than the international expert, who often knows little about Indonesia.

If the international expert is paid in U.S. dollar, the Indonesian expert should also be paid in U.S. dollar. This is very important especially during these uncertain economic conditions. With the same payment, regardless of domestic or foreign status, the Indonesian skilled workers can better compete with the foreign workers. For both skilled workers there is already a global need and, hence, there is no need to make a distinction between the local and international technician. If the current practice continues, Indonesian will suffer from an inflow of skilled workers.

Indonesia should also consider allowing the use of the U.S. dollar, the Euro, the yen, or other strong world currencies, for everyday business. This step would increase the feeling of economic certainty for Indonesians, amidst the high inflation rate and continuously weakening rupiah. The Government of Indonesia should not feel that their sovereignty is lost if one day people no longer have any faith in rupiah at all. Liberalization may mean a smaller number of currencies in the world in the long term.

In short, from an economic point of view, consistent international economic liberalization will benefit all economies, including the industrialized economies. The issue is then more political than economic.

CONCLUDING REMARKS

This chapter presents recommendations for the achievement of long-run and sustainable economic development. One cannot ignore the importance of short-run macroeconomic stabilization and financial restructuring, but it is necessary to consider sustainable economic development. By doing this, the risk of another crisis can be reduced. But the crisis itself can be converted into a golden opportunity to make drastic reform towards long-run, sustainable economic development. Recovery, for example, should not be measured by simply citing that the "Indonesian economy has achieved a 5 per cent growth rate", for example. In summary, policy must include the considerations of: people-centred development; a change in statistical indicators; human capital development; a freedom-from-fear based economy; a health-based economy; a knowledge-based economy; domestic market-led development; the strengthening of economic institutions; domestic regional development; and consistent liberalization.

Lastly, the current crisis provides Indonesia an opportunity to change its development orientation towards a people-centred development. It may lead to a slower economic growth rate, but with strong economic institutions and a consistent economic integration, Indonesia will have greater sustainable competitiveness and prosperity.

Notes

1. Earlier drafts of this paper have been presented at conferences in Indonesia and Singapore.
2. Robert J. Samuelson. "Great Depression", in *The Fortune Encyclopedia of Economics*, edited by David R. Henderson (New York: Warner Books, Inc., 1993).
3. Hilton L. Root. "Distinctive Institutions in the Rise of Industrial Asia", in *Behind East Asian Growth: The Political and Social Foundations of Prosperity*, edited by Henry S. Rowen (London: Routledge, 1998).
4. Kim Quaile Hill, *Democracies in Crisis* (Boulder and London: Westview Press, 1988).
5. Paul Krugman, *The Return of Depression Economics* (New York: W. W. Norton and Company, 1999).
6. United Nations Development Programme. *Human Development Report 1992* (New York: UNDP, 1992).
7. The discussion of human capital as consisting of education, health, and freedom from fear originated from Siti Oemijati Djajanegara and Aris Ananta, *Mutu Modal Manusia: Suatu Pemikiran Mengenai Kualitas Penduduk* [Quality of Human Capital: A Note on Population Quality] (Jakarta: Demographic Institute Faculty of Economics University of Indonesia, 1986). The phrase "freedom from fear" was made popular by Aung San Suu Kyi's book of the same name (Penguin, 1996).
8. Anis Chowdhury and Iyanatul Islam, *The Newly Industrializing Economies of East Asia* (London: Routledge, 1993).
9. Gerald Tan, *The Newly Industrializing Countries of Asia* (Singapore: Times Academic Press, 1995).
10. Clarence J. Enzler, *Some Social Aspects of the Depression* (Washington, D.C.: The Catholic University of America Press, 1939), p. 164.
11. Douglas C. North, *Institutions, Institutional Change and Economic Performance* (Cambridge: Cambridge University Press, 1990), pp. 107, 100.
12. Hilton L. Root, "Distinctive Institutions in the Rise of Industrial Asia", in *Behind East Asian Growth: The Political and Social Foundations of Prosperity*, edited by Henry S. Rowen (London: Routledge, 1998).
13. Michael Beckman, *Asian Eclipse. Exposing the Dark Side of Business in Asia* (Singapore: John Wiley & Sons Pte Ltd, 1999).
14. Root, op. cit.
15. Beckman, op. cit., pp. 373-78.
16. Ibid.
17. Ibid.
18. Ibid.

19. Ibid.
20. Hal Hill, ed., *Unity and Diversity. Regional Economic Development in Indonesia since 1970* (Singapore: Oxford University Press, 1989).
21. 1980, quoted in ibid.
22. Hal Hill and Anna Weidemand, "Regional Development in Indonesia: Patterns and Issues", in Hal Hill, ed., *Unity and Diversity. Regional Economic Development in Indonesia since 1970* (Singapore: Oxford University Press, 1989).
23. Ibid.
24. Asian Development Bank, *Asian Development Outlook 1999* (Hong Kong: Oxford University Press, 1999).

SECTION V
The Microeconomy in Year 2000

13

Investment and State Enterprises

Laksamana Sukardi

Usually when people do an assessment of a government's first 100 days, they are not presented with a situation such as one finds in Indonesia today. Under the circumstances when a mere change of government has occurred, for instance Republicans replaced by Democrats in the United States, or the Conservatives replaced by Labour in the United Kingdom; it is a shift in parties, not a change in the whole governmental structure. Thus an assessment after only 100 days of a major transformation will be quite different from an analysis for countries where the basic institutional architectures of government is already in place and there is established legitimacy.

This makes it impossible to make conclusive judgements about what the new Indonesia will be like in the years to come based on just the first few months. One cannot talk about the situation in Indonesia today without mentioning the difficult challenges faced during this period of transition to democracy, and one should bear in mind how far Indonesia has come from just a short time ago when the consensus amongst the population was that the authoritarian regime would continue indefinitely. Soeharto had built a corrupt dynasty that he intended to hand down to his progeny — his children and grandchildren. We have successfully blocked that agenda and are charting a new and legitimate course into the future. This new path is not only good for Indonesians, it is also good for foreign investors. A legitimate government brings with it the rule of law, stability, accountability, and predictability. As we put all these elements in place it is an ideal moment for foreign investors to get in early and show their goodwill. Despite all the turmoil of recent years Indonesia remains a rich country with tremendous potential. Setting up a democratic system is the first step towards unleasing Indonesia's full potential. On behalf of the Indonesian Government I warmly welcome all the business and investors, and give my personal pledge to use every resource of my Ministry to create a favourable climate for this.

Some of the important actions we have taken recently to improve the political and economic situation in Indonesia need to be mentioned. First, Indonesia has a stable and constitutionally democratic government in power for the first time in decades. This government is led by the two most influential people on the Indonesian political stage — Gus Dur and Megawati. Both enjoy tremendous support across the whole of Indonesian society as the legitimate leaders of the people. Given this situation no one would dare make an unconstitutional move against them, the protests of unsatisfied people who lost in the last election notwithstanding.

Second, there are now more checks and balances in the system. In the not too distant past, everything happened according to the whim of the president and his cronies. Now, Indonesia's legislature has a new lease of life as a representative of the people. The parliament is working hard on a range of deep judicial and legal reform as a top priority. To be frank, the Indonesian judicial system under Soeharto was rotten to the core with corruption. Although legal and institutional reform is a long process, Indonesia has already taken a critical first step — the creation of a more independent judiciary. The Wahid government has now transferred all administrative responsibility for judges to the Supreme Court. Formerly, judges were under the aegis of the Ministry of Justice in the Executive Branch, which actively assisted in the "distortion" of the Soeharto regime. The Wahid administration also changed the Ministry of Justice into the Ministry of Law and Regulation. This Ministry is working in tandem with the newly established Ombudsman, supported by an independent committee for the review and development of laws.

Third, Indonesia has freed all political prisoners. This, combined with our solid commitment to a free press, is an important element in building the foundation of rule of law. As everyone knows, the genuine rule of law is not possible in a political climate marked by fear and intimidation. The new cabinet also symbolizes an end to discrimination, particularly against Indonesians of Chinese heritage. Indonesia has come a long way since the days when Chinese written characters were routinely censored from any publication entering Indonesia. President Wahid has made it clear that no country can fight against corruption and other abuses of power without strong guarantees of free expression and a free press. For the first time in decades, critiques are viewed as both healthy and useful for moving the country forward on the right path. Naturally it would be nice if we were not testing our "new wings of freedom" in the middle of a "tropical storm". Nevertheless, there is no such thing as a bad time for freedom, and Indonesians welcome this democratic era and fully recognize all the responsibilities that come with freedom.

Fourth, there are important changes that are of particular interest to potential investors. We have streamlined and decentralized the investment approval authorities to local government. This means the regions will increasingly compete to attract investment and this is a very positive development for the investors. Indonesian embassies have now been authorized in major countries to approve foreign investment. The direction the government is moving in is towards good governance of the investment climate, not control and allocation. New investment laws are being drafted that ends all discrimination between foreign and domestic investment. In this respect we are already ahead of the Multilateral Agreement on Investment (MAI) which is gridlocked by international negotiations. The Wahid government is showing its fundamental commitment to preserving the integrity of fair contracts in Indonesia. For example, in the dispute between Perusahaan Listrik Negara (PLN), the state power corporation, and independent power producers, cabinet sought to preserve the contractual integrities and honour all past commitments — which demonstrates the commitment of the Wahid administration to the rule of law.

The government is also combating corruption by conducting investigative efficiency audits on strategic government institutions, under the auspices of the IMF and the World Bank. So far audits have been conducted into Badan Urusan Logistik Nasional (Bulog), Pertamina, Bank Indonesia, PLN and the reforestation funds.

A final area in which we have made major strides is in empowering Indonesian civil society. One way is through the parliament, but the Cabinet is also giving solid backing to independent commissions investigating human rights violations, even to the extent of questioning senior military officers. International observers have given this process effort high marks for its integrity and willingness to confront difficult issues left over from the previous dictatorship. As a government, we are very proud of this achievement and there are many more that could be mentioned. However, in a difficult and deep transition there is no time for feeling satisfied about what has been done. There is much more that remains unfinished.

Perhaps the one most pressuring is the whole issue of regional autonomy. We inherited a very difficult set of regional issues, due to the abuse of the Soeharto period. The complaints of our Indonesian brothers and sisters in Aceh, West Papua and Ambon are valid and are being taken very seriously by this government. The Cabinet is fully aware that achieving a peaceful and negotiated solution is a crucial ingredient for Indonesia's economic and political future. The Wahid government has demonstrated a clear commitment to avoid using repression, which was always the first reflex of Soeharto's regime. Indeed, the automatic recourse to repression is one of the reasons the regional problems are now so insoluble. This has caused the regions to distrust the central government. Their anger is not directed at "Indonesia" or "fellow Indonesians", but as victims of repression and torture, they have directed their hatred to the central government. The changing nature of government gives cause to be optimistic over this problem.

The new government is open and flexible to restructuring the legal and institutional relationship between the centre and the regions. Indonesians are daily engaging in healthy public debate on whether, for instance, we should adopt a federalist structure or find other options. There are other aspects of the regional challenges that make one optimistic that Indonesia will weather this storm and remain unified. The international communities, and in particular Indonesia's ASEAN neighbours, remain uninvolved with the regions demanding autonomy and independence. Unlike East Timor, the current regional issues are rightly judged to be solely the domestic domain of Indonesia. It is also important that the regional problems have not yet crystallized into unified movements. They remained highly fragmented in every case. And with the partial exception of Ambon, the regional complaints are not directed against fellow Indonesians, but rather against an overly centralized and exploitative regime of the past. Although future negotiations will require elements of passion, compromise and creative thinking on all sides, the regional challenges will be solved peacefully. Indonesia is not on the verge of a civil war, and except for a few limited areas, the country is in an excellent and profitable location for economic activities.

Aside from these basic political factors, the top priorities for accelerating our economic recovery include management of the Indonesian Bank Restructuring Agency (IBRA), banking recapitalization, the privatization of state corporations, corporate debt-restructuring, and fiscal decentralization.

President Wahid has already changed IBRA's top management and thereby sent a clear signal that he wants more initiative. Meanwhile Bank Indonesia has issued a much more stringent requirement to banks. High on the agenda is to move forward aggressively with the privatization of state firms. As Indonesia restabilizes state enterprises following the Asian financial crisis, privatization will gain momentum in the next twelve to eighteen months. Corporate debt restructuring is obviously a high priority. The government has announced it is able to apply special treatment for nearly 170,000 IBRA cases involving small firms without "writing them off". The government recognizes that restoring Indonesia's economic health depends on facilitating a restructuring of the remainder of the corporate sector. The Singapore Government has committed to allocate US$500 million for a corporate debt-restructuring fund. This can be seen as "seed capital" for more investment, with the Singapore Government as the anchor, with other investment banks also contributing to the overall fund.

Finally, fiscal decentralization and greater compliance with tax laws are necessary ingredients for a stable and healthy fiscal base for the Indonesian Government. Although the headlines are full of very disturbing news about Indonesia, we have turned a very important corner in our nation's history with what should be regarded as a minimum of bloodshed and destruction. This does not mean that we do not honour those who passed away in the violence, but for some countries, a major regime change is horribly violent with far greater human suffering. One need only look back to the hundreds of thousands killed during Indonesia's last major regime change in 1965 to see how much worse it could have been. As a committed democrat, from an emerging democracy, for the first time in my life I can honestly say that I have great optimism for Indonesia's political and economic future.

In conclusion, the difference between an optimist and pessimist is illustrated by a famous saying: "An optimist sees an opportunity in every disaster, and a pessimist sees a disaster in every opportunity." Despite the challenges facing Indonesia, there is good reason to be an optimist and see the opportunities that now exist. A pessimist will be defeated before he or she even starts. Having the right outlook is the first challenge. Napoleon once said, "Victory belongs to the most persevering". I would only add to those wise words that victory also belongs to those who stand for genuine democracy, justice, fairness and prosperity.

14

Industry and Trade

Jusuf Kalla

Indonesia's problems since 1998 mainly revolve around three interlinked areas — economics, politics and social structure. In 2000, this has manifested as religious and regional upheavals, as can be seen everyday on CNN. Aceh is proving to be a particularly difficult issue. For the Indonesian Government there are no easy answers to settle all these problems. In January 2000, when the Singaporean Prime Minister, Goh Chok Tong, came to Jakarta, he explained that the major problem in Indonesia is "political instability". However I question what is meant by political instability in this context because, in the case of Indonesia, we are also seeing political dynamism. Compared to 1998 and 1999, the overall situation has vastly improved, and is presided over by a legitimate government. Unlike in Singapore where a protest rally may seem out of place, there are protest marches everyday in Jakarta, albeit often small. This type of activity is equally common in Seattle, Tokyo, Seoul, and many other major cities. This is the natural consequence of greater democratic pluralism. The protests do not change the fact that the situation is much better than before. In fact, it proves the opposite. Admittedly there are inter-religion problems in some parts which, hopefully, we can be settled this year, particularly with the dialogue with the protagonists in Maluku who started negotiations in Jakarta in January 2000. Regional problems will be alleviated as parliament debates, over the next six months, to change the constitution to foster greater regional autonomy.

For now, our leading agenda is economic recovery. The chapters of this book, penned after Wahid's first 100 days, echo press questioning about achievements in that period. It is unrealistic to expect miracles to happen in 100 days when the problems have accrued over 30 years of mismanaged government. In the Department of Trade and Industry, the problems are categorized into three areas: (1) exports, (2) the industrial sector, and (3) small and medium enterprises (SMEs). In a country like

Indonesia, the economy must be increasingly export-orientated because this is the means to improve the industrial and agricultural sectors through the access to wider markets.

Last year oil export returns increased by 1 per cent because of slight price increases, but non-oil export returns declined by 6 per cent. This is because the global price of primary agricultural products, like cocoa and coffee, took a fall. However, the returns are still high as farmers received more money than before because the exchange rate worked in their favour. The agricultural sector is not as easily expanded as the industrial sector. If demand for industrial products increases more products can be produced quickly. However, there are greater limitations to increase agricultural production.

The industrial sector also faces difficulties in export expansion because of the lack of capital due to the economic crisis. Trade financing was restricted as a result of the capital crisis in the banking institutions. During the Soeharto era, the economy was slanted towards favoured conglomerates. But this strategy was a failure and it culminated in the capital flight of the late 1997. What worsens the social and political problems was the perception in the outer provinces that all overseas trade came to Jakarta, and the social and economic problems all stem from the same core problem.

It is not so easy to solve any of these problems when the banking systems are essentially not working. It will take time before this can be rectified. As I travel in many provinces to visit exporters, it is apparent that there are many and varied problems to be solved. There are some interesting examples of how regional exports can be increased from the provinces such as Medan, Sulawesi, or Bali, and the problems they face. In Medan, there is a major problem with security. In many palm oil estates, it is not possible to provide tight security, such that many people steal from these estates at will. Furthermore, some tankers became victims of piracy in the Malacca Straits. In some parts, exporters risk highjackings on the road. The solution is to travel in convoy, or to step up protection in the harbour to facilitate exports. The lack of market information is another problem faced by many regions. One solution is to provide Internet access. The promotion of products is also an issue, so we will facilitate associations to enhance promotion abroad. Industries on the whole would be well served by the streamlining of regulations.

It has been argued that the real sector has already collapsed, but this is not true. The Chamber of Commerce recently complained that the interest rate is very high. I responded by saying, "are you paying the interest?" I believe that not a single businessman in Indonesia pays 50 per cent interest. Even though the interest rate is high, the businessmen do not pay the interest. Therefore, high interest rates have little effect on the businessmen. They also complain about the lack of working capital, but none of the Indonesian businessman will pay off a loan even within two years. They still have money which is deposited in a bank. When the interest rate is 50 per cent, the economy collapsed because all the businessmen put their money in the bank to take advantage of the high interest rate.

A visitor to Jakarta will notice that the traffic jams have returned. This is not because of the protests or the rallies, but because the economy is starting to pick up. This shows that businessmen have enough money, but because they do not pay their debts, their debts remain. Industrial production has reached a current level of 45 per cent per annum on average. Some commodities have done well, such as paper (90 per cent), textiles (80 per cent), while others, like cars (10 per cent) have not done so well. Again a visitor to Jakarta, before the end of the month of Ramadan, will notice that all supermarkets are full, and transport must be booked well ahead. That said, there are still problems. While the businessmen have capital (maybe in Jakarta or in Singapore) other sources are helpful. The key problem here is the banking sector. As banks will be guaranteed by the government through Bank Indonesia, this means the whole crisis of the economy is borne by the government, or by the Indonesian people who generate the revenue, not by businessmen. The economy is running along neo-conservative or neo-classical lines. In the whole of Indonesia, the commercial sector has diverted from bank guarantees and modern instruments to a "cash and carry" basis, which characterised the 1960s, whereby goods were obtained through cash or by trust for one month. In this case, there is no need for a bank guarantee if economies can run on trust. Compare this to the situation two years ago. When a big project is underway, a bank would give credit (though sometimes misused for buying luxury items). Now things have changed. Indonesia does not need big investment projects anymore. We had a rapid expansion of investment over ten years. For example, Indonesia does not need so many hotels, which now have an average 40 per cent occupancy rate. Indonesia already has big chemical factories, steel companies, and high-value real estate — what we need are more corporations. That is the reason we invite investments to Jakarta. The assets are already there, and often at a very cheap price. Coupled with investment is the exploitation of natural resources. The vastness of Indonesia's resources cannot be fully tapped until the security situation is resolved, for example, in Sumatra or Kalimantan. Gus Dur's government is working hard to find solutions.

This new government must be able to achieve consistency in policy and unity of purpose. The changes in Indonesia have led to a very strong parliament and a number of very vocal newspapers that will not hesitate to remind the government if it is inconsistent. "Our friend", the IMF, is also always there to check rigorously on our policies. This is all beneficial of Indonesia. It is important to have critics to respond to such issues as higher salaries for top-ranking civil servants. This environment means we cannot make sudden and unreasonable policy changes. It also means we have to be more realistic about what we can achieve. Can we increase our exports by 50 per cent? Realistically, we cannot. The banks are not in a position to provide the capital necessary for this expansion. The recovery will be slow, but steady, and I can conclude that there are many positive developments in Indonesia which signal a brighter future.

15

Key Principles for the 2000 Budget

Noor Fuad

This short chapter was presented as a paper on behalf of the Minister of Finance when I was just three days in my new position. Previously I was working for the state budget preparation to parliament, and I have also been the Secretariat General of the Indonesian Economists Association. This chapter presents briefly the key principles of the fiscal year 2000 budget.

The key principles include the following aspects. The first principle is the medium-term fiscal framework, on which I am working with the IMF team to good effect. The civil service salary issue remains a significant problem however. The government has adopted a multi-year framework to achieve its fiscal objective. Over the medium-term, the government budget will be restructured as follows: first of all, the tax system will be reformed to enhance the equity and raise revenues in an efficient manner; and second, civil service remuneration will be steadily increased to narrow public–private salary differentials, and thereby help reduce corruption among public officials.

The civil service salaries have become a big debate in Indonesia, particularly after somebody told the press that the president already earns more than Rp100 million per month. Another crucial issue is that of subsidies on basic commodities. The subsidies will be gradually reduced to protect low-income families and avoid disturbing social stability, particularly in the first year. This issue is also much debated by a very active parliament. Then the funding for the development plans will be progressively reoriented away from the wasteful expenditure of previous administrations towards the efficient: in particular we wish to focus on the poverty alleviation scheme, the traditional sector, and the small and medium enterprises (SMEs).

The overall budget deficit will be steadily lowered in order to reduce dependence on foreign assistance. The Ministry recognises the need for domestic bank financing, thereby ensuring the sustainability of the public debt. It is also a very important policy for the central government to try to keep the budget deficit for 1999 to 6.8 per cent, then in 2000 we aim to lower this to 5 per cent, and in 2001, to less than 4 per cent. Beginning from 1999 the government has tried to change the format of the state budget from a reliance on credit. Following international formats, we are hopeful that fiscal policy and fiscal management will become more transparent over time. This will allow parliament, in the short-term, to have an oversight function on the development of expenditure, where the development spending is allocated, and the transparency of local budgets.

The 2000 budget framework represents an initial step towards the above fiscal objective. This budget attempts to strike a balance between: (1) supporting economic recovery, (2) beginning of the process of fiscal consolidation, and (3) reducing the high public debt. The budget is based on the following assumptions, already published in the press, that the GDP growth will be 3.8 per cent, the average CPI inflation will be less than 5 per cent, the exchange rate will average Rp7,000 per U.S. dollar, the average oil price will be more or less US$18 per barrel, and the nominal GDP is valued at Rp910.4 trillion. The overall deficit will be targetted at 5 per cent of GDP, based on revenue earnings of 15.1 per cent of GDP and an expenditure of 20.1 per cent — hence the 5 per cent deficit. Hopefully by the end of 2002, it will be lower, which would be a strong indication that the transparency of the fiscal management is on the right track. Economists and members of the parliament, under the transparency method, will be able to exercise influence, but also understand the government's intention to cover the deficit, and free up long-term funds for the domestic sector and end the reliance on foreign loans. The revenue projection would depend largely on the taxation reform programme, which is being launched right now in order to improve the efficiency and equity of the system. During the fiscal year 2000, many tax exemptions will be removed and the overall tax administration will be strengthened, which will significantly assist value-added tax and import duties collection. Clearly, amendments will be made to this proposal, possibly by April 2000. The tax rates themselves are expected to remain unchanged. There will be an average 25 per cent increase in tobacco excise starting in April 2000, and a narrowing of the tax differential between the white and *kretek* cigarettes. Improvements in the excise regulation will see, before the end of 2002, a lot of revenue created by taxes on the *kretek* cigarette.

In terms of expenditure projection within the fiscal year 2000, this is all in the Letter of Intent with the IMF. At the time of writing, it is impossible to give an exact figure on this. The cost of the bank reconstruction is a nightmare for the Republic of Indonesia. Within the fiscal year 2000 budget will be incorporated the cost of bank reconstruction of around 4.7 per cent of GDP, which is a substantial sum of around Rp40 trillion. This is based on the assumption that the government will issue Rp625 trillion in bonds by the end of March 2000, carrying an average interest rate during the fiscal year of 8.6 per cent. Indonesian Bank Restructuring Agency (IBRA) has said that recovery is recorded as a financing item within the budget in order to cover this item at around Rp44 trillion to Rp45 trillion. In the expenditure projection for the fiscal year 2000, wages and salaries are a large item. Civil service wages will be increased in two amounts involving a 10 per cent increase in the base wage on 1 April and again on 1 October. The Minister of Finance has said that the best option is for the government to improve income of the higher ranking officials to a level close to the private sector, but at the same time, the sudden increase will fall flat until 2002 when it may be reconsidered.

At the same time, the lower level civil servants will see improvements in their additional salary to supplement the structural salary, then they may see an increase from the beginning of 2000 up to the end of 2002. This is the "dream" of the Cabinet and parliament, particularly those from Partai Demokrasi Indonesia-Perjuangan (PDI-P, or Indonesian Democratic Party-Struggle), Partai Amanat Nasional (PAN, or National Mandate Party) and Partai Kebangkitan Bangsa (PKB, or National Awakening Party). They expect the salaries, including those for the parliament, to be increased substantially. However, they have to ask an important question: can you guarantee the increasing expenditure for the enhanced civil service salary? Perhaps the answer is "yes" but there are limitations. One suggestion is to implement a 5 per cent increase in personal income tax or even impose a value-added tax.

With regard to subsidies, we have a petroleum subsidy, and we hope to introduce the coupon scheme for those with lower incomes. With the removal of subsidies, the best way to target the lower income kerosene users would be through coupons. The electricity subsidy, under some discussion with the IMF, does not involve a large expenditure, but the rice subsidy is a much larger item. A crucial item for the poorer people is the development of the social safety net expenditure, which will probably be supported by the IMF.

The fiscal autonomy for local authorities will be increased through a well-sequenced devolution of expenditure and revenue responsibility. This is also part of the road to decentralization based on Laws Number 22 and 25. Probably the year 2000 will be spent in preparation for 2001, when Law Number 25 on expenditure will be fully implemented. Naturally, this will follow keen debate in the parliament.

The framework of decentralization might pose one of the most serious problems for the next budget as we try to alter the central budget, with its development spending, and move to fiscal decentralization. This involves enormous expenditure which cannot be known fully until the Dewan Perwakilan Rakyat (DPR, or People's Representative Assembly) makes the final decision. The capital transfer to regions will increase substantially but Law Number 25 is still not fully implemented because the law takes effect in April 2001. Therefore, Indonesia is in a transition period. The revenue-sharing programme cannot be directly implemented this fiscal year. The Minister of Planning and the Minister of Finance are seeking to set up revenue-sharing whereby the central government might transfer funds to the regions of Aceh, Riau, East Kalimantan, and Irian Jaya. It is possible that 1999 might see an increase in the nominal budget spending for development funds through a block grant. The issue of decentralization is the subject of so much debate on top of warnings from international organisations, and of course we realise that this is not easy. The transition period of only two years is very crucial. The Minister of Finance has surveyed 340 of the second level districts and this database indicates that 60 to 80 per cent of the local state budget was supported and transferred by the central government. Therefore the 340 local districts, or the second level, have salary expenses that outweigh their own income by more than 125 per cent. This means that in the short-term, the government should support the local authorities before trying to implement the grand allocation resources to decentralize funding.

With regard to budget financing, the Cabinet has told the public that Indonesia is going to reduce its foreign debt and we are still hoping for that outcome in 2002. The new format of public expenditure is that if the expenditure is bigger than revenue, then we have a deficit. How can we overcome the deficit? I am going to try financing this budget from the proceeds of privatization and IBRA's asset-recovery programme. However, to meet the shortfall the net foreign financing could be around the Rp20 trillion to Rp25 trillion mark. First, the gross disbursement of the foreign loans will amount from Rp30 trillion to Rp35 trillion, bulk of which will come from the existing commitment of the World Bank, the Asian Development Bank, and Japan. It is estimated that there will be a small residual financing need around Rp0.5 billion to Rp0.75 billion which is expected to be covered by new commitment from the Consultative Group of Indonesia (CGI) — a multilateral aid consultation group. On the basis of the quasi-Paris Club re-scheduling will revolve around Rp10 trillion to Rp15 trillion.

All domestic arrears are a very important aspect of the budget. For Indonesia we have arrears, especially for Badan Urusan Logistik Nasional (Bulog, or National Logistics Board), Perusahaan Listrik Negara (PLN, or National Electricity Company) and Pertamina. In conjunction with the IMF team we expect that by the end of March 2000 all domestic arrears will be cleared. Whatever the case may be, there will be no accommodation of domestic arrears beyond 2000.

SECTION VI
Bank Restructuring

16

An Overview of Bank Restructuring in Indonesia

Farid Harianto

INTRODUCTION

From September 1999 to the time of writing not much has happened with bank restructuring. This report is about the work-in-progress in terms of bank restructuring in Indonesia. This involves looking into some of the structural issues that the Indonesian banking sector was facing prior to the crisis, and then the work-in-progress in terms of bank recapitalization. This chapter will conclude by alluding some of the important policy issues that need to be addressed for the future.

WHAT WENT WRONG: STRUCTURAL ISSUES

In the banking sector, prior to 1997, the large number of banks and financial institutions resulted in steep competition, which saw many ignore both quality and prudence in banking practices. The balance sheet of the banking sector showed an asset-liability mismatch of many years standing. Capital liquidity has always been low, compounded by massive lending to "related parties". In fact on the data that Indonesian Bank Restructuring Agency (IBRA) holds, there is almost a near perfect correlation between ownership and lending that resulted in non-performing loans. The correlation is so close that it is reasonable to cite this as the most substantial cause of "bad loans". Furthermore, the banks that are controlled by one single party, private or government, specifically had the highest non-performing loans in the country. Many banks also held high off-balance sheet liabilities. All these factors cited above were made worse by the near total lack of regulatory enforcement.

The financial crisis severely exposed the banking sector's poor risk management and hedging practices. Similar structural weaknesses are also evident in the corporate sector. The overall leverage, asset-liability mismatch, poor risk management, and poor disclosure practices have resulted in poor asset quality in both the banking and corporate sectors. It must also be understood that the banking sector dominates the financial systems of Indonesia. The importance of restructuring the banking sector cannot be underestimated.

WORK-IN-PROGRESS: BANK RESTRUCTURING PHASE 1

The government, through IBRA, has consolidated the industry. The closing of one third of private banks — sixty-six banks in all — also represented about one third in terms of total sector assets and one third in terms of deposit base. This has been supplemented by the merger of four state banks into one, and the merger of ten banks into Danamon. The next step has been the recapitalization of banks. Several private banks, including Bank Mardiri, have completely recapitalized. There are still six remaining banks that are awaiting government bonds, three state banks and three other private banks or ex-private banks. These include Bank Bali, Bank Niaga and Bank Dagang Indonesia (BDI). For unclear reasons, the bonds never come out to these banks but IBRA fully expects this to be issued after the reopening of parliament in 2000. IBRA hopes to conclude the recapitalization of those six banks as soon as possible.

The third progress is toward finalization of corporate debt restructuring under IBRA, subject to final documentations. IBRA announced in January 2000 that (face value) debt amounting to Rp35 trillion has been restructured. But a careful reading of the Letter of Intent indicates that, by the end of June, there will be 50–70 obligators involving about 200 to 250 companies which will come to the final stage of the debt-restructuring process with the face value of somewhere between Rp90 trillion to Rp110 trillion.

One particular aspect of bank restructuring in Indonesia, which is unique to Indonesia, is the whole issue of shareholder settlement, and this particular experience is being observed by IBRA's counterpart organizations across the Southeast Asia region. Seven previous bank owners, including Bank Central Asia (BCA), BDI, and Danamon, have settled with the government to pay either the group lendings that they took from their own banks in the past, or in the case of bank closures, the shareholders take the resulting loss. That particular shareholder settlement resulted in the transfer of good assets, with a market value of somewhere around US$10 billion, now under IBRA's aegis. IBRA can claim that this is, as far as I know, the only aspect of bank and corporate restructuring in Indonesia where we are one step ahead of South Korea, Thailand or Malaysia. Some of the conglomerates of Indonesia have faced their problems and have restructured. This has resulted in the Initial Public Offering (IPO) of BCA in the first quarter of 2000, as well as the IPOs of seven companies under the Salim group. The Salim group is basically the only company in Indonesia, and in the region, that has been able to restructure itself fully and return to something approaching business as usual. This is one particular aspect that many have overlooked. The *Asian Wall Street Journal* is now hailing the Salim group as an Indonesian success.

ENTERING INTO BANK RESTRUCTURING PHASE 2

The balance sheet of the banks is still very fragile. Seventy per cent of third-party funding is in the form of one-month Certificates of Deposit (CDs) against only less than Rp50 trillion of liquid assets in the system. The aggregate equity is only less than Rp30 trillion while assets largely consist of government bonds, about Rp400 trillion, and the remaining loans of about Rp300 trillion. So the balance sheet is still on a knife-edge. If something further happens to the system, the Rp50 trillion of liquid assets will not be able to cover the Rp400 trillion to Rp500 trillion of one month CDs. This is why there is a need for the government guarantee programmes.

There is the strong need for a secondary market for government bonds to restore the liquidity in the system, in tandem with the need for long-term funding for the bank. The idea that IBRA is now working on is to convert the Rp400 trillion government bonds into productive yielding assets. By the end of June 2000, IBRA plans to inject the restructured debts back into the system. The new debts, with expected market values of between Rp35 trillion to Rp50 trillion, will be injected. The low-pace equity in the system is another hurdle, and IBRA will run into the problem of legal lending limit and capital adequacy requirements.

What is needed in Indonesia is an increase in equity, which means a second phase of recapitalization. This is exactly what we are going to do with the BCA. In the IPO of BCA, half of the proceeds will still be put into the bank to enhance capital while half of the proceeds will be used to buy government shares. Likewise I can also report that Franky Widjaja's bank, Bank Internasional Indonesia (BII), plans to go ahead to raise money for the bank and, at the same time, to buy back the government shares within the next few months. This type of action is necessary; otherwise the banking system will be very prone to any future events in the market.

Looking into the future, there will be a full consolidation, and in IBRA's opinion, five or six large national banks are all that are needed. These five or six banks, run efficiently, will need to face the ASEAN Free Trade Area (AFTA) post-2003 commodity trade liberalization when the financial sectors will be included. It is the obvious conclusion that what Indonesia needs is a better regulatory framework and enforcement of that framework, because the problems of the past have been allowed to happen due to the weakness in supervision and enforcement.

REMAINING POLICY ISSUES

There are several policy issues that will be very important over the course of the year 2000. First of all, the cost of bank restructuring is large — IBRA estimates somewhere between 60 to 80 per cent of GDP (Joshua Felman's figure in this volume of 90 per cent seems too high). Nonetheless, the cost of bank restructuring in Indonesia is the highest in the world, regardless of the figure that one accepts. This highest cost of bank restructuring in the world is due to government "over-guarantee" programmes. These programmes not only guarantee but "over-guarantee" what amounts to a "blank cheque". The annual interest charges that IBRA expects are somewhere in between 2.5 to 3 per cent of GDP. The net cost after IBRA's contributions through asset disposal will only amount to 0.5 per cent of GDP for the next four years. The remaining question is what will happen after four years when almost all of IBRA's assets are depleted? The implications are that, by 2005, the 2.5 to 3 per cent of GNP cost of bank restructuring will be borne entirely by the fiscal budget.

The second issue, and a rather serious one for Indonesia, is the question of out-of-court settlements. There is an attempt within some quarters of government to open up the "old wounds" and punish past crimes. There is certainly merit in this approach but is needs to be balanced with the need for a speedy and cost-effective recovery. What will happen then if the shareholders' debts have been settled but some wish to pursue the "sins of the past". For example, if the Salim group paid about US$7 billion in shareholder debts, what will happen if the government opens up a legal case for those shareholders settlements? In this instance, the desire for justice (or retribution) needs to be addressed with considerable care.

The third policy issue is the need for market clearing of both financial and corporate assets. Price formation does not take place both in the financial and real assets as sellers are playing the waiting game. While there is a lot of talk about the need to dispose of properties in Jakarta and Bali, not a single major transaction has happened. The same thing has occurred with regards to the need to have transactions of distressed assets. Unreasonable assumptions about the future are compounded by differing discount rates across asset classes (for example, bank investors versus distressed assets investors). Part of the strategy of IBRA is to create a market clearing that will facilitate price formation, to provide a benchmark for assets such as property. Indeed this is a trade-off between maximizing the value of their invested properties and, at the same time, fulfilling the goal of corporate debt restructuring.

The fourth issue, and admittedly this author's favourite cause, is the subject of restoring the incentive regime, to get the right balance. Attention must be given to both non-compliance behaviour as well as good corporate governance. Again, this relates to the question about the out-of-court settlements. The incentive for co-operative debtors and bank shareholders need to be addressed, as well as the need for severe punishments for non-compliance or non-co-operative behaviour. In the past, Soeharto's New Order gave incentives for co-operative behaviour for the shareholders settlements but the government did nothing to punish bad behaviour. A balanced situation would be a sense of reward and punishment based on compliance. At the heart of the matter is the need to restore the culture of creditor-debtor relations into a normal working relationship.

The fifth issue, mentioned earlier, is the need to reduce the overdependency of the financial system on the banking sector. Statistics show that corporate funding from the banking sector, prior to the crisis, is somewhere between Rp800 trillion and Rp900 trillion (including the non-performing loans) compared to the capital market capitalization of only Rp400 trillion to Rp450 trillion. The insurance and pension fund industries only represent less than Rp40 trillion.

Looking forward, there is every reason for the optimist assessment that the government bonds (practically at fixed rate) now floating around, will provide the much needed yield for Indonesian domestic rupiah bonds. With the establishment of a secondary market for the government bonds in the near future, this will be a critical ingredient for the development of a domestic bond market in Indonesia.

Right now there has been a lot of discussion in Indonesia about emulating the Employees Provident Fund (EPF)/Central Provident Fund

(CPF)[1] model for domestic resource mobilization. However, these models cannot be neatly transferred. Out of about 30 million paid employees in Indonesia, only 16 million are wage earners. Out of this 16 million, 5 million are civil servants and armed forces personnel, while 11 million are private sector employees. Another 14 million are non-fixed income earners such as part-timers (*upah*). To mobilize resources, given the structure of employment, Indonesia will have to use different rules, programmes and policies, and even different institutions, to mobilize funds. CPF and EPF models can only be applied for the 11 million people that are working for the private sectors but not for the majority of Indonesians.

CONCLUSION

There are still considerable challenges that need to be addressed. The five remaining policy issues outlined here are critical aspects that must be resolved in order to restore the dangling corporate sectors to economic health.

Note

1. Malaysia's Employees Provident Fund (EPF) and Singapore's Central Provident Fund (CPF) involve retirement savings through regular deductions of workers' salaries.

17

Indonesian Bank Restructuring
A Practitioner's View

Gunarni Soeworo

INTRODUCTION

This chapter examines banking restructuring from the point of view of a practitioner. While others in this volume discussed, in a very systematic way, the crisis itself and the impact of the crisis on the banking industries, I will give a different perspective on the impact of the crisis on the Indonesian banking sector, government responses, and what is needed to go forward.

THE IMPACT OF THE ASIAN FINANCIAL CRISIS ON INDONESIA'S BANKING SECTOR

To be frank, most of the domestic banks in the banking sector are technically insolvent (see Table 17.1 and Figure 17.1 for total credit portfolios). This is because of the negative spread, foreign exchange losses, and the very high ratio of non-performing loans (NPLs). In terms of negative spread, in 1997/98, the interbank interest rate reached around 80 per cent at its highest and the deposit rate reached 50–60 per cent, causing the banks to suffer. The negative spread is not only the result of the high interest rates on the liability side, but also due to the very high NPL ratios on the asset side. To compound all of this, the structure of the funding is very unfortunate because all of the banks were suffering from a mismatched maturity and a mismatched currency. So the cross-currency funding has further aggravated the funding structure, resulting in the very high negative spread. The whole banking sector is facing a huge debt problem — almost 60–70 per cent of the asset side are NPLs. Offshore credit basically disappeared

TABLE 17.1
Total Credit Portfolio (Rupiah and Foreign Currency) by Group of Banks
(In Rp billions)

Group of Banks	1992	1993	1994	1995	1996	1997	1998	1999[a]
State banks	68,236	71,543	80,010	93,480	108,925	153,266	220,747	127,914
Regional govt banks	3,015	3,554	4,201	5,242	6,457	7,539	6,570	6,560
Private national banks	42,337	60,441	86,303	111,644	149,955	168,723	193,361	58,483
Foreign and J.V. banks	9,330	14,733	18,366	24,245	27,584	48,606	66,748	50,022
All commercial banks	122,918	150,271	188,880	234,611	292,291	378,134	487,426	242,979
Conversion rate US$/Rp (Mid-rate)		2,110	2,200	2,308	2,383	4,650	8,025	6,900

1998 Positions

Group of Banks	Jan	Feb	Mar	Apr[b]	May	Jun	Jul	Aug	Sep	Oct	Nov[b]	Dec
State banks	203,303	196,765	202,569	202,585	219,752	256,354	241,625	230,329	231,292	208,434	212,118	220,747
Regional govt banks	7,630	7,412	7,181	6,709	7,045	7,009	8,898	6,812	6,769	6,706	6,699	6,570
Private national banks	208,528	196,982	192,076	186,870	209,389	241,833	226,946	214,411	209,107	189,428	187,042	193,361
Foreign and J.V. banks	91,671	78,811	75,015	72,551	91,269	121,269	106,181	92,424	88,807	66,800	63,712	66,748
All commercial banks	511,132	480,080	476,841	468,715	527,455	626,465	581,650	543,976	535,975	471,368	469,571	487,426
Conversion rate US$/Rp (Mid-rate)	10,375	8,750	8,325	7,970	10,525	14,900	13,000	11,075	10,700	7,550	7,300	8,025

1999 Positions												
Group of Banks	Jan	Feb	Mar[c]	Apr[c]	May	Jun	Jul	Aug	Sep	Oct	Nov	Dec
State banks	226,788	225,514	154,377	144,816	141,720	131,791	130,222	132,241	135,539	127,914	N/A	N/A
Regional govt banks	6,655	6,782	6,977	7,334	6,756	6,134	6,255	6,342	6,476	6,560	N/A	N/A
Private national banks	199,10	197,832	138,358	75,837	71,715	64,164	64,176	64,555	62,515	58,483	N/A	N/A
Foreign and J.V. banks	71,739	69,810	66,831	59,890	57,411	49,173	48,775	54,437	58,732	50,022	N/A	N/A
All commercial banks	504,282	499,938	366,543	287,877	277,602	251,262	249,428	257,575	263,262	242,979	N/A	N/A
Conversion rate US$/Rp (Mid-rate)	8,950	8,730	8,685	8,260	8,015	6,726	6,875	7,565	8,386	6,900		

[a] Per October 1999.

[b] Closure of 7 private banks in April and 3 private banks in August.

[c] Transfer of assets to IBRA and closure of 38 private banks.

Source: Bank Indonesia Weekly Report, No. 2093, 30 November 1999, and *Bank Indonesia Annual Report 1998/99.*

FIGURE 17.1
Credit Portfolio

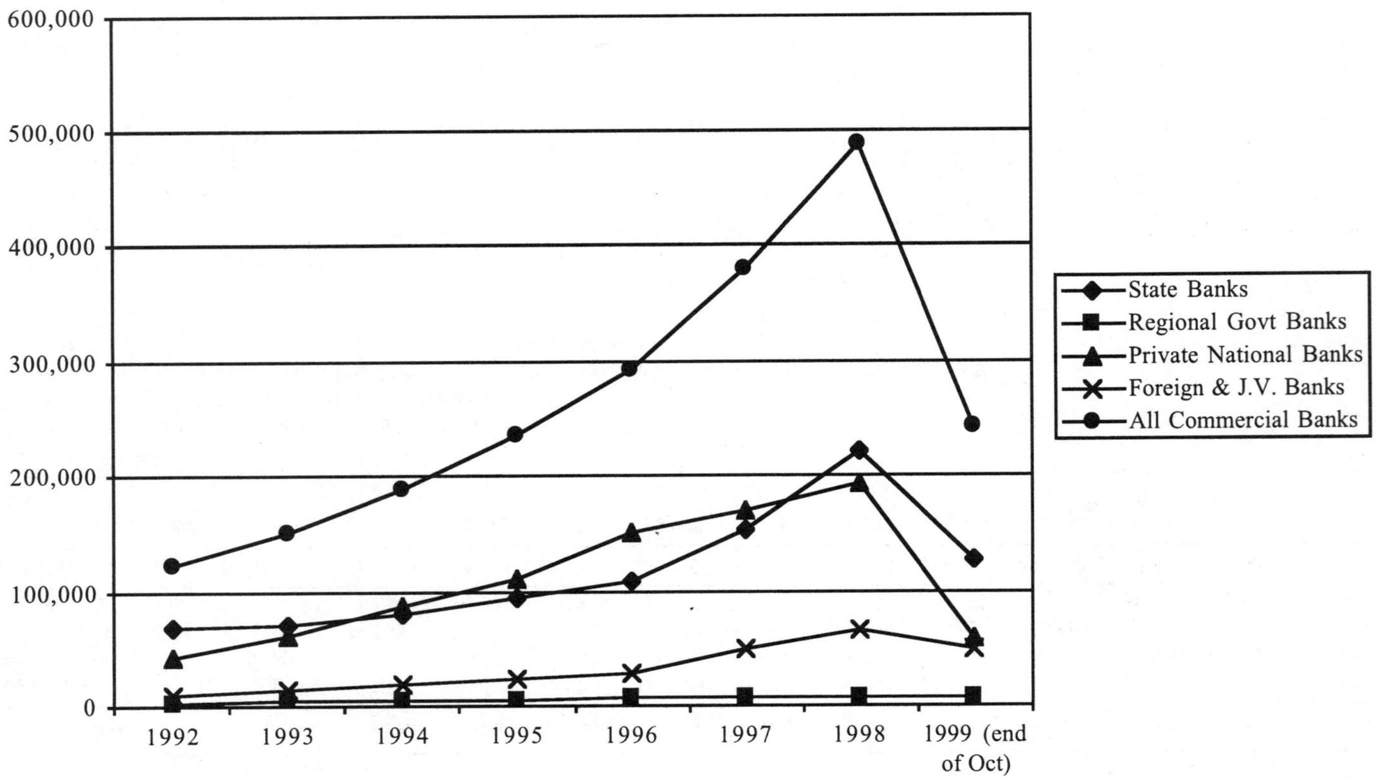

immediately after the crisis. Before the crisis, foreign creditors had been very generous to the players in the market. On a weekly basis, they visited Indonesian banks offering extended facilities. The reality is, however, that once the crisis happened, the notion of relationships in banking was little more than lip-service. Foreign investors could accurately be described as "fair weather friends". Even after the government's issuance of a blanket guarantee, foreign creditors are still not comfortable with the risks involved in extending credit to the Indonesian banking sector.

The foreign banks and the state banks (because of their status) actually benefited from the crisis on the deposit side (see Figure 17.2) — but this is thanks to the high interest rate. While others in this volume point out that while bank liquidity has declined, total deposits have in fact increased tremendously (see Table 17.2 and Figure 17.3). The reason for this is self-evident. Customers, including the corporate clients, are keeping their money in bank deposits because of the high interest rate, while at the same time they are not fulfilling their debtor obligations.

GOVERNMENT RESPONSES

First, to restore public confidence, the government has issued a blanket guarantee, thereby guaranteeing all the depositors and the creditors. This has been achieved at a very high cost to the government, and constitutes a big blunder as guarantees have been issued to all the creditors. When the government issued the blanket guarantee, it expected foreign lenders to continue to provide the credit facilities to the banking sector. In reality, not too many foreign creditors are willing to provide facilities to the banking sector. So the cost borne by the Indonesian government is not well compensated. This policy initiative needs to be revisited.

Other important government initiatives have been the creation of Indonesian Bank Restructuring Agency (IBRA) to rehabilitate ailing banks and improve prudential regulation. Although the banking sector is still far below the Bank for International Standards (BIS) requirements on the capital adequacy ratio (CAR), the government has enforced the CAR of 4 per cent in the banking system. This is a very hard target to reach, as most of the banks are insolvent. However, IBRA's recapitalization programme on behalf of the government and the new bankruptcy law may help the banks to reach this target. There are some problems on this last point because the bankruptcy law is not actually working properly and needs to be visited. The government outlined in its "Jakarta Initiative" its intention to restructure debt.

FIGURE 17.2
Foreign Currency Deposit

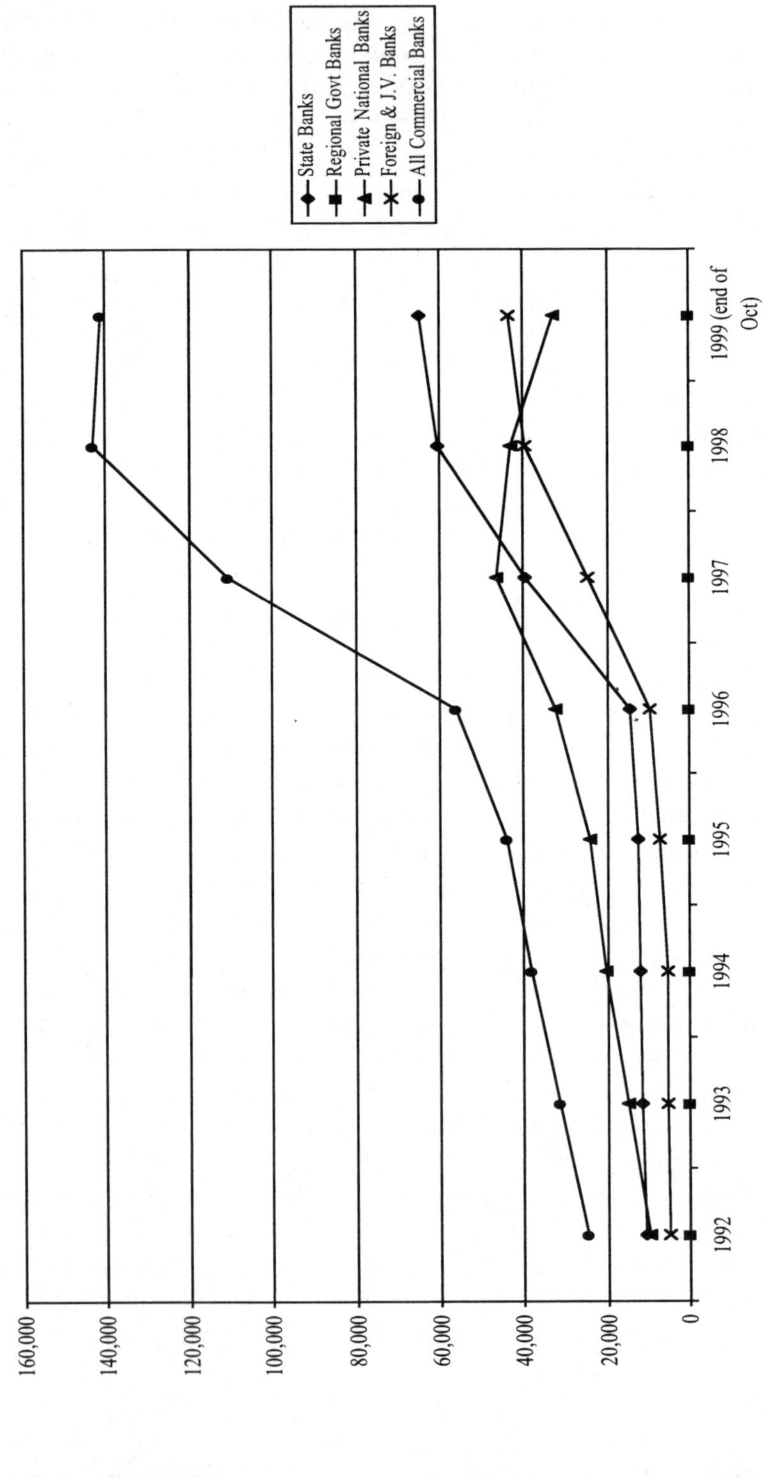

TABLE 17.2
Total Commercial Banks' Deposits by Group of Banks
(In Rp billions)

Rupiah Deposits

Group of Banks	1992	1993	1994	1995	1996	1997	1998	1999[a]
State banks	42,161	50,258	52,394	63,385	76,165	93,249	211,087	236,247
Regional govt banks	3,684	4,740	6,142	7,766	8,470	8,739	10,876	13,761
Private national banks	41,401	52,605	68,431	93,318	132,797	130,777	192,558	214,307
Foreign & J.V. banks	2,869	3,497	5,484	6,178	8,115	14,071	15,870	24,283
All commercial banks	90,115	111,100	132,451	170,647	225,547	246,836	430,391	488,598

Foreign Currency Deposits

Group of Banks	1992	1993	1994	1995	1996	1997	1998	1999[a]
State banks	10,439	11,425	11,889	12,535	14,269	39,793	60,467	64,823
Regional govt banks	13	33	41	46	52	57	56	53
Private national banks	9,678	14,936	20,494	24,133	32,182	46,416	43,047	33,078
Foreign & J.V. banks	4,605	5,185	5,531	7,401	9,668	24,511	39,563	43,322
All commercial banks	24,735	31,579	37,955	44,115	56,171	110,777	143,133	141,276
Conv. rate US$/Rp (Mid-rate)		2,110	2,200	2,308	2,383	4,650	8,025	6,900
US$ eqv. (in billion)		15	17	19	24	24	18	20

Interest Rate (end of period) (% per annum)	1993	1994	1995	1996	1997	1998	1999[b]
Bank Ind. Certificate	9.08	11.59	13.34	12.26	17.38	37.84	13.06
Interbank call money	8.72	9.87	13.62	14.13	30.52	39.45	12.29
3 months T/D	11.79	14.27	17.15	17.03	23.92	49.23	13.43

[a] As per end of October 1999.

[b] The interest rate for interbank call money during the period ranged between 39.45 per cent (lowest) and 80.64 per cent (highest), while the interest of 3 months T/D ranged between 22.86 per cent (lowest) and 54.67 per cent (highest).

Source: Bank Indonesia Weekly Report, No. 20995, 15 December 1999.

GOING FORWARD

Much discussion about the banking sector paints an exceedingly gloomy picture, but as a practitioner this author is not so pessimistic. There is good reason to argue that the outlook for the banking sector in Indonesia is still reasonable. But first, Indonesia needs to expedite the restructuring of the banking industry by recapitalizing the banks (coupled with corporate restructuring) in an accelerated manner to facilitate a sustainable recovery.

FIGURE 17.3
Rupiah Deposit

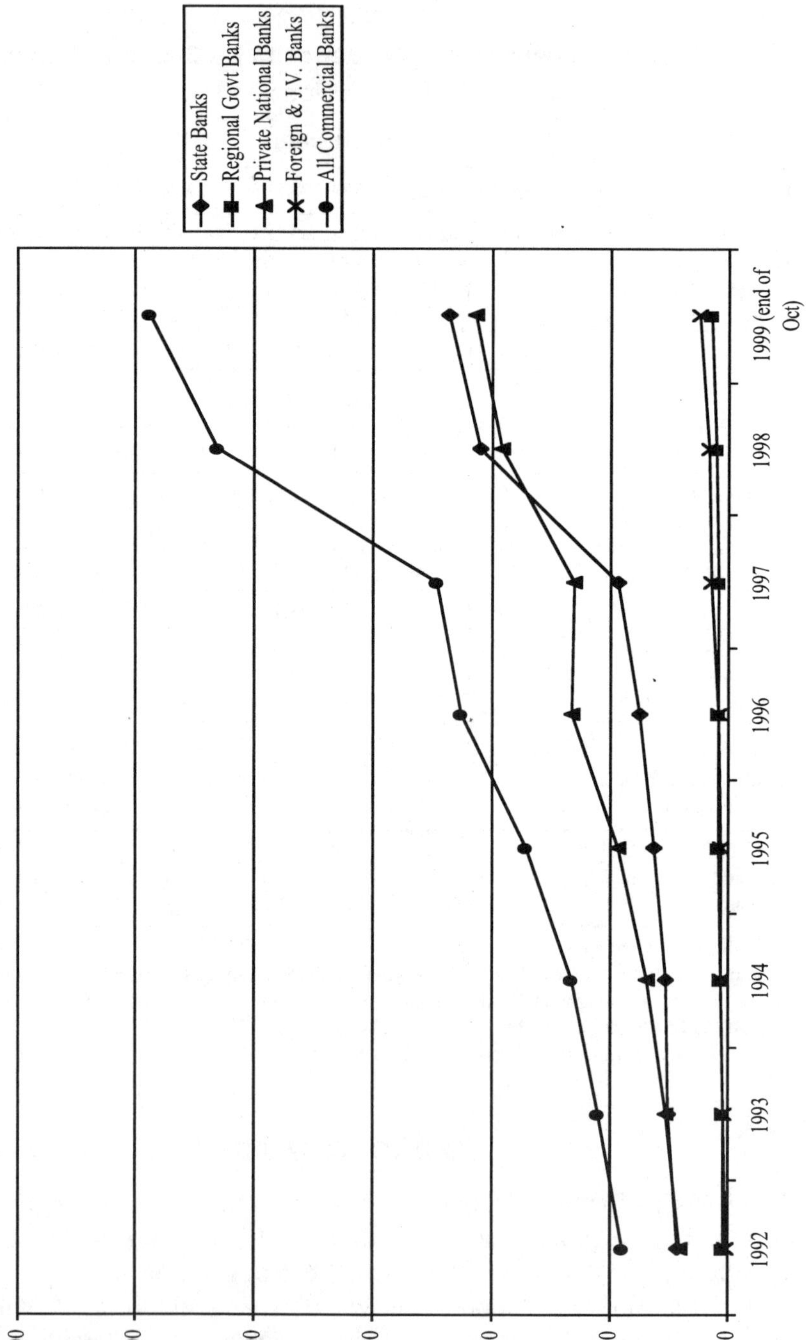

The fact that significant loans are yet to be made available has raised concern for economic recovery, but this author anticipates that in the second half of 2000 the banks will probably start re-lending — which would be of significant help to the real sector. Although there are some political and social uncertainties, Indonesia has a strong basis for recovery and future growth due to abundant natural resources, physical infrastructure, and production facilities, which are still under-utilized. In the past, domestic savings have helped to support economic growth and investment. Furthermore, Indonesia has, to a certain extent, benefited from the IMF programme with regard to the economic and political reforms. Significant support from the donor countries is still there too.

EXPECTED TRENDS

In the long run the banking sector is likely to evolve into a much more efficient structure. One expected trend is the further consolidation in the banking sector through merger acquisition or further liquidations. It is further expected that foreign players will have a much bigger role. There will be increasing foreign ownership or stakeholdings within domestic banks, strategic alliances with the foreign partners. In terms of lessons learned, the banking supervision will be rigorous and, with the support of IMF, the banking supervision system will be much more professional in the future. With the enforcement of prudential banking regulations, especially with regard to the group-related lending, better asset-liability management, better risk management, and an international audit system, the industry is in a better position to avoid similar crises in the future.

The government guarantee scheme, which is very important at this time, will eventually be replaced fully by a deposit insurance scheme. However the government should not lift the guarantee scheme immediately because on the liability side the depositors are still easily panicked with even the hint of unfavourable news. So great care is needed in this regard. Until the CAR of the bank is above 10 per cent, then the government is on safe grounds to lift the guarantee scheme.

Another expected trend is that banks will have better quality management systems. The government, through the central bank, has introduced fit and proper tests mandatory for banks. So banks have appointed compliance directors, and many local banks, especially the private banks, have asked foreign banks to manage their banks through technical assistance arrangements.

IBRA will have greater knowledge and statistics on this, but when one looks at the business plans that have been submitted by the banks, probably almost all banks, because of their bad experiences, switched their business strategy from corporate banking to retail banking. This is not only difficult, but also dangerous, as it risks creating a credit crunch for the corporate sector. Eventually the corporate client has to rely on the capital market, while the retail banking and the consumer banking markets will be crowded with the new players creating heavy competition. For example, Bank Mandiri, one of the biggest banks, is shifting its strategy towards retail and consumer banking.

I am confident, however, in predicting that the banking sector will start providing the credit liquidity to the market, especially for working capital later in 2000. Investment or the long-term or project financing, however, will still have a fair distance to go. The working capital, on the other hand, will filter through soon because the banks cannot just allow the Sertifikat Bank Indonesia (SBI, or Bank Indonesia Certificates) to remain idle, as this will not provide sufficient return. The obvious limitation remains limited capital. If the banking sector is to grow, with an important knock-on effect for the real sector, the second recapitalization probably cannot be avoided. But will the government provide the second recapitalization? At this juncture, it does not seem likely. So the capital market then becomes the only solution to further recapitalize the banking sector. However it remains to be seen who is going to buy the banking sector shares. Problems are bound to resurface after restructuring as banks start providing substantial credit liquidity to the real sector.

IBRA estimates that there will be around 5 or 6 core banks in the future, although this is still to be determined. What is important is that review of the banking structure need to be undertaken very carefully. The central bank is drafting a blueprint of what the banking architecture will look like in the future. At the moment there are 7 state banks, around 27 regional government banks, 48 foreign exchange private national banks, 45 non-foreign exchange private banks, 33 joint-venture banks, and 10 foreign banks (see Table 17.3). Looking at the composition, this author would concur with IBRA that there are still too many banks, but there will still not be too many core banks that can play a bigger role in the banking sector.

It is very interesting to note, based on the statistics, that the foreign banks now have a bigger role in the industry. The financial statements of Citibank place their assets at around Rp20 trillion. Most of the assets are in terms of the SBI and interbank borrowing. On the liability side, Citibank

TABLE 17.3
Total Number of Commercial Banks by Group of Banks

Group of Banks	1997/98	1998/99
State banks	7	7
Regional government banks	27	27
Private national banks (forex licence)	77	48
Private national banks (non-forex licence)	67	45
Joint venture banks	34	33
Foreign banks	10	10
Total	222	170

has actually benefited from the crisis. Citibank, in terms of profitability is probably the best bank in Indonesia. This is a clear indication that Indonesian banks will have to compete with the likes of Citibank, Deutsche Bank, Standard Chartered Bank, and ABN-Amro to take just some examples. So all the domestic banks increasingly face strong competition or pressure from foreign banks. This process is unavoidable, so further consolidation is necessary for local banks. In the future, whether banks like it or not, management improvement and prudential banking practices will become a matter of survival.

That said, with government assistance, including supervision, there is still reason to believe that the local banks will still be dominant players in the industry, or at the very least, major contributors.

FINANCIAL ASPECTS

The banking industry expects a turning point at some point in the second half of 2000 from gradual loan growth and the recovery of loan losses that have been written-off and the sale of foreclosed assets. The banks' balance sheets will be stronger with adequate loan provisioning, lower NPLs, lower interest rates, improved liquidity (10 per cent of government bonds are tradable) and moderate loan growth. With the support of IBRA and Jakarta Initiative, corporate debt restructuring could be accelerated, thus generating new income streams task force. However, the reality is that lack of capital could be a constraint for sustainable growth, and this makes the issue a crucial one for the Wahid administration.

18

Restructuring the Banking System
Indonesia's Challenge

Sri Adiningsih

INTRODUCTION

The financial and economic crisis that afflicted Thailand on 2 July 1997 ultimately hurt the economies of all the ASEAN tigers. The crisis subsequently spread to Indonesia and effectively destroyed the Indonesian economy. The crisis has also destroyed the Indonesian financial market, especially the banking industry. The market has "disciplined" the Indonesian financial market and the banking industry, causing it to suffer a near meltdown. Consequently, the Indonesian financial market, including the banking industry, has had to carry out total restructuring. The financial crisis indicates that the financial market in the country is fragile and remains weak. For this reason, the financial market has to totally restructure in order to develop a healthy financial market on a domestic, regional, and global scale.

Indonesia needs to have a strong financial market. The role of the financial sector is essential for the economic development of a country. Banks and financial institutions under the capital market have important roles in facilitating financial intermediation from those with a surplus to those with a deficit. Douglas Diamond has said that the financial intermediation could reduce the cost of monitoring funds used by the debtor: "diversification is the main reason delegating monitoring is superior to direct lending and borrower".[1] Furthermore, the existence of financial institutions will also increase the cash flow with cheaper transaction costs.[2] Thus the existence of financial institutions will raise the overall access to capital and improve society's welfare.

Banks have a very important role in Indonesia's financial market. Banks were the first financial institution to appear in the society, and their numbers grew in recent times. Hence, the condition of banks will greatly influence the financial markets and general economic condition. A sound banking industry is one of the conditions for economic recovery in Indonesia. A healthy banking industry will support monetary stability, an effective and competitive financial system, and gives solid guarantees to the depositors and consumers.[3]

THE DEVELOPMENT OF THE BANKING INDUSTRY

The financial markets have developed markedly since Indonesia's deregulation policy in 1983, known as "Paket Kebijakan Juni 1983". However, the financial market really developed much faster since the release of Pakto 88 (1988) which eased restrictions on the establishment of banks. The number of banks doubled within ten years, increasing from 111 in 1988 to 238 on July 1997 (before the crisis in Indonesia). This development also saw the rise in bank assets, the ability of the bank to gather credit, and the ability to channel that credit to society, which increased more than 500 per cent from 1989 to 1996.[4] The data indicates that banks, as financial institutions, were playing an increasingly important role in Indonesia's economy.

Other financial institutions had also developed fast in the same period even though their role in the economy was still small. The development of other financial institutions in Indonesia since 1989, until just before the crisis, was at a faster rate than the banking industry. This trend indicated that their role in the financial market was becoming more important. The capital market, which started developing in Indonesia since the end of the 1980s, developed very fast in Indonesia until about 1996, as did the finance companies. However, their roles in the financial market in general were still small compared with the banking industry (see Table 18.1).

In the past, the development of the banking industry in Indonesia was not supported by the infrastructure that is needed to develop a sound and efficient banking industry. The regulation, supervision, and the regulators themselves were not prepared to ensure the development of a healthy banking industry. Likewise, lack of human resources has not helped develop a health banking industry in Indonesia. This can be judged by looking at how weak the risk management analysis undertaken by Indonesian bankers was.[5] This exposed many banks to foreign exchange, interest rates, liquidity, maturity, and off-balance sheet risks, if not managed properly. The weaknesses were made worse by wholesale corruption,

TABLE 18.1
Asset Value and Average of Financial Sector Growth in Indonesia in 1996
(In Rp billions)

Financial Activities	Asset Value in 1996	Average of Financial Sector Growth in 1989–96 (%)
Bank	328,600	26.16
Insurance company	17,269	23.07
Finance company	33,591	43.58
Pawnshop	14,300	24.65
Capital market		
— Stock	36,800	68.02
— Obligation	8,700	36.86
Money market		
SBI (Issuing)	111,201	33.01
SBPU (Buying)	124,995	167.24
Interbank transaction	218,367	53.59

collusion, and nepotism, either in government or private institutions. This caused much credit to be lent to improper borrowers. Many violations of the banking laws, for example, going above the legal lending limit, were never controlled firmly by the regulators. A depreciating rupiah, increasing interest rates, and decreasing economic growth placed banks in extremely difficult positions where the non-performing loans (NPLs) increased dramatically. The existing weaknesses of the Indonesian financial system grew rapidly in a short time, culminating in the banking crisis of 1998 (see Table 18.2).

THE BANKING CRISIS

The problem in the banking industry was not handled properly in Indonesia at an early stage. The problem in the banking industry grew worse in late 1997, such that the government took hard measures to resolve the banking problem. The government disciplined the banking industry by liquidating sixteen banks on 1 November 1997 without appropriate preparation. The lack of explanation over the chosen policy shocked public confidence in banking industry and created "bank panics". Depositors took out their money from the banking industry, making the banks illiquid. Consequently, most of them could not even pay to the depositors. This situation meant the central bank, as a lender of last resort, had to provide the funds for the

TABLE 18.2
Development of Commercial Bank Asset and Equity in Indonesia June 1998 to March 1999
(in Rp trillions)

Month	Asset	Equity
June 1998	1,013.94	54.37
July	954.49	32.94
August	894.82	21.45
September	883.63	10.83
October	777.83	–28.55
November	777.77	–43.59
December	762.43	–98.54
January 1999	786.30	–112.89
February	704.192	–198.02
March	594.911	–244.55

Source: Bank Indonesia.

banking industry as liquidity support (Bantuan Likuiditas Bank Indonesia or BLBI). The loss of confidence in the banking industry was very costly for Indonesia because the government finally provided BLBI of around Rp16,450 trillion.

Because of the crisis, the banking industry increased interest rates to around 70 per cent. The increasing interest rates put the corporations under more pressure, already in trouble because of the overall macroeconomic problem, and this dramatically increased the NPLs. It estimated that the NPLs rose to around 60–70 per cent (see Table 18.3). The NPLs and

TABLE 18.3
Non-Performing Loans in Commercial Banks 1995 to January 1999
(%)

Bank Category	1995	1996	1997	1998	Jan 1999
Persero	16.6	13.4	11.1	51.7	55.6
BUSN Devisa	3.7	4.3	3.2	72.0	76.0
BUSN Non-devisa	13.8	11.1	6.4	16.5	47.3
BPD	16.2	13.5	10.9	14.8	16.5
Joint venture	7.1	7.1	5.4	56.3	59.5
Foreign	2.0	2.7	3.3	44.4	45.4
Total	10.4	8.8	7.2	57.2	61.1

Source: Bank Indonesia.

negative burden of net interest margins, the banking structural problems, and the economic, social and political environment that was not conducive for business, gave rise to a banking crisis and the need for total restructuring.

The crisis in the banking industry can also be seen from the decrease of bank capital which experienced a free fall. The bank capital was still positive at Rp10.83 trillion in September 1998 and decreased to Rp244.55 trillion at the end of March 1999 (a fall of Rp255.38 trillion). The decrease of bank capital was partly caused by the negative impact of interest rates. Another cause of decreasing bank capital were losses from its other risk investment, such as credit risks, that can be seen from high number of NPLs (61.1 per cent in the end of January 1999, see Table 18.4), foreign exchange risks, and off-balance sheet risks.

The free fall in the banking industry should stop soon since postponing the restructuring only means that the cost of restructuring is higher. As mentioned by the Indonesian Banking Restructuring Agency (IBRA), the cost of bank restructuring in Indonesia had almost tripled as the programme had moved too slowly. Therefore, the 13 March 1999 policy, which was launched by the government, was expected to include an earlier schedule in order to avoid conditions becoming worse.

The problem of the banking industry in Indonesia has meant there is a need to take simultaneous policies to fix the banking and the corporation problems. The research which has been done by the World Bank shows that Indonesia's real sector declined in the same period. The crisis across all sectors makes it impossible to solve each problem separately. Therefore, it needs an integrated banking and corporate sector restructuring plan in order to achieve an optimal result. Bank restructuring has been undertaken by the government using both IBRA and Bank Indonesia, and the real

TABLE 18.4

Percentage of Non-Performing Loans Based on Collectability by Commercial Banks in Indonesia 1996 to May 1999

(%)

Criteria	Dec 96	Dec 97	Dec 98	Mar 99	Apr 99	May 99
In special attention	0.00	0.00	8.70	7.80	9.34	8.72
Less current	2.58	2.62	10.35	9.06	10.26	11.05
Doubted	3.34	2.51	15.22	14.34	16.44	16.67
Bad debt	2.87	2.03	22.98	27.46	14.02	13.18
Total	100.00	100.00	100.00	100.00	100.00	100.00

Source: Bank Indonesia.

sector restructuring is done through the Jakarta Initiative, the Indonesian Debt Restructuring Agency (INDRA), and IBRA's Asset Management Unit. But the real sector restructuring will not yield optimal results if there is no integrated plan with the financial sector restructuring.

BANKING RESTRUCTURING AND MASTER PLAN IN DEVELOPING FINANCIAL SECTOR

The financial market in Indonesia is still dominated by the banking industry. This means that the stability of the market is determined mostly by the stability of the banking industry. Hence, Indonesia needs to resolve the banking problem first to start the recovery of Indonesia's economy. However, the degree and coverage of the financial crisis requires Indonesia to take an integral solution to solve the banking problem. The bank sector restructuring has to be placed in an integrated financial market master plan to develop a healthy and efficient financial market. The integrated solution is important because there are many overlapping regulations and supervision among the financial institutions. The integrated plan is important to solve incentive problems, especially that of "moral hazard". An integrated plan will be able to develop a healthy and efficient financial market in Indonesia.

Indonesia needs to restructure its banking industry in order to solve the insolvent banking problems, increase its profitability, operate its intermediary function, and restore public confidence.[6] Bank sector restructuring does not only include recapitalization, but also relates to the stability of the macroeconomic and microeconomic conditions. The bank recapitalization is only part of bank restructuring programme. The World Bank definition about banking restructuring is:

> Bank restructuring can be defined as the package of macroeconomic, microeconomic, institutional, and regulatory measures taken in order to correct incentives and to restore problem banking systems to sustainable financial solvency and profitability. Consequently, bank restructuring must tackle the causes and the effects of individual bank problems, or of widespread bank distress.[7]

According to the World Bank definition, it is known that the recapitalization programme, or banking liquidation, is only a part of bank restructuring. Banking sector restructuring is a large and expensive programme for any country, and hence it needs good planning, co-ordination and sound policies.

Bank restructuring can be categorized into three instrument groups as the base keys to restructure the banking industry. They are financial instruments, operational instruments, and structural instruments.[8] Financial instruments are used to solve solvency problems through directly injected funds. These instruments are usually done in a short time-frame. This is the easiest way to implement the programme. The second instrument is operational restructuring which is applied in order to improve the bank's profitability and efficiency. It covers many aspects such as business strategy improvement, management and accounting system improvement, approval of sound creditworthiness, and decreasing operational cost with reducing in bank staff and branch offices. The last instrument is the structural instruments which are focused on increasing international competitiveness and soundness. The last two instruments are the difficult ones to achieve in that it takes time. The success of bank restructuring depends on the salience of the policies in order to achieve optimal and sustainable results.

THE DEVELOPMENT OF THE BANKING RESTRUCTURING

After two years of bank restructuring, there has been no significant progress in the banking industry in Indonesia. The policies have been done too slowly and incomprehensibly — something noted by both the IMF and the Co-ordinating Minister of Economics, Finance and Industry. In general, the banking sector has not functioned well even though the government liquidated 66 banks, took over 11 banks, and recapitalized 9 banks. The government also acted the Act Number 10 of 1998 about Commercial Bank and Act Number 23, of 1999 about Central Bank. IBRA was set up in January 1998. However, almost none of the banks under IBRA supervision have graduated successfully from the scheme.

The government also gives guarantees to almost all bank obligations since January 1998, for a two-year period to stop "bank panics". Bank Indonesia determines the highest deposit interest rate that is guaranteed, since the guarantee has been launched. Bank Indonesia is now independent since the establishment of the Habibie administration in May 1998. Bank Indonesia finally spent Rp164.5 trillion to help the banks in terms of BLBI since the central bank is the lender of the last resort for banks in Indonesia that have liquidity problems.

All of the indicators show that the government lacks concepts and programmes to restructure the banking industry. The lack of appropriate and timely programmes in restructuring has also caused the cost of bank restructuring to increase dramatically — both the direct costs (recapitalization and liquidation costs) and indirect costs (unemployment and social-political costs). The estimated total of the direct cost increased from around Rp250 trillion to around Rp550 trillion, according to IBRA, from 1998 to mid-1999. Even IBRA has recently admitted that the cost is estimated around Rp643 trillion. In addition to the direct cost, the indirect cost also increases significantly because the wrong options continue to postpone Indonesia's economic recovery.

TRENDS IN THE DEVELOPMENT OF THE FINANCIAL SECTOR

The development of a country's financial sector is influenced by the development of the global and regional economy and financial markets. Likewise, the development of Indonesia's financial sector will be influenced by the development of ASEAN and the global financial economy and this will continue to be the case.

The financial market dependency on the global market was the result of the increase in financial market liberalization over the last decade. Financial market integration, in the future, will be accelerated by the integration of financial markets under ASEAN Free Trade Area (AFTA), Asia Pacific Economic Co-operation (APEC), and World Trade Organization (WTO). This means that the financial markets in Indonesia may be more volatile since the global financial market tends to be more volatile. Therefore, Indonesian financial markets must be ready for this development if they want to survive in the future.

The financial sector controls around the world have generally become more liberal. The operational restrictions on financial institutions tend to be reduced over time. The kinds of financial institution, and differences between financial institutions, occur because there is regulation which limits the financial operation in a financial market.[9] The Indonesian government also limits the operations of each financial institution in the market. However, the development of a global financial market shows that there are more countries that deregulate their banking industries by giving more freedom to the banks undertaking non-banking activities (underwriting insurance, for example). Universal banking is more developed in West Europe, and in Japan (under the "Big Bang" policy) has given more banks more freedom to enter the capital market. In America, the deregulation of banking systems is also underway. This trend is expected to come to

Indonesia sooner or later. Therefore, it will be beneficial for Indonesia to anticipate these trends in its financial market policies.

CONCLUSION

Banking sector restructuring has not been done thoroughly in Indonesia at this time. After two years the recapitalization programme is not finished. Indonesia must fix the operational instruments and structural instruments, which are not easily done. The banking restructuring problem in Indonesia was threatened by the emerging Bank Indonesia scandal and the replacement of IBRA's management. Bank Indonesia and IBRA play very important roles in the bank restructuring in Indonesia. Bank Indonesia as the regulator and supervisor of the banking industry has been guilty of misconduct, according to Badan Pemeriksa Keuangan (BPK, a State Auditing Agency). It also found that the central bank had negative equity. So, Bank Indonesia may also need to be restructured and recapitalized to enhance its performance. IBRA, which was founded two years ago, has not been able to solve the banking industry problem thoroughly. Even the cost of bank restructuring has increased almost three times over the first estimation. In the surrounding controversy of IBRA's ability to solve the banking problems appropriately and in a timely manner, the government appointed a new management, but it has not been demonstrated that they are fit and proper to be in the position. The Indonesian public knows that the new head of IBRA is not an independent professional. Indonesia must make IBRA transparent. The government, as the people's representatives, needs to monitor IBRA better so that it can minimize the moral hazard problem. The success of the bank restructuring in Indonesia also depends on how well the government can move clear of banking scandals, like the Bank Bali and Texmaco scandals. The key to achieve all this is to properly enforce the rule of law. This enforcement needs to be firm in the banking industry to give positive signals in the market that the authorities are serious about resolving this very serious problem.

Notes

1. Douglas W. Diamond, "Financial Intermediation and Delegated Monitoring", *Review of Economic Studies* (1984), pp. 393-414.
2. Anthony Saunders, *Financial Institutions Management A Modern Perspective* (USA: Richard D. Irwin Inc., 1994).
3. Kenneth Spong, *Banking Regulation Its Purposes, Implementation, and Effects*, 3rd ed., (Federal Reserve of Kansas City, 1990).

4. Bank Indonesia, *Indonesia Economic and Financial Statistics*, various editions.
5. Djiwandono, J. Soedradjat, "Banking System Soundness and Macroeconomic Management: The Recent Indonesian Experience", in Symposium Towards the Restoration of Sound Banking Systems in Japan — Its Global Implication (IMF's Research Institute for Economic and Business Administration, Kober, 14 July 1998).
6. Dziobek and Pazarbasigln, *Lessons from Systemic Bank Restructuring* (IMF, 1998).
7. World Bank, "*Restructuring Banks*" (a Multimedia Guide).
8. Dziobek, Claudia, *Market Based Policy Instruments for Systemic Bank Restructuring* (IMF, 1998).
9. Smith, Gary, *Financial Assets, Markets, and Institutions* (Washington, D.C.: Houghton Mifflin Company, 1993).

SECTION VII
Corporate Debt Restructuring

19

Indonesia's Corporate Debt
The Role of the Jakarta Initiative Task Force

Jusuf Anwar

The Government of Indonesia, in September 1998, announced a strategy to stimulate restructuring and recovery of the Indonesian private sector. Called the "Jakarta Initiative", this programme sets out principles that will facilitate out-of-court corporate restructurings. These principles will apply to both domestic and foreign creditors in a non-discriminatory manner. The Jakarta Initiative also provides for the establishment of a government task force, officially called the Jakarta Initiative Task Force (JITF), whose mandate will be both to facilitate out-of-court negotiations and remove the regulatory obstacles to restructuring.

The Jakarta Initiative, which is supported by the International Monetary Fund and the World Bank, will accelerate Indonesian economic recovery by increasing employment, promoting the recovery of the banking and financial sector, and generating tax revenue. It is designed to complement the newly amended bankruptcy law and use of the exchange rate mechanism provided by the Indonesian Debt Restructuring Agency (INDRA). Furthermore it will be implemented in concert with banking sector restructuring, which is being undertaken by the Indonesian Bank Restructuring Agency (IBRA).

The Jakarta Initiative sets forth guidelines for negotiations that draw upon strategies that have proven successful in other countries. These guidelines are designed, among other things, to promote the availability of interim financing to companies being restructured. It also obtains information from these companies so that their restructuring proposals can be effectively evaluated by creditors.

The Jakarta Initiative Task Force will include the representatives of relevant ministries and agencies, and is managed by professional staff with experience in facilitating negotiations. In addition to facilitating out-of-court negotiations, the Task Force will have the power to recommend to the public prosecutor that negotiations have failed and case should go to a court-supervised process under the bankruptcy law.

The Task Force will also provide a forum for the "one-stop" facilitation of regulatory applications required for restructuring plans, and will work actively to eliminate any additional regulatory or administrative obstacles to restructuring. Indeed, the government is in the process of adopting regulatory changes to facilitate restructurings, including the removal of tax disincentives and the elimination of limitations on debt-to-equity conversions. The Task Force will work in conjunction with a Corporate Restructuring Advisory Committee, made up of a representative group of domestic and foreign creditors and Indonesian companies.

Since its inception in September 1998, the Jakarta Initiative Task Force has received a positive response from debtors and creditors. It is currently assisting in the restructuring of not less than 323 companies, involving more than US$25 billion of debt and potentially affecting 268,000 employees. Of this number, over fifty-seven of these companies have reached some form of an agreement with their creditors involving approximately US$3.3 billion debt and securing the positions of over 86,000 employees. These companies have bad debts ranging from less than US$30 million to over US$1.2 billion.

A number of issues are faced in these restructuring efforts, usually in the form of commercial, administrative and regulatory impediments. Commercial issues are being resolved through the implementation of a number of solution schemes. In this regard, steps are taken to speed up private sector's corporate restructuring. To complement the implementation of the Jakarta Initiative, an enhanced facilitation service was formed. The service is going to be provided by a unit, designed to provide one-stop facilitation in conjunction with the Jakarta Initiative Task Force. The main objective of the One-Stop Facilitation Group (OFG) is to help solve administrative and regulatory impediments to corporate restructuring. By alleviating hindrances posed by existing bureaucracy, the service will help speed up the restructuring process. As neutral mediators and facilitators in debtor–creditor negotiations, the Jakarta Initiative Task Force hopes to enhance its role with the formation of the OFG. In my capacity as Chairman of the Jakarta Initiative task Force, I have argued that performance in implementing the Jakarta Initiative will improve with the formation of the

OFG, in addition to the enhancement of resources and facilities of the task force.

In addition to both public and large enterprises, corporate restructuring efforts will also increasingly include small and medium enterprises (SMEs). This will also occur outside Jakarta, as other cities cannot be ignored. The Jakarta Initiative Task Force plans to co-operate with various consulting firms and professional organizations, including the Indonesian Accountants Association and universities. Restructuring clinics, especially for SMEs, will be set up in a number of cities throughout Indonesia.

On the formation of the OFG, the Co-ordinating Minister of the Economy, Finance and Industry stated that the on-going bank restructuring programme will only effectively push Indonesia's economic recovery when implemented together with the recovery of the real sector through corporate restructuring. JITF plans to revive the commercial sector and, at the same time, directly improve the employment sector. Similarly, the Minister of Finance has expressed his hope that negotiations between debtors and both local and foreign lenders could result in timely private sector debt restructuring. This will help achieve economic growth and open up employment prospects. Chairman of the Public Sector Debt Restructuring Team, which co-ordinates the corporate restructuring effort, has stated that a functional combination of the JITF, INDRA, and the OFG will produce timely results, so that the Indonesian economy may quickly recover.

In support of the foregoing efforts, and in keeping with its integrated approach to the economic crisis, the Government of Indonesia has implemented, and continues to implement, a number of legal and regulatory changes. Most importantly, a new bankruptcy law has been adopted and the bankruptcy court has become operational. The next step in this process is to review the new bankruptcy law and other regulatory changes in light of actual case experience and to determine what, if any, remedial actions are necessary, including the appointment of ad hoc judges. Additionally, as task force has encountered individual debt-restructuring transactions, it has become apparent that additional education of both creditors and companies regarding efficient debt-restructuring practices is necessary. In the future, the success of this educational process will be critical to widespread restructuring success.

In conclusion, the various co-ordinated measures taken by the Government of Indonesia are beginning to show results. There is increasing evidence that Indonesia is reaching the bottom of the economic downturn and laying the foundations for renewed economic growth in the near future. As mentioned earlier, results are being seen from new measures in monetary and fiscal policies and, as indicated by many, the success of the Jakarta Initiative. Companies and creditors are beginning to face up to the new economic reality, which has done more than anything else to foster discussion on issues of debt restructuring. A full recovery will take time but with the process of change and reform established, there is strong evidence for the hope that the worst of the economic crisis is behind us.

20

Corporate Debt Restructuring

Franky Widjaja

INTRODUCTION

This contribution is an overview of what I believe is the best approach to corporate debt restructuring. If one reads newspaper articles on Indonesia, the common perception runs something like this: corporate debt restructuring is a process whereby lenders sit down with borrowers to discuss how the owners can keep their business and the bankers can keep their jobs. However, in all seriousness, business leaders must understand that there is not just one rule that applies to all debt situations. The bankers are well aware of this and are trained to recognize the characteristics, which will govern the direction of any restructuring exercise. It is time that business leaders become aware of this process to conduct the negotiations on a level playing field. This chapter is divided into two parts: an overview of corporate activity and the debt crisis. The aim of this paper is to convey the options for corporates in terms of debt restructuring.

THE CORPORATE ACTIVITY

The business leader must know that a crucial part of the process is understanding the status of the borrower's business. If the financial crisis creates a temporary dislocation in the volume of sales, margins, or operations, then there is comfort that normalcy will bring the original business and profits which will service the restructured debt in the future. If, however, the crisis has made significant and structural changes in the business and its profitability, such as, unfavourable foreign exchange or change of customer preferences, then the process will be a difficult one for both the borrower and the lender.

As a rule of thumb in most developing countries, an export-orientated company will be more favourably viewed in a restructuring exercise than a domestic or service-orientated business. In Indonesia, however, the large domestic market can be a positive negotiating point for a sound business.

Each industry has its own unique characteristics, which may be positive or negative factors in the negotiation process. In the short-term, real estate suffers a lot more in its ability to service its debt. However, over a longer period, real estate, by its very nature, provides assurance of a solid source of repayment over time. Of course, as they say in this industry, it all depends on three factors: "location, location and location". For the manufacturing industry, demand is a reflection of the state of the economy. Therefore, difficulties can be considered to be of a temporary nature that will vanish with an upturn in the economy. It will not be the same for the service industry. Likewise, trading companies are less likely to be favourably viewed, especially if their customers are seriously affected by the economic downturn. Their advantage though is that their conversion cycle (financed assets to cash) is shorter. Thus it can be argued that with proper systems and controls, a lender may continue to support deserving companies in this industry. It is important to note that in Indonesia's case its large domestic market provides a solid business base. It is also necessary for companies to focus on their strengths and divest unrelated activities.

THE DEBT CRISIS

Most Asian companies (including those in Indonesia) have had traditionally high debt-equity ratios. This has been fuelled by continued economic growth in the region where local companies did not want to pass up new business opportunities. This resulted in additional leverage, thereby overextending a corporation's financial resources, leaving very little reserve for any sudden financial setback. With scarce local currency availability, some corporations boldly took unhedged foreign currency borrowings. With the regional crisis, this scenario evolved into the current situation requiring corporate debt restructuring for a number of companies.

Two issues are important to focus on when talking about debt. The first is the issue of matching and the second is the issue of the lender.

Most borrowers, in their desire to obtain project funding, ignored the rule that you should match tenders and currencies. Unmatched loans create a difficult environment for restructuring negotiations since in most cases it involves "haircuts", "equity injections", or both. This is also true when high leverage exists.

The source and nature of the lenders make for very interesting negotiating process. On the issue of debt restructuring, the old saying "the more the merrier" should be modified to "the more, the longer it takes". It is evident that a one-on-one discussion will be faster and more productive than one conducted with multiple creditors. The process becomes more complex when bonds traded in public are part of the liabilities to be restructured. It is likewise complicated when export credit agencies are involved in the discussions. Then again, trade creditors are to be considered as part of any debt restructuring negotiation.

The two most difficult items to reconcile in the final negotiations are first, the issue of security or collateral, and second, the terms for the interest and principal repayment under the restructured loan. Here, there is significant room for give and take depending on the relationship of the various parties involved. This is where historical experience (from the origin of the relationship, the ease or difficulty of the negotiations on the original loan, and the frequency and openness of the communication during the term of the relationship) plays a very important role. A relationship marked by a well-conducted, professional, and congenial atmosphere will make this part of the process less acrimonious. Obviously, the reverse can also be true.

The restructuring exercise can result in any or a combination of the following:

- rescheduled principal payments;
- reduced interest or interest forgiveness;
- reduction in the principal (or "haircuts");
- balloon payments;
- earnings recapture arrangements;
- debt for equity swaps;
- temporary lock box arrangements;
- selective asset sales;
- restrictive covenants on financing and operations; and
- management changes.

In the end, the negotiations should result in a situation where both parties feel that they have achieved the intended result, which is that the company remains in business and the lenders keep a good loan asset. The ideal outcome is the establishment of a "win-win" solution.

CONCLUSION

In conclusion, the collective challenge in Indonesia is more than just a financial restructuring exercise. The goal is to keep the wheels of industry running to return economic health to Indonesia. Today, even a so-called "healthy Indonesian company" has formidable financial hurdles. The overall country rating for Indonesia restricts continued inflow of funds from private lenders and investors. To this end, a restructured loan does not resolve all our problems, as repayment does not mean availability of funds for future operations and expansion. When a working capital loan is converted into a term loan, the company becomes limited to doing business with its own resources. Clearly, this is not a formula that will speed up Indonesia's economic recovery. Unfortunately, we in the private sector alone cannot provide the whole solution. The private sector's job is the orderly and realistic restructuring of corporate debt. Wider solutions will need to come from the government and other sectors of the economy.

SECTION VIII
Trade, Manufacturing, Agriculture, and SMEs

21

The Crisis and Agriculture Policy

H. S. Dillon

THE LEGACY OF THE NEW ORDER

During the high growth phase of 1986–96, fuelled by massive investment into industry and urban infrastructure, public policy on food and agriculture became increasingly irrelevant to agriculture. There was a great deal of discussion about agribusiness development and a need to develop a more commercial, "modern", farm sector. Indonesia's traditional donors — the World Bank, the Asian Development Bank (ADB) and Japan — largely abandoned agriculture. For the most part, the bureaucracy went along with the donors for the ride. Adopting a "borrow to plunder" attitude, the reality is that the bureaucracy enjoyed the perks that came from wasting economic donor spending.

Furthermore, discrimination against agriculture was indicated by measures such as low investment incentives compared to other sectors of the economy. Near the onset of the New Order (1969/70), 35 per cent of total investment credit was allocated to agriculture. However, this number declined drastically in subsequent years. For the fiscal years 1979/80, 1989/90, and 1997/98, investment credit allocated to agriculture was only 17 per cent, whereas the allocation for the industrial sector increased to 34 per cent, 42 per cent, and 40 per cent for the three years, respectively.

The 1993 census indicated that about 22.8 million households owned less than one hectare of arable land, while about nine million were landless. The economic crisis has further exacerbated inequity in asset ownership. Arable land continues to decline as well. For example, the total irrigated paddy field area converted yearly to other uses is estimated to be about 30,000–40,000 hectares. This hopeless situation in agriculture induced massive migration from rural to urban areas. The five-yearly population census (SUPAS) in 1995 indicated that the urban population had increased by as much as 35.9 per cent under the New Order, with the bulk in the informal sector earning very low incomes. Out of the 80.1 million-strong labour force in 1995, only about 31.4 per cent were employed in the formal sectors, leaving the rest with no other recourse save the informal sector.

Despite the strong growth, serious structural problems still lurked beneath the cloak of national prosperity, namely:

(a) fragmentation of landholding further increasing the number of landless rural households;
(b) conversion of 45,000 hectares of prime land each year into non-agricultural use;
(c) the gap between rural and urban incomes widened sharply;
(d) massive scale land-grabbing outside Java fomenting social unrest, and privatizing what were fragile natural resources carefully tended by local communities; and
(e) abuse of rural property rights (no clear land title and legal framework for commercial business).

High economic growth during the New Order was also achieved at the expense of the environment. The growth had been supported mainly by oil, gas, and timber (logging) revenues. The latter has had a profound effect on the environment, despite the huge amount of funds (dana reboisasi) set aside to restore the environment (forest) to its original condition. These funds have never been used as originally planned, but were siphoned off to other strange ventures such as for the development of the national aircraft industry.

Marine exploitation in the past left behind devastated marine resources. The existing resources had been tapped indiscriminately, using destructive technologies such as dynamite fishing, and cyanide fishing for the sake of economic development without any regard to sustainability. As a consequence, many inshore waters have now reached the level of overexploitation, such as the North Coast of Java, the Malacca Straits, and Arafura Sea. Another negative impact of the overuse of marine resources is the destruction of the ecosystem. A recent study on coral reef condition in 421 stations, located in 43 different areas, revealed that only about 6.41 per cent of reefs are in pristine condition, 24.23 per cent are good, 29.22 per cent fair, while 40.14 per cent are in very poor shape.

THE CRISIS, AGRICULTURE AND RURAL WELFARE

The financial crisis changed food and agriculture decision-making in three very important ways:

(a) government policies were not concerned with agriculture per se, but with macro-implications of food availability and food prices (the IMF, with the World Bank came to the table to negotiate macro and structural reform);
(b) the government entered into partnerships with international institutions that were largely uninformed about food and agriculture; and
(c) the "old guard" ministries were somewhat stuck in the past, as they were so accustomed to enriching themselves that they began to look "out of place" when the economy declined.

After the crisis hit, no clear strategy was pursued in relation to agriculture. From September 1998 to January of 1999, food and agriculture policy lurched from one ad hoc decision to another:

(a) trade in all food stuffs was liberalized;
(b) in November 1998, fertilizer subsidies were removed all at once, forcing prices to double and causing supply to disappear from domestic markets;
(c) in November and December 1998, seventeen new cheap credit schemes for small enterprises were established to help new cooperatives get off the ground;
(d) in December 1998, subsidized farm working capital credit allocations were raised from under Rp1 trillion for 1997/98 to Rp7 trillion for 1998/99;
(e) in December 1998 the government liberalized licensing for palm oil plantations;
(f) in January 1999, the government raised the rice floor price by 50 per cent;
(g) to compete with Chinese food traders, the Indonesian Distribution co-operative was founded and supplied with cooking oil from Badan Urusan Logistik Nasional (Bulog) (in the first five months of operation, under this urban food marketing co-operative, about Rp1 trillion managed to "disappear"); and
(h) in agriculture, the central government continued to announce food self-sufficiency campaigns, and instruct the farmers to plant rice, corn and soybeans.

The crisis has revealed the continued importance of agriculture as both a productive sector and as a source of income and social benefits for the poor. There were some positive developments in food and agriculture. First of all, the agricultural sector did not shrink in 1998. In fact it grew at a modest rate, meaning that this sector was able to absorb an additional five million workers, implying that labour productivity fell by nearly 10 per cent in the sector in that year. Second, rice production seems to have bottomed out in 1998 and 1999. Despite input supply disruption and the lack of decent seeds, food production should grow at about the same rate as population growth. Third, export-orientated agricultural regions are generally better off than the other parts of Indonesia.

The New Order developed various rural institutions to support agricultural development. However, these institutions have played a minimal role in providing the necessary support for the farmers. Designed for the all-out push towards rice self-sufficiency, these institutions were ill-equipped to respond to the challenges posed by globalization.

THE WAHID–MEGAWATI ADMINISTRATION'S POLICY RESPONSE

For any meaningful analysis into Gus Dur's government, it is important to realize that Gus Dur has been trying to give some meaning to democratization. In his understanding, this means that one man does not make all the decisions, and that are run by their ministries, while technocrats give independent advice to the government. It also means that presidents (former and current) and generals are accountable to rule of law. We have seen that even the high and mighty of the New Order regime are not beyond public scrutiny. As a result, Indonesia is starting down the road from authoritarianism to democracy, and while there is a loss of speed and stealth in government decision making, gains are made in terms of checks and balances on authority and ultimately, on taking policies that are in the best interests of the citizens as a whole.

In the first 100 days, Gus Dur has demonstrated that economic reform is about more than just the business interests of Jakarta. The IMF, the U.S. Government, and a number of the Ministry of Finance technocrats argue that there be free trade in rice and that a tariff, if any, be set at a very low level. Gus Dur knows that some twenty million families make their living by growing rice, and that the farm sector is highly depressed. This demonstrates yet again that Wahid thinks beyond the interests of the "centre" to the many millions who are working for next to nothing to keep the country both fed and secure.

Preliminary figures indicate that since the fourth quarter of 1998, agriculture has shown strong signs of recovery. This recovery is driven by the recovery of food crops, which constitutes 52.6 per cent of GDP. The

Ministry of Agriculture (MOA) has announced several policies in an effort to promote agricultural development. The whole policy approach is focused on food security, but not necessarily rice self-sufficiency. However, in order to protect the welfare of rice farmers, who constitute the major proportion of Indonesian farmers, the Ministry proposed high rice import tariffs. Preliminary observations of the impact of the tariff on domestic inflation seem, to date, to have been minimal.

The MOA, as an institution, appears to endorse the national agenda for democratization and decentralization, on the whole. It is committed to minimizing the direct intervention of the government in order to leave it up to the people to determine and decide what they consider to be the best for them. However, there are a number of high-ranking officials still espousing the defunct command and country mode. This ideological struggle appears to be running throughout the various agencies dealing with agriculture.

The government seems committed to the Kredit Usaha Tani (KUT) credit scheme to support farmers. However, this scheme is currently facing major difficulties as a result of trillions of rupiahs handed out to Habibie supporters under the guise of KUT support. Furthermore, according to the new banking law, the central bank can no longer issue the Kredit Likuiditas Bank Indonesia (KLBI, or Bank Indonesia's Special Credit Scheme) such as the KUT of the past. Now the KUT must follow the ordinary commercial credit scheme.

THE UNFINISHED AGENDA

A number of serious problems still remain:

(a) real wages for unskilled labourers have collapsed;
(b) input markets are not working;
(c) government support services for agriculture have all but collapsed;
(d) the breakdown in law and order is raising agricultural marketing costs and leading to wide gaps between consumer and farm prices;
(e) the donors are trying to design social safety net efforts that, in practice, will be so institutionally complex that they won't be implemented; and
(f) the IMF carries on trying to ensure that whatever ad hoc decisions the government takes are enshrined in stand-by agreements, regardless of possible long-term negative consequences for the nation.

Food and agriculture have an important role to play in the Indonesian recovery. This would require a paradigm shift of going back to basics in agriculture, based on community needs. Such a shift should, at least, aim to:

(a) restore food security;
(b) harness rural growth capacity;
(c) create a transformational policy environment;
(d) promote decentralization and enhance local government capacity; and
(e) forge new partnerships between government, civil society, and the donor community in the domestic food and agriculture decision-making process.

There is an emerging consensus that overall policy priority would be to re-embark on the path of high growth by bringing the debt burden to a more manageable level without inflicting undue hardship on the poor and underprivileged. Most of the players realize that Indonesia's economic future depends upon growth that is socially, environmentally, and politically sustainable. There is greater recognition that agro-industry and rural development are essential for generating broad-based economic growth. In this respect, one should not lose sight of the fact that Indonesian already has more than a million small agro-industries, providing a means of livelihood for not less than two million people at the present. It is estimated that 88 per cent of total agro-industrial output and 92 per cent of added value is generated by the medium-to-large industries, which only comprise 5 per cent of the total number of agro-industries.

The government should ease regulatory and public enterprise impediments to a more business-orientated rural agricultural environment. In food crops, the co-operatives providing seed, fertilizers, pesticides, and marketing services should be transformed into market-orientated businesses. Public investment in rural economic and rural social infrastructure should be increased, but uneconomic public investment should no longer be tolerated. Completing and then capitalizing on past investment in rural infrastructure and services is the immediate public investment challenge. Institutional reform should be launched to enhance the operation of rural factor and product markets, most notably the rural land, labour, and capital markets. Special attention should also be provided to augmenting the shelf of relevant rural technology. And finally, the downward spiral of rural resource degradation should be reversed.

In the past, the government assumed the "commanding heights" of economic activity to provide key agro-inputs and services in the rural areas. At an earlier stage of agricultural development, this served to "get markets going" and to encourage technological innovation. But now, many of these interventions act only to restrain competition and to shield public enterprise inefficiency. New public and private roles are required to facilitate investment and equity needs. Transforming public enterprises responsible for delivering agro-inputs into private enterprises will inspire more competition in the delivery of agro-inputs.

The government has to undertake an important policy in abolishing the Bulog monopoly rights on food imports. Further, the government should consider limiting Bulog to their core business as a state logistics agency. This new role should be established based on the resources (human and investment) that Bulog has throughout Indonesia. Bulog resources in the region should be directed to meet the storage and marketing requirements of farmers. A recent audit has revealed that reportedly large inefficiency of Bulog is more of a management problem.

Indonesian farmers have adopted a vast number of new technologies during the past three decades, and have demonstrated their willingness to assume new risks and innovate. In the past five years, the rate of technological progress in Indonesian agriculture has demonstrably slowed, while technological progress in other competing (and land constrained) Asian states has continued at a brisk pace. The dearth of suitable innovations in technology can be explained by several factors. The most important are the high fragmentation of the agricultural research and development effort (with a very limited involvement of the many universities in the process), an erosion in the linkages between Indonesia's own research and development effort and those of international research and development providers, persistent under-funding of the public sector research and development effort, and the disruption of AARD's research efforts resulting from the 1995 restructuring of the research service. Other factors, such as the weak enforcement of intellectual property rights registration for improved seed varieties, constitutes a barrier to the entry of foreign seed companies and dampens incentives for private agricultural research.

Agricultural biotechnology merits special attention, if for no other reason than the pace of developments in the area are expected to radically alter the technological frontier for tropical agriculture. Indonesia has mounted an aggressive biotechnology effort, through Lembaga Ilmu Pengetahuan Indonesia (LIPI, or the Indonesian Academy of Science), the universities and the agricultural institutes, and expends approximately US$4 million per annum on some 300–400 experiments in agricultural biotechnology. But biotechnology efforts are extremely fragmented and very few of the research activities are in "near-to-the-market" technology. In Singapore, the Institute of Molecular Biology is an excellent example of the public-owned agricultural biotechnology institute that has built a critical mass of biotechnology capacity, sells its services to the private sector, focuses on market-orientated commodities and stays at the cutting edge of technology developments. Not only should Indonesian consider buying research services from Singapore's Institute of Molecular Biology, but LIPI's own agricultural biotechnology institute could follow a similar path and become a private-sector orientated centre of biotechnology excellence.

The cheap food policy, especially in rice, adopted in the past, must now be abandoned. Cheap rice allows low industrial wages which in turn will promote industrial development, but cheap rice will also mean that labour is pushed out of the villages for lack of decent jobs. Most of the labour does not get pushed or pulled into industry, but into the informal services sector. With pervasive low wages there cannot be an improvement in the quality of human resources. Farm families do not have enough discretionary income to invest in schooling. Those who work for low industrial wages also have few savings to put into further education. Those who are pushed into the urban services sector barely make enough to meet their needs on a day-to-day basis. So Indonesia has become trapped in a system with low wages, low levels of human resource development, and low labour productivity. In order to get out of this vicious circle, farmers must be paid a decent price for the food they produce. They will use their higher incomes for better health care, nutrition, and education for their children. This strategy may well raise industrial wages, but the labour force will be better nourished, better educated and more productive. In short, Indonesia needs to compete globally by being more productive rather than being the cheapest source of labourers on this planet.

Considering the drawbacks of the KUT scheme in the past, farm credit in the future must be redesigned in such a way that it can be accessed directly by farmers and all rural households. A drastic shift away from disbursing credit packages to creating working rural capital markets is called for. Then, and only then, will credit prove instrumental in transforming farmers into traders, entrepreneurs, and rurally-based agro-industrialists.

CONCLUSION

To sum up, in the Wahid–Megawati administration, economic development in general, and agriculture development in particular, must be people driven. This means that the development effort must be based on existing realities. The fact of the matter is that about 70 per cent of Indonesians reside in the rural areas, 50 per cent of the national labour force earn their living from agriculture, and 80 per cent of the total population have only finished, at best, primary school. The "trickle down effect", preached by the Soeharto Regime, has brought Indonesia into economic and political chaos. There need be no trade-off between growth and equity as the new millennium calls for a development paradigm espousing growth through equity.

22

Industrial Policy for Indonesia

Faisal Basri

First of all I would like to posit a question: does Indonesia need an industrial policy similar to what had been implemented for the last 30 years in Indonesia? To answer this question, it is important to examine what has happened, during the crisis, to the structure of the Indonesian economy. One of the most important facts about the economic crisis in Indonesia is the significant change of the economic structure, as well as the structure of the components within it. The share of the agricultural sector has increased from 16 per cent before the crisis to almost 20 per cent today. The other sector that has also increased significantly is mining, from only 7 per cent before crisis to almost 12 per cent after the crisis. These two sectors, collectively called the non-oil primary sector, now account for one-third of Indonesia's GDP, which demonstrates the important contribution of agriculture and mining. The share of the manufacturing sector has decreased slightly but the biggest loser is the services sector. The trend for the next couple of years will be the increase of the agriculture sector to the maximum of 20 or 21 per cent, following which time, this sector will decrease (a standard pattern in many countries). The manufacturing sector should increase again to 30 per cent, which would be the normal course of events for the Indonesian economy.

The changing structure of the GDP is mainly caused by the changing of the incentive structure, the depreciation of rupiah, and the elimination of entry barriers. This opens Indonesia to strong competition and issues a warning to local businesses to improve their competitive advantage. Assuming that banking and corporate restructuring has been done properly to lay the foundations, the task of the government, especially the Ministry of Trade and Industry, the Ministry of Agriculture, and other relevant ministries, is to concentrate on creating a conducive environment to accelerate the structural adjustment in order to strengthen Indonesia's comparative advantage and to strengthen its economic foundations. H. S. Dillon's suggestion to concentrate more on agriculture, I would argue, is a jump from one extreme to the other. Shifting from manufacturing to agriculture and mobilizing resources in that direction will create a distortion — a different distortion from the interventions of the past, but a distortion nonetheless. What are really needed is what this author would term "neutral incentives". A good example of this is found in the Letter of Intent (LoI). In the sugar industry, the government and the IMF will restructure the domestic industry by consolidating the number of sugar factories on Java and promoting a private sector-led investment in the industry. Unlike the previous government, which implemented a ban on imports of sugar, or a high tariff for imported sugar, the current government realized that the heart of the problem is inefficiency — in part fostered by protection — and it is not feasible anymore to protect sugar factories in Java. The LoI offers a kind of transitional measure to smoothen the process of changing the attitude and activities of the farmers. To achieve this the government will replace the previous decree that limited imports to selected traders with a 20 per cent tariff to be phased out over several years. At the same time, the sugar trade will open to all general importers, which is why it is a more neutral policy. The government will most likely also prepare a strategic plan to consolidate the Java-based industries. The government must reiterate its commitment to farmers, but equally farmers must be free to make their own crop choices as a reflection of their freedom as individuals. That has not happened in the past when there was little leeway in this regard.

In dealing with trade many entrepreneurs and exporters are concerned with the issue of trade financing. Lack of trade financing is one of the major obstacles for companies trying to expand into export markets. It has been argued that ensuring trade financing should be a policy of priority given the importance of Indonesian manufacturers to secure the importation of spare parts and materials. Efforts must be made to overcome persisting troubles related to the letter of credit issued by Indonesian banks. However, for a very credible exporter, with a good track record, financing is not a big hurdle because such an exporter can find alternative sources of financing either from foreign buyer or foreign supplier. Naturally businesspersons are always interested in obtaining the cheapest source of funding. The Ministry of Trade and Industry should concentrate more on a comprehensive policy with comprehensive design to empower small and medium enterprises (SMEs) — a policy promoted by the current Minister, Jusuf Kalla. An example of what is meant by a comprehensive policy is, for example, the automotive industry. The government is committed to reduce tariffs on assembled cars from 200 per cent before the WTO decision in the Timor-Kia car case, to only 60–80 per cent. The previously high cost was the price Indonesians had to pay to allow Tommy Soeharto, owner of the Timor venture, turn his "dreams" into reality. Now the decision makers up to the ministerial level, especially in the Ministry of Trade and Industry, want to reduce the tariff rate as soon as possible. There is a strong need to allow the car industry to recover, while at the same time improve the public transportation. There is also no support for infrastructure. The poor quality of the roads in Jakarta reduces the lifetime of a car and lowers the service that Indonesians can get from public transportation. A reduction in the price of cars is not so important, as it may be important to let the price of cars stay high in order to finance public transportation and the maintenance and construction of new infrastructure. The sorts of infrastructure needed are projects that will serve the lower income group in the community. What Indonesia does not have is a comprehensive set of policies across all government ministries and departments, which sometimes lead to conflicting policies.

An important facet within this discussion is how to strengthen the role of SMEs in Indonesia as a foundation for recovery. As a liberal, this author would argue that there are three factors for SMEs. First, SMEs must have access to capital facilities. Equality to larger corporations on issues such as banking, taxation, and services provided by the government is a matter of survival for SMEs. Second, a reduction in transaction costs is important as SMEs are already at a disadvantage over unit costs, compared to big industries with their enormous output. This makes the average cost of SMEs' product high and the government, as an institution, has to create the facilities for reducing transaction costs for these industries. Third, the proposal to give autonomy to local government will create more opportunities for SMEs to emerge and to grow more rapidly by strengthening their own uniqueness compared to other regions. I am very optimistic on the subject of empowerment of SMEs through the use of market mechanisms rather than through direct, and selective, intervention which was used to pick favourites in the past. The government should set the framework of neutral incentives, but then allow the commercial sector to operate under real free market principles.

SECTION IX
Principles for Stabilization and Reform

23

Comments on Indonesia's Economic Reform

Emil Salim

Indonesia has experienced a deep crisis since late 1997, in which we experienced a drop in growth rates and by 1998 the contraction was as low as –13 per cent. The first comment to be made about Indonesia's economy is that there is improvement across the economic indicators: rising inflation is now under control; the exchange rate is down to a more manageable level; interest rates are down; while GDP growth has returned. The 1999 rate of growth was 1–2 per cent. Economic indicators show that the inflation rate of 77 per cent in 1998 dipped to 2 per cent in 1999. The exchange rate is now stable — initially it was around Rp10,000 to the U.S. dollar in 1998 and is now around Rp7,000. The message is that 1999 was far better than 1998, and that gives cause for confidence that 2000 will be better still. What is noteworthy here is not the achievement of Gus Dur government, which is still in its infancy at the time of writing, but the achievements of the previous Habibie government. Special mention goes to the achievements of Boediono as the Minister of State for National Development Planning (Bappenas), and Bambang Subianto as the Minister of Finance. The Habibie administration made substantial gains in economics, but ultimately failed politically. What is significant is that Habibie's economic policy has a political flavour as expansion of farmers' credit was almost four-fold. Although H. S. Dillon, of the Centre for Agricultural Policy Studies, has argued that there was no credit, this was not the case. But, the problem was that such schemes were under the banner of a populist economic policy, used for the most part for political advantage: "money politics". Redirection of the recapitalization funds of Bank Bali for non-economic purposes, and what might be termed "neo-KKN" (corruption, collusion, and nepotism), had started to emerge around cronies linked to Habibie. Habibie lost the popular election and the presidency because of two issues: the East Timor crisis and KKN. Now that Habibie has been replaced by the Gus Dur–Megawati government, it is important that the economic policies, which are now being drafted, are based on economic rationalism. Implementation of the sometimes hard economic measures is very much constrained by the prevailing political conditions and pressures from a revived polity.

However, the general policy direction is straightforward, and there is continuity between the changes brought by the Habibie government and Gus Dur. Gus Dur has been strongly influenced by the Letter of Intent (LoI) concerning bank restructuring, corporate restructuring, the removal of subsidies, and so on. Many wonder whether this economic direction is the government's own policy or one imposed by the IMF policy. Perhaps a polite way to view it is to see it as a combination of both. On 20 January 2000, the signing of the LoI between the Indonesian Government and the IMF firmly established the general economic direction. It is a straightforward policy aimed at a budget but with an overall deficit of around 5 per cent of GDP. It aims to redress the balance of payments problem increasing reserves over time. Based on economic rationality, the goal is to get the economy out of the trough of the crisis.

However, the most substantial new element in Gus Dur's economic policy is the role of decentralization, which has gained momentum. Since Independence, Indonesia has followed a centralization policy but now it is moving towards decentralization, meaning that the central government will be rather lean, giving up many responsibilities to the districts in twenty-six provinces. So there is a trend towards decentralization which will open up to new opportunities. For example, Riau is clearly in a position to co-operate much more closely with Singapore to its north, and perhaps even with the Southern Philippines. Because of the LoI and the decentralization process, Gus Dur's economic policy must be market friendly and outward looking with emphasis on the small and medium enterprises (SMEs). A policy of economic rationalism, however, must work within political constraints, which are largely determined by the new political parties represented in Cabinet. Gus Dur puts heavy emphasis on institutional change, bank reforms, corporate reforms, state enterprise reform, administrative reform, as well as political reform. The Indonesian parliament will most likely see a decrease in the current twenty-seven parties and the emergence of two major political parties or alliances broadly grouped around the nationalist social democrats and inclusive Islamic parties. In the past there was a central government dominated by a hegemonic executive which could alter policy at will. The separation of power between executive, legislative, and judiciary has altered the political landscape.

Another political issue which constrains the movement of economic policy is the civil-military relationship, in which the pendulum is now swinging to the civilian authorities. But civilian control of the military will not be completely smooth. Further constraints on economic policy are the three arms of the government. Indonesia's judiciary is, to be blunt, very poor. The major stumbling block for a sound economic policy is the need to strengthen the legal system, while the legislature is also not yet firmly established and the executive is, at times, rather confused. Therefore the economic policy, although rational, is constrained by these bottlenecks, which are political by nature. In fairness, little more could be expected. The Gus Dur administration is new and many of the ministers, for example the academics from Gadja Mada University, have never been in the government before and, therefore, have little experience. The new reform government will still need some time to adjust itself in order to co-operate, but generally there is broad agreement on the direction of an open and market-friendly economy.

The first diplomatic act of President Wahid was to visit ASEAN, including Singapore and Malaysia. This visit is a symbol that the first circle of economic co-operation and political co-operation is ASEAN. And ASEAN will conclude the ASEAN Free Trade Area (AFTA) in 2003 and hopefully that will be just the first step towards greater unification or integration of ASEAN in the year 2020. ASEAN is the first and foremost circle. In that context, what does it mean for Indonesia's close neighbour, Singapore? Singapore is far more than Habibie's dismissive "red dot on the map". Singapore is in fact well recognized as a major engine of economic growth in the region. For example, the Prime Minister of Singapore, Goh Chok Tong, visited Bangalore to open up a hi-tech centre that is a joint venture between India and Singapore. Singapore has that kind of capacity to broaden its economic activities and influence on a regional and global level. If Singapore can co-operate successfully with India, then such arrangements are also possible with Indonesia. Singapore's arrangements with Shanghai and the Southern coastal area of China are well known, and Riau and other parts of Sumatra could be seen in the same light. In brief, it is the intention of the current administration to look upon Singapore as a co-operative partner in arrangements in which both countries gain. The second circle, Asia, is wider, and Gus Dur has also visited China, South Asia, and the Middle East. The third circle is the region encompassed by the Asia Pacific Economic Co-operation (APEC) grouping. The fourth circle is the European Union. These are the circles in which Indonesia wants to play a role and hopes to be assisted by the countries in the circle.

The major focus of Gus Dur's preoccupation is capacity-building to create employment. Gus Dur is not someone who wants public ownership. He is a far cry from Habibie's erstwhile ambition of creating Indonesian-made passenger aircraft and ships. While Gus Dur would not oppose heavy industries of this nature, they would not necessarily have to be owned by Indonesians. The key is that these industries employ Indonesians, and that will be the main interest of the government, not ownership per se. From the early days of this administration, it is evident that Gus Dur is market friendly and not opposed to foreign interests. The current administration is keenly aware that foreign governments and corporations are in a position to provide investment, technology, and development assistance. It is in this context that economists can play an important role. The economics of the future will be more globally-orientated as economic nationalism becomes less useful. Discussion on the first 100 days of Gus Dur must inevitably include envisioning an integrated ASEAN in 2020. ASEAN in 2003 will see the creation of an AFTA through the removal of tariffs, but by 2020 ASEAN may be a Union of Asian countries. In this context, research institutes, like the Institute of Southeast Asian Studies, can play a significant role in using combined "brain power" of ASEAN economists to move the co-operative elements of the Indonesia-Singapore economic relationship into an ASEAN relationship striving forward towards ASEAN 2020.

24

Comments on Indonesia's Economic Reform

Mohammad Sadli

Although I write one of the concluding sections, the perspective will be rather different. Emil Salim, the author of the previous chapter, has become rather influential in the current government, some would say the "prime minister" of Gus Dur's "evening" or "informal" cabinet, and is thus a very close advisor to Gus Dur. My own position is rather more independent, or that of a bystander, looking at things from afar. I would judge that the first 100 days of Gus Dur be awarded a "B grade" for its economic agenda. That grade is an average between a "B+" in the macroeconomic policy agenda, a "B–" in the bank restructuring agenda, and a "C+" in corporate restructuring; overall a "B". There is every prospect that the grade will improve over the coming year to a "B+" average.

How do I defend this grade? Many contributors write about the potential forcefulness and effectiveness of government as the leading agent in the reform process in the economic agenda, which depends on "consensus" as a political force. As Boediono argues, the most important consensus process will be within the Cabinet itself, with its different political factions. In addition to this, consensus is needed among the political parties. If there is consensus, with respect to policies and concepts, that may be 80 per cent of the battle won. But clearly, there is hope in the process of consensus. In this volume alone, I have gratification to see the two ministers, Laksamana Sukardi and Jusuf Kalla, and Noor Fuad as Secretary-General of the Ministry of Finance in place of the minister, demonstrate but professionalism and board consensus on the issues at hand. The Minister of Finance, my junior at University, an accountant from Gajah Mada, has worked out well. He has not made many great mistakes, except one small mis-statement about politics. All of these ministers are under the co-ordination of Kwik Kian Gie. This inner circle of economic decision-makers is not experienced or even professional. The common complaint has been that Gus Dur failed to put in a professional technocratic Cabinet during political compromises he made. However, we see these ministers working well together based on a common consensus. But this is only half of the picture, as Wahid has instituted an alternative source of economic policy advice. He has instituted his "shadow" or "evening cabinet" where the technocrats, led by Emil Salim, exert great influence. In this sense, history is being repeated because thirty-two years ago Emil Salim and myself were part of an informal team that advised Soeharto behind the scenes. Soeharto became comfortable with us and trusted our advice. From then on, every time he needed a new executive in an important situation, or a new Cabinet minister, one of us was picked. Increasingly, it looks as though this process may repeat itself and in the next six months the "shadow Cabinet" will fold as they are appointed to the formal government executive. This would be a very good development for Indonesia. What also impresses me about the decision-makers in Jakarta — the ministers, the shadow Cabinet, the top bureaucrats, the technocrats, and the IMF and World Bank — is that they all work very well together. There are no major ideological problems that threaten the process. These are the building blocks of consensus which are driving the reform process. The real question mark hangs over progress in the banking corporate restructuring efforts over the next six months.

Despite that, I am very much "upbeat" for the next six months, but equally the whole thing can be de-railed by politics if, for example, the republic becomes inflamed because Gus Dur cannot control the problems in Ambon, Maluku, or Aceh. However, Gus Dur has a good feel for these issues and is not standing idly by. With the help of God and providence, these problems will be averted. Most crucial of all is Gus Dur's ability to control the military (Tentara Nasional Indonesia (TNI)) because, at times, the armed forces are not part of the solution but very much part of the problem. Now Indonesia has the prospect of Gus Dur being able to control the military and subordinate it to civilian authority. If he has the military under his control then he will have gone a long way towards solving the major political problems that beset Indonesia.

25

Conclusion

Anthony L. Smith

Indonesia has gone from one of Asia's high growth economies to the worst affected Asian economy of the financial crisis that gripped the region from the latter half of 1997. What went wrong for Indonesia? How could a country that was capable of double-digit growth, a balanced budget, a positive balance of payments, and a proven track record in inflation control, crash in such a dramatic fashion? Clearly there are some lessons to be taken from this.

The actions of the Soeharto regime continue to loom large over Indonesia. While the Soeharto regime will be remembered in history as facilitating one of the worst cases of high level corruption and cronyism in living memory, it should be remembered that this same regime had earlier made spectacular gains in economic growth and the provision of social services. The earlier Sukarno regime failed to make substantial improvements to the lives of ordinary Indonesians. The Soeharto Government understood that trade and investment links with the outside world, primarily the developed countries, was the only way to improve the country's economic performance. Improvements not only came for the wealthy few, but dramatic gains were made by those living above the poverty line, education and general literacy improved, population levels were controlled, and the average life expectancy (a good litmus test of an improving standard of living) increased from less than 55 years old to 65 years old by the 1990s. Unfortunately, the Soeharto regime demonstrated a growing tendency over time to use economic growth, fostered by foreign investment and the export sector, to reward his family and supporters in a very obvious display of patron–client relations. Economic bad times forced Soeharto to turn to the so-called "technocrats", U.S. trained academics like Widjojo Nitisastro, Ali Wardhana, Emil Salim, and Mohammad Sadli, to implement sound macroeconomic policy. Once a crisis had been ridden out, the Soeharto regime would typically grow complacent and allow for elements of protectionism to surface.

Although Indonesia was unlucky enough to be affected by a regional contagion, domestic factors compounded the problem. With the onset of the financial crisis, the Indonesian people, perhaps at one stage grateful for social gains, overwhelmingly turned against Soeharto, blaming him squarely for the depression and for squandering the gains of economic growth. The regime had shamelessly farmed out enterprises and licences to family members and favoured conglomerates. While there has been much discussion on the Asian model of development, pioneered by Japan and South Korea, whereby the market was guided by government, in Indonesia this idea transmogrified into one where cronies were put in charge of strategic enterprises. Much public money had been wasted on "white elephant" projects such as aircraft and automobile industries which could not be competitive, the economy had become high-cost due to the number of rent-seeking industries established to generate revenue for Soeharto family members, and conglomerates seemed unregulated and unstoppable.

Governments have always had to make decisions to balance the objectives of wealth creation and wealth distribution. The free market principles of free trade and investment flows will allow for the creation of wealth, but that wealth will most likely benefit the upper classes, even if the "rising tide lifts all ships" according to the trickle-down theory of increasing welfare leading to the multiplier effect throughout society. The distribution of wealth is also something that governments must take into account, and understandably many Indonesians feel that they are long overdue for a redistribution of the country's wealth. The Wahid administration must contend with this dilemma. The Soeharto regime showed that the generation of wealth was possible, but then proceeded to limit the gains to society by allowing those close to him to take control of various economic sectors. An important lesson to be learned from the New Order is that openness to the global economy brings important socio-economic gains, but efforts must be made to ensure that those gains do not just accrue to the privileged élite. While there will always be economic inequality under such an arrangement, the extremes of wealth and poverty were not avoided by the Soeharto administration. For example, establishing state monopolies over primary commodities which returned little to rice, sugar, wheat and clove growers, but made enormous profits for the President's cronies, also denied rightful income levels to vast numbers of Indonesians.

The use of political power to establish "crony capitalism" heavily distorted the economy and alienated vast numbers of Indonesian people. This was not a failure of capitalism *per se*, but the use of government interference to block the market mechanism and divert riches to the élite. Elsewhere (but not everywhere by any means) government interventions have been used for the more laudable goals of establishing long-term viable infant industries and/or the extension of social services, notably education and health. While many are right to point to the limitations of a free market in a globalized world, it would be a mistake for Indonesia to establish barriers, Sukarno-style, to commercial contact with the outside world. Indonesia's dramatic growth levels since 1965, and its failure before that time, bear out this point.

It is easy to write out a prescription for the ills of the Indonesian economy. The authors in this volume, collectively, give their views on what needs to be done — with some disagreement. Clearly a host of problems confront the Wahid administration: ending corruption and establishing the rule of law; adequate capital adequacy ratios for the deeply indebted banking sector; the sale of assets taken over by the government; the reduction of the deficit; keeping inflation low; providing social services including health and education; and so on. Putting these plans into practice is proving to be no easy task.

However, there is no reason to think that previous levels of economic growth cannot return to Indonesia. Foreign capital at one time flocked to Indonesia for, *inter alia*, natural resources, labour supply, regional access and domestic market access. These conditions are still present and so foreign investors could be attracted back again. By and large, however, this has not yet happened. The problems of corruption, a lack of the rule of law, instability in parts of Indonesia, and uncertainty over regional autonomy, have meant that foreign investors have not regained confidence. Thus the Wahid administration will need to alleviate these problems. Unfortunately the major domestic source of foreign capital, the ethnic Chinese community, has also lost confidence in their physical security and the security of their assets. The flight of capital of the Indonesian Chinese has been an enormous drain on the economy (because of liberalized currency movements there is no record of exactly how much). Those who joined the mobs in destroying Chinese-owned businesses achieved a pyrrhic victory that served to lower the living standards of many Indonesians. The Indonesian Government needs to ensure that the Chinese community are not scape-goated in the future as the contribution of Indonesian Chinese businesses is essential.

Another lesson to be taken from the Soeharto regime involves the nature of the political system. It has been pointed out that Wahid now lacks the central authority to undertake a number of speedy decisions. The Wahid administration operates in an environment of political pluralism that the Soeharto regime never faced. Wahid will find it difficult to remove subsidies on food and fuel. Given the ability of authoritarian regimes to mobilize resources and undertake decisive economic policy without substantial opposition, something known as the "authoritarian advantage thesis", some commentators have wondered if democracy is really the best option for a state like Indonesia. However, it is important to note that authoritarian regimes are essentially uncontrollable in how they manage the resources of that nation/state. There is no check on executive power, and thus macroeconomic decision-making becomes reliant on a small élite. Indonesia followed the path well-trodden by its neighbour, the Philippines, whereby an authoritarian leader used his strength to mobilize resources overwhelmingly to a favoured élite. Democratization is, demonstrably, already having an impact. Scandals and incidents of corruption are routinely exposed by a free press, taken up by members of parliament, and are noticeably unpopular with the masses. None of the contributors, significantly, advocates a return to authoritarianism, which reflects a consensus that this form of government has not been helpful to Indonesia in the past.

Index